A SCEPTIC'S GUIDE TO ATHEISM

'The argument with faith is the foundation and origin of all arguments, because it is the beginning – but not the end – of all arguments about philosophy, science, history, and human nature.'

Christopher Hitchens, God is Not Great
(New York: *Atlantic, 2007*), *p. 12.*

'Recent history suggests strongly that religion is going to garner more and more attention, not less, in the immediate future. If it is going to receive attention, it had better be high-quality attention, not the sort of hysterics, paranoids, and boodlers on all sides engage in.'

Daniel Dennett, Breaking the Spell (London: *Penguin, 2006*), *p. 49.*

'We desperately need a public discourse that encourages critical thinking and intellectual honesty.'

Sam Harris, Letter to a Christian Nation
(London: *Bantam, 2007*), *p. 87.*

'all who have secure grounds for their views should not be afraid of robust challenge and criticism.'

A.C. Grayling, Against All Gods
(London: *Oberon Books, 2007*), *p. 9.*

'Of course, dyed-in-the-wool faith-heads are immune to argument . . .'

Richard Dawkins, The God Delusion (London: *Bantam, 2006*), *p. 5*

A SCEPTIC'S GUIDE TO ATHEISM

Peter S. Williams

Paternoster:
thinking faith

MILTON KEYNES ● COLORADO SPRINGS ● HYDERABAD

Copyright © 2009 Peter S. Williams

15 14 13 12 11 10 09   7 6 5 4 3 2 1

First published 2009 by Paternoster
Paternoster is an imprint of Authentic Media
9 Holdom Avenue, Bletchley, Milton Keynes, Bucks, MK1 1QR, UK
1820 Jet Stream Drive, Colorado Springs, CO 80921, USA
Medchal Road, Jeedimetla Village, Secunderabad 500 055, A.P., India
www.authenticmedia.co.uk

Authentic Media is a division of IBS-STL U.K., limited by guarantee, with its
Registered Office at Kingstown Broadway, Carlisle, Cumbria CA3 0HA.
Registered in England & Wales No. 1216232. Registered charity 270162

British Library Cataloguing in Publication Data

A catalogue record for this book is available from the
British Library

ISBN-13: 978-1-84227-617-4

Cover design by James Kessell for Scratch the Sky Ltd.
(www.scratchthesky.com)
Print Management by Adare
Printed and bound in Great Britain by J.H. Haynes & Co., Sparkford

Contents

Preface

In a strained reference to the poet W. B. Yeats,[1] the New Atheists may well dub this book a 'flea'.[2] But if I may offer an insect allusion of my own, I would rather aspire to be 'a sort of gadfly'.[3] As neuroscientist Mario Beauregard observes: 'the term "sceptical" has developed a rather restricted meaning. It no longer means "applying rigorous critical judgement" so much as "defending materialism."'[4] This book aims to apply rigorous critical judgement to contemporary popular defences of metaphysically materialistic atheism, especially defences arising out of the so-called 'New Atheism'. With Dinesh D'Souza I contend that the 'difference between me and my atheist opponents is that I am sceptical not only of the allegedly irrational claims of religion but also of the irrational claims made in the name of science and of scepticism itself.'[5] I agree with the late Carl Sagan that it is better 'to embrace the hard truth than a reassuring fable'.[6] But what if atheism is the 'fable', and the 'reassuring fable' of theism is actually the 'hard truth'? What if Christianity is, as C.S. Lewis thought, 'myth become fact'?[7]

My thanks must go first of all to the staff of Paternoster Press, especially to commissioning editor Dr Robin Parry (who invited me to take a thematic approach to my subject) and to my copy-editor, Kate Kirkpatrick. Thanks are also due to my colleges at *Damaris* (www.damaris.org) – especially Robin Collins for his comments on chapter five – and to all those who support me through their prayers and other encouragements. Last but not least, a special thank you must go to Luke Pollard for his comments on the book. Any remaining mistakes are of course wholly my own.

Southampton, Summer 2008

1.

Atheism is Dead . . .

'The question of God ... has returned to the contemporary conversation.'
– Roy Abraham Varghese[1]

God is back, and this time it's personal. Recent years have seen a rising tide of public debate about the existence of what Richard Dawkins calls 'a supernatural creator that is "appropriate for us to worship"'.[2] God, as 'he'[3] is otherwise known, has permeated the media – from the internet to print, from television and film to radio and pod-casts, as well as the bestseller shelves of book stores. As David Robertson comments, 'Richard Dawkins' *The God Delusion* [has] been joined in the bestseller lists by Christopher Hitchin's *God is not Great*, Sam Harris's *Letter to a Christian Nation*, A.C. Grayling's *Against all Gods* and a host of other books [e.g. Daniel Dennett's *Breaking the Spell*] extolling the virtues of atheism and the dangers and follies of religion.'[4]

Perhaps more surprising than the fact that we have started thinking publically about God again is the ironic fact that this conversation was started by atheists. As Madeleine Bunting observes,

> It's an extraordinary publishing phenomenon – atheism sells. Any philosopher, professional polemicist or scientist with worries about their pension plan must now be feverishly working on a book proposal . . . The science writer, Matt Ridley, recently commented that on one day at Princeton he met no fewer than three intellectual luminaries hard at work on their God books . . . Surely not since Victorian times has there been such a passionate, sustained debate about religious belief.[5]

The motivation of those who have put God in the spotlight isn't only intellectual (or financial), it is also intensely political: 'After more than six years of a Republican administration that has been identified more closely with Christian conservatives than any other in American history, there was bound to be a backlash . . . Add to that the unpopularity of the current administration's policy in Iraq and you have a combustible mix of political and cultural hostility . . .'[6] God's *existence* is of course the central issue at stake in every debate about theism; but the current 'sizzle' surrounding this 'stake' is the proclamation that faith isn't merely *intellectually* mistaken, but *morally wrong* to boot. Hence, Christopher Hitchens writes, 'I'm not even an atheist so much as I am an antitheist; I not only maintain that all religions are versions of the same untruth, but I hold that the influence of churches, and the effect of religious belief, is positively harmful.'[7]

Wired Magazine dubbed the rising tide of popular antitheism 'The New Atheism' in a November 2006 cover story written by agnostic contributing editor Gary Wolf. He wrote that 'The New Atheists will not let us off the hook simply because we are not doctrinaire believers. They condemn not just belief in God but *respect* for belief in God. Religion is not only wrong; its evil. Now that the battle has been joined, there's no excuse for shirking.'[8] The New Atheism combines a naturalistic worldview with a moral imperative to eradicate religion (or at least *theistic* religion); a rhetorical 'call to arms' fuelled by the intellectual and moral failings of Christian and Muslim fundamentalism. Indeed, one of the primary arguments advanced by the New Atheist movement is that faith is either directly or indirectly the cause of such suffering that it should be spurned by all right-thinking people. The New Atheism is thus as much of a political *riposte* to monotheistic religion (especially the American 'Christian Right', on the one hand, and 'Jihadist' Islam on the other) as it is an *intellectual* riposte to the God hypothesis. As agnostic John Humphrys observes:

> The twenty-first century came of age on 11 September 2001. Nineteen Muslims, with the name of their God on their lips, murdered three thousand Americans . . . Whatever else they may have achieved, the zealots have given militant atheists yet more

ammunition. Isn't this what religion does, they say, create endless conflict in the name of God? So the atheists are on the march armed with logic and even more righteous indignation at the horror of religion and determined, at the very least, to weaken its grip on the national debate.[9]

Thus vocal antitheists have launched a political-cum-intellectual movement that has precipitated not only a raft of replies from believers, but which has simultaneously ignited a heated debate among atheists about the tactical merits of telling the faithful that they are all brainwashed idiots who pose a threat to public safety. And just as the New Atheism has provided theists with an expanded 'route to market', so it has stirred up renewed expressions of more tentative forms of non-theism, as exemplified by the publication of Humphrys' *In God We Doubt: Confessions of a Failed Atheist* (2007) and David Berlinski's *The Devil's Delusion: Atheism and its Scientific Pretensions* (2008). As secular philosopher John Gray observes: 'there has been a sudden explosion in the literature of proselytising atheism . . . For the first time in generations, scientists and philosophers, high-profile novelists and journalists are debating whether religion has a future. The intellectual traffic is not all one-way.'[10]

Three Responses

Jeremy Stangroom complains that 'It's obvious that God doesn't exist and that religion is bunk. But irritatingly this is not the view of some ninety percent of the world's population.'[11] The typical response to the God hypothesis is 'theism' (an ancient Greek term meaning 'god-ism'). For the monotheist (one-god-ist) 'God' means: 'a supreme personal being – distinct from the world and creator of the world.'[12] There are two atypical responses to the God hypothesis: atheism and agnosticism.

Atheism

Atheism is the denial that the proposition 'God exists' is true. Like many whose 'atheism is motivated at least in part by their naturalism',[13] philosopher Julian Baggini, editor of *The*

Philosopher's Magazine, calls upon naturalism ('a belief that there is only the natural world and not any supernatural one'[14]) to provide an alternative 'positive world view'[15] to that of theism. Equating atheism with naturalism secures Baggini a big bunch of denials, all grounded in the denial that there is anything more to reality than the physical. As Baggini explains: 'The atheist's rejection of belief in God is usually accompanied by a broader rejection of any supernatural or transcendental reality. For example, an atheist does not usually believe in the existence of immortal souls, life after death . . . or supernatural powers.'[16] Indeed, the atheist's rejection of theism is often *produced* by the presupposition that naturalism is true. As Corliss Lamont says: 'naturalistic metaphysics . . . considers all forms of the supernatural as myth [because it] regards Nature as the totality of being . . .'[17]

In recent decades, naturalism has come under an unprecedented barrage of high-calibre intellectual fire on multiple fronts.[18] As John G. West reports: 'A growing number of scientists and other scholars . . . say that recent developments in biology, chemistry, physics and related sciences undermine the . . . materialist worldview . . .'[19] Sociologist Steve Fuller admits that: 'naturalism remains a controversial position within academic philosophy. In fact, it is probably still a minority position.'[20]

According to many commentators, atheists in society at large are a shrinking minority. Paul M. Zulehner, a distinguished sociologist of religion, says that European atheists are: 'an infinitesimally small group [such that there] are not enough of them to be used for sociological research.'[21] A worldwide poll taken in 1991 put the global figure for atheists at just 4.4% of the population.[22] By 2006 it was estimated that only 2% of the world population were atheists.[23] As Phil Zuckerman acknowledges: 'the nations with some of the highest degrees of organic atheism (such as Great Britain, France, and Scandinavia) have been experiencing a steady increase of atheism over the past century, an increase which shows no indication of abating . . . On the other hand, worldwide atheism overall may be in decline.'[24]

Agnosticism

The more popular atypical response to the God hypothesis is *agnosticism* (from the Greek *gnosis*, meaning 'knowledge', and the alpha 'a,' which negates its subject). As a general term, agnosticism expresses: 'any conscious attitude of doubt, denial, or disbelief, towards some, or even all, of man's powers of knowing or objects of knowledge.'[25] Applied to religion, agnosticism is: 'The position that neither affirms belief in God (theism) nor denies the existence of God (atheism) but instead suspends judgement.'[26]

Strictly speaking, an agnostic claims that we *cannot* know whether God exists ('hard' agnosticism); but the term is often used to mean someone who says that we (or they) simply *do not* know if God exists ('soft' agnosticism). The soft agnostic may claim that *no one* has been able to resolve the question of God's reality one way or the other, and that therefore 'suspension of judgement is the only reasonable stance'[27] (corporate soft agnosticism); or merely that *they* have been unable to resolve the question of God's reality, and are currently suspending judgement (individual soft agnosticism). While theists believe that the proposition 'God exists' is true, and atheists believe that this proposition is not true, agnostics believe that 'God exists' is a proposition with a truth-value that either they or we *do not know* (perhaps because we *cannot* know).

General agnosticism 'reduces to the self-destructing assertion that: "one knows enough about reality in order to affirm that nothing can be known about reality."'[28] In any form of *limited* agnosticism 'the door remains open for some knowledge of reality',[29] and this is of course compatible with 'finite knowledge of an infinite God.'[30] As agnostic-turned-theist Francis Collins warns, 'To be well defended, agnosticism should be arrived at only after a full consideration of all the evidence for and against the existence of God. It is a rare agnostic who has made the effort to do so.'[31]

Many agnostics are practical atheists. As atheist George H. Smith writes, 'One either accepts the proposition "god exists" as true, or one does not . . . The self-proclaimed agnostic must still designate whether he does or does not believe in a god . . . Agnosticism is not the escape clause that it is commonly thought to be.'[32] We all live either as if God exists, or as if God doesn't exist, and agnostics usually live as if he doesn't. As agnostic Somerset Maugham acknowledged: 'the practical outcome of agnosticism is that you act as though God did not exist.'[33]

Philosopher Stephen D. Schwarz comments that the supposedly neutral position of agnosticism:

> is certainly a position, but is it really neutral? What does this position entail for one's life? Does it not entail the same thing as atheism: that one does not live before God, that one does not reckon with God, that one does not pray to God, does not thank him? Whether one does not reckon with God because one says, 'God is not,' or because one says, 'I don't know that he is,' makes no practical difference . . .[34]

Interesting Times

> *'Doubt that a supernatural being exists is banal . . .'*
> – John Allen Paulos[35]

A reputedly Chinese curse runs: 'May you live in interesting times.'[36] The last century was an 'interesting time' for those concerned with the God hypothesis: 'in the 1960's . . . in the affluent West, at least, there emerged a "radical godlessness" that was, by historical standards, unique.'[37] Naturalistic atheism remains the orthodox worldview of Western intellectual culture, despite the fact that its advocates constitute 'a tiny minority of the world's population'[38] with a disproportionate amount of influence in and through the academy. As Keith Ward reports:

> In the first decades of the twentieth century, idealism was almost taken for granted among English-speaking philosophers . . . In the latter half of the twentieth century, some of the very best professional philosophers opted for materialism. But most of them would concede that their view is provocative, and that there are deep and unresolved puzzles . . . I have taught philosophy professionally in British universities for at least twenty years and am on the committee of the Royal Institute for Philosophy. Looking around at my philosopher colleagues in Britain . . . I would say that very few of them are materialists. Some . . . are idealists. A good number are theists. And most seem to be generally sceptical or agnostic about all worldviews, preferring to deal with specific tricky problems case by case . . .[39]

Nevertheless, recent decades have seen affiliation with theistic religion suffering a marked decline in many countries.

> [N]ations with the highest degrees of organic atheism (atheism which is not state-enforced . . .) include most of the nations of Europe, as well as Canada, Australia, New Zealand and Israel. There also exist high degrees of atheism in Japan, Vietnam, North Korea, and Taiwan. Many former Soviet nations . . . contain significant levels of atheism . . . In some societies, particularly Europe, atheism is growing. [40]

In a 2004 MORI poll conducted for the BBC, '12% said they were sure there was no God and another 14% said they're unconvinced that one exists. Between them, it looks like 26% are agnostic or atheist, and in a similar question (phrased differently) 29% said that they do not believe in God.'[41] British lives actively centred on God are undoubtedly atypical; in fact, according to recent findings:

> About half of the British believe in God, yet about 72% told the 2001 census that they were Christian, and 66% of the population have no *actual* connection to any religion or church, despite what they tend to write down on official forms. Between 1979 and 2005, half of all Christians stopped going to church on a Sunday. Religion in Britain has suffered an immense decline since the 1950s, and all indicators show a continued secularisation of British society . . .[42]

Jonathan Petre reports that in Britain, 'While 1,000 new people are joining a church each week, 2,500 are leaving.'[43] The 2005 English Church Census found that 'Sunday churchgoing continues to fall at a rate of 2.3 per cent a year, an improvement from the 2.7 per cent decline in the 1990s but still a very alarming slide.'[44] According to Peter Brierley:

> While the apex for church membership in 1930 in the UK topped ten million people (29% of the population), by 1980 the number had dropped to 7.5 million people (just 13% of the population). In the interim, overall population in the UK had increased by ten

million . . . If we are to follow this trend, the total decrease from 7.5
million in 1980 to 4.6 million in 2020, and from 13.4% of the population to just 7.2% leads to an average rate of decline of 1.2% per
year.[45]

It would be a mistake to extrapolate from this decline the eventual death of Church attendance in the UK.[46] As of 2005, 34% of
Churches were growing (compared to 21% in 1998), while 16%
were stable (compared to 14% in 1998). One quarter of churches
in decline during the 1990s have turned things around.[47] Figures
published in 2006 showed that: 'Evangelicals account for a rising
one-third share of the 870,000 regular attenders remaining in the
Church of England.'[48] At some point, then, the two graphs are
going to intersect, and a growing, mainly evangelical church will
emerge. And none of this addresses the state of British non-
Christian theists, including approximately 1.6 million Muslims.

The Rise of Positivism

The intellectual roots of Britain's slide into secularism can be
traced to a time in the early twentieth century when God was
almost banished from the intellectual scene by the idea that talk
about 'God' was *literally meaningless*. This view was rooted in the
'verification principle' of the 'logical positivists'. Kelly James
Clark explains that positivism 'began in the early 1920s in an
informal discussion group in Austria called the Vienna Circle. The
original members, led by physicist Moritz Schlick, included math-
ematicians, physicists, sociologists and economists but no professional philosophers.'[49] This omission was unfortunate, because
'United by their passionate dislike of the metaphysical . . . the
group developed a unified philosophy that embraced science and
attempted to destroy philosophy.'[50] Attempting to develop a philosophy that dispenses with philosophy makes about as much
sense as Groucho Marx's comment that he wouldn't belong to any
club that would have him as a member.

The positivist's verification criterion said that the meaning of
any statement that wasn't true by definition (e.g. $2 + 2 = 4$) lay in
its ability to be empirically verified (at least in principle). To
'empirically verify' something means to check it out with the
physical senses (sight, hearing, touch, etc.). In other words, the

statement 'This is a book' is meaningful *because you can verify it* by seeing, touching and even smelling this book. But 'God exists' is a meaningless statement, *because you can't verify it* by seeing or touching or smelling God. According to positivism, 'God exists' isn't a meaningful statement that's either true or false, but a use of language on a par with nonsense poetry (like the parts of 'Jabberwocky' Lewis Carroll didn't define). It may have emotional resonance, but it has no rational content that can be understood and judged. Oxford philosopher A.J. Ayer – whose 1936 publication *Language, Truth and Logic* popularized positivism in Britain – proclaimed:

> 'God' is a metaphysical term. And if 'God' is a metaphysical term, then it cannot even be probable that a god exists. For to say that 'God exists' is to make a metaphysical utterance which cannot be either true or false . . . If a putative proposition fails to satisfy [the verification] principle, and is not a tautology, then . . . it is metaphysical, and . . . being metaphysical, it is neither true nor false but literally senseless.[51]

As Ayer admitted, 'If the assertion that there is a god is nonsensical, then the . . . assertion that there is no god is equally non-sensical.'[52] Ditto agnosticism! Ironically, given that many who embraced positivism were materialists: 'materialism would have to be rejected as nonsense by a strict interpretation of logical positivism..[53] The mind-independent reality of matter is neither true by definition, nor something that can be empirically verified!

William Cash calls Ayer 'arguably the most influential 20th-century rationalist after Bertrand Russell'.[54] As Catholic philosopher F.C. Copleston observed, 'Ayer's writings [have] exercised a widespread influence, particularly perhaps on university students, for whom it possessed the charm of novelty and an atmosphere of daring.'[55] Ayer's declaration that God-talk was nonsense influenced many.

> It was one of those books that galvanize a whole generation. Ambitious undergraduates commonly read it at a sitting. Their elders were appalled. When students tried to discuss the book at an Oxford seminar, the Master of Balliol flung it through the

window . . . Asked what came next, the young iconoclast [Ayer] said cheerfully: 'There's no next. Philosophy has come to an end. Finished.'[56]

The Fall of Positivism

Sir Anthony Kenny recalls how 'Philosophers of religion were in a pretty shattered state when I first came to the subject, and thought it would be wonderful if they could prove that religious propositions had meaning, let alone that they were true.'[57] However, Kenny observes, 'In the fifty years I've been in philosophy I think there's been a great revival of confidence among philosophers of religion.'[58] Julian Baggini comments, 'Although Kenny has moved from faith to agnosticism, in the discipline as a whole, he has witnessed a remarkable rehabilitation of religious belief.'[59] As Paul Copan and William Lane Craig observe, 'Over the last forty years there has been an ongoing revolution in Anglo-American philosophy. As the old, anti-metaphysical prejudices have waned, there has been a renaissance of Christian philosophy.'[60] Indeed, just two decades after *Language, Truth and Logic* was published, Copleston wrote that 'there are few British philosophers who willingly accept the title of "positivists" or who make open profession of applying the principle of verifiability as a criterion of meaning . . . [positivism] is no longer fashionable.'[61]

Several factors conspired to render positivism unfashionable. For example, philosopher John Hick pointed out that, when made sufficiently precise, the statement 'God exists' *is* empirically verifiable (at least in *principle*, which is all the verification criterion requires): 'A set of expectations based upon faith in the historic Jesus as the incarnation of God, and in his teaching as being divinely authoritative, could be so fully confirmed in *post-mortem* experience as to leave no grounds for rational doubt as to the validity of that faith.'[62] That is, if one was to die and find oneself in a Christian afterlife, one could count this as an *indirect* verification of God's existence; 'the existence or non-existence of the God of the New Testament is a matter of fact, and claims as such eventual experiential verification.'[63]

Hick's argument didn't challenge the verification principle, but its capacity to draw a line of demarcation between 'scientific' claims on the one hand and 'metaphysical' claims on the other. Unless positivism is framed broadly enough to allow the sort of *indirect* verification utilized by Hick, many explanatory claims within science would lack meaning, because they concern entities that are verified indirectly from observation of their hypothesized effects. This being so, it may be argued that the God hypothesis is not only verifiable *in principle*, but also *in practice*, since several arguments for God can be framed using the same scientific form of indirect verification. As Basil Mitchell comments:

> the Logical Positivist movement started as an attempt to make a clear demarcation between science and common sense on the one hand, and metaphysics and theology on the other. But work in the philosophy of science convinced people that what the Logical Postitivists had said about science was not true, and, by the time the philosophers of science had developed and amplified their accounts of how rationality works in science, people discovered that similar accounts applied equally well to the areas which they had previously sought to exclude, namely theology and metaphysics.[64]

As George Schlesinger argues, 'Theism is in principle confirmable by all sorts of possible observations and is in fact confirmed by some actual observations.'[65]

Richard Dawkins objects strongly to 'the erroneous notion that the existence or non-existence of God is an untouchable question, forever beyond the reach of science . . . Either he exists or he doesn't. It is a scientific question; one day we may know the answer, and meanwhile we can say something pretty strong about the probability.'[66] In *The God Delusion* Dawkins defines science as simply 'the honest and systematic endeavour to find out the truth about the real world'.[67] Such a definition provides no grounds for the sort of air-tight distinction between metaphysical philosophy and natural philosophy (as science used to be called) sought by positivism. In practice, however, Dawkins uses 'science' as a term of endearment restricted to any critical investigation of the 'real world' *grounded in empirical evidence*; and as a naturalist he assumes that the 'real world' can be described in exclusively naturalistic terms. By way of contrast, Intelligent Design (ID) theorists[68] refuse to allow *a priori* assumptions to pre-determine the conclusions natural philosophy reaches. Instead, they follow Scottish philosopher David Hume in distinguishing between conclusions science can and can't support without purely metaphysical extension.[69] Dawkins is less nuanced than Hume. Nevertheless, bearing the above in mind, ID theorists can give a qualified welcome to Dawkins' affirmation that 'the existence of God is a scientific hypothesis . . . God's existence or non-existence is a scientific fact about the universe, discoverable in principle if not in practice.'[70] And all ID theorists (theists and non-theists alike) can give an unqualified welcome to his statement that: 'The presence or absence of a creative super-intelligence is unequivocally a scientific question . . . The methods we should use to settle the matter . . . would be purely and entirely scientific methods.'[71] As William Lane Craig explains:

> Dawkins . . . implicitly rejects methodological naturalism and treats intelligent design as a scientific hypothesis which should be assessed like any other scientific hypothesis . . . Dawkins does not reject the inference to a cosmic designer *tout court*: he recognizes that we might be products of some super-human designer, and he offers no in principle objection to inferring such an intelligent designer of the universe. What Dawkins objects to is identifying that super-human designer with God . . . Thus, whatever the merit of Dawkins' objection [to the God hypothesis], design theorists will be unfazed by it, since it is strictly irrelevant to a design inference . . . Dawkins, then, finds himself in agreement with the most fundamental tenets of intelligent design theory: (i) that intelligent design is a scientific hypothesis which should be assessed as such, (ii) that it is illegitimate to exclude *a priori* from the pool of explanatory options hypotheses which appeal to final causes or even super-natural beings, and (iii) that the design inference is not to be equated with an inference to theism . . .[72]

A positive answer in respect of the existence of 'a creative super-intelligence' (a scientific conclusion, as Dawkins confirms) would nevertheless provide obvious grist for the metaphysical mill of arguments for theism. The point of most immediate relevance here, of course, is that *Dawkins' atheism, no less than the theism he opposes, is built upon positivism's grave.*

Chief among the woes of positivism, as R. Douglas Geivett explains, was the fact that the verification principle: 'was neither empirically verifiable nor tautological'.[73] The principle *'failed its own requirement* for factual meaningfulness', notes William P. Alston, 'and thus was self-refuting'.[74] Keith Ward reports the following conversation with Ayer:

> A student once asked [Ayer] if you could make any true general statement about meaningful statements. 'Yes,' he replied. 'You can say that all meaningful statements must be verifiable in principle.' 'I see what you mean,' said the student. 'But how can I verify that?' 'I am glad you asked that,' said the philosopher. 'You cannot verify it. But it is not really a meaningful statement; it is just a rule for using language.' 'Whose rule?' 'Well, it's my rule, really. But it is a very useful one. If you use it, you will find you agree with me completely. I think that would be very useful.'[75]

If we adopt the rule, then of course we will agree with Ayer, who will find that useful! But he can't give us a *reason* for adopting his rule that doesn't contradict the rule he wants us to adopt. Hence James Kelly Clark describes the verification principle as a piece of 'unjustifiable philosophical imperialism that, in the end, could not survive critical scrutiny.'[76] Ayer himself mused, 'I just stated [the verification rule] dogmatically and an extraordinary number of people seemed to be convinced by my assertion.'[77] In 1973 he admitted that 'the verification principle is defective . . .'[78] Discussing positivism in 1978, Ayer conceded, 'Nearly all of it was false.'[79] Ayer wrote the obituary for verificationism: 'Logical Positivism died a long time ago. I don't think much of *Language, Truth and Logic* is true. I think it is full of mistakes.'[80]

UCLA philosopher Tyler Burge writes that 'the central event [in philosophy during the last half-century was] the downfall of positivism and the re-opening of discussion of virtually all the traditional problems of philosophy.'[81] Including, of course, the God hypothesis. As Craig explains,

The collapse of verificationism was undoubtedly the most important philosophical event of the twentieth century. Its demise meant a resurgence of metaphysics, along with other traditional problems of philosophy that had been suppressed. Accompanying this resurgence has come something new and altogether unanticipated: a renaissance in Christian philosophy. The face of Anglo-American philosophy has been transformed as a result. Theism is on the rise; atheism is on the decline.[82]

Plantinga's Impact

'**planting**, v. To use twentieth-century fertilizer to encourage new shoots from eleventh-century ideas which everyone thought had gone to seed; hence *plantinger*, n. one who plantings.'
– Daniel Dennett, *Philosophical Lexicon*

In 1967 American philosopher Alvin Plantinga (b. 1932) published *God and Other Minds*, which 'applied the tools of analytic philosophy to questions in the Philosophy of Religion with an unprecedented rigour and creativity'.[83] He argued by analogy with the rationality of belief in other minds (whose non-tautological existence can't be empirically verified) that 'if my belief in other minds is rational, so is my belief in God.'[84] If belief in God is meaningless because he can't be empirically verified, then so is belief in other minds. But positivists believe in other minds . . . Then, with the 1974 publication of *The Nature of Necessity*, Plantinga kick-started a philosophical re-evaluation of the traditional arguments for God by using modal logic to lay out a valid version of the 'ontological' argument (originally formulated in 1078 AD by Anselm).[85] Plantinga's work on the ontological argument (which will be briefly examined in chapter seven) got a theistic foot in the newly re-opened door of metaphysics and served, as Roger Scruton acknowledges, 'the useful purpose of showing the rumours of God's death to be greatly exaggerated'.[86]

One could think of *God and Other Minds* and *The Nature of Necessity* as tackling both prongs of the positivist's proposed dilemma: show that theism is verifiable or tautologically true, or else accept banishment to the outer darkness of meaninglessness. In effect, Plantinga responded to the first prong that the demand for verification renders positivism self-contradictory, and to the second prong that although he can't prove that God's existence is tautologically true, he can prove that it is *rational to think that God's existence is tautologically true*, and that this is sufficient to demonstrate that God-talk is meaningful. For how can a truth-claim be rational yet meaningless?

Plantinga also had a massive effect on the philosophical standing of one of the few arguments *against* the existence of God, the 'problem of evil'. Sam Harris remains impressed by the so-called 'logical problem of evil', that is, that 'If God exists, either He can do nothing to stop the most egregious calamities, or He does not care to. God, therefore, is either impotent or evil.'[87] (Note that, even if it worked, this is only an argument against the existence of a deity who is all-powerful *and* all-good, not an argument against the existence of a deity *per se*.) However, atheist William L. Rowe observes that few contemporary philosophers believe there is a logical contradiction between God's existence and evil.

> Some philosophers have contended that the existence of evil is *logically inconsistent* with the existence of the theistic God [who is all-powerful and all-good]. No one, I think, has succeeded in establishing such an extravagant claim. Indeed . . . there is a fairly compelling argument for the view that the existence of evil is logically consistent with the existence of the theistic God.[83]

Rowe is referring to Plantinga's 'free will defence', namely that it is *logically possible* (albeit implausible) that all evil is caused by the misuse of libertarian free will given by God to various creatures as the necessary means to a sufficiently greater good. '[M]any contemporary philosophers believe that the Free Will Defence . . . is a strong and effective response to the logical problem of evil . . . Plantinga . . . and other theistic philosophers have cast serious doubt on the viability of all formulations of the logical problem of evil . . .'[89] In essence, the logical problem of evil is based upon the assumption that it is *impossible* for God to have a morally sufficient reason for permitting evil. But as Craig explains:

> there is no reason to think that God and evil are logically incompatible. After all, there is no *explicit* contradiction between them.

And if the atheist means that there is some *implicit* contradiction between God and evil, then he must be presupposing some hidden premise to bring out this implicit contradiction. But . . . no philosopher has been able to identify such premises . . . more than that, we can actually prove that God and evil *are* logically compatible. You see, the atheist presupposes that God cannot have morally sufficient reasons for permitting the evil in the world. But this assumption is not necessarily true. So long as it is even *possible* that God has morally sufficient reasons for permitting evil, it follows that God and evil are logically consistent.[90]

Agnostic Paul Draper concedes that 'it is possible that there is some good reason (perhaps a reason too complicated for humans to understand) for God to permit tragedies. So tragedies don't conclusively disprove God's existence.'[91] Primarily because of Plantinga's analysis, 'informed philosophers of religion today acknowledge that the logical problem of evil is not a good argument against God's existence. Whether among theists or atheists, there is something of a consensus that the logical problem of evil is not a problem.'[92]

The typical atheistic claim today is not that evil *disproves* God, but rather than evil *counts against* God (the New Atheist argument that the evil done by theists counts against the rationality and/or morality of theistic *belief* is a separate issue). However, even if evil counts against God – an assumption Plantinga (along with many other philosophers) questions by noting the difficulty of extrapolating from our inability to propose reasons justifying the existence of evil in all instances, to the conclusion that there are instances of evil that probably lack any justification[93] – one must still take into account the grounds *for* belief before deciding if evil counts *decisively* against God. As Plantinga argues:

suppose evil does constitute evidence, of some kind, against theism: what follows from that? Not much. There are many propositions I believe that are true and rationally accepted, and such that there is evidence against them. The fact that Peter is only three months old is evidence against his weighing nineteen pounds; nevertheless I might rationally (and truly) believe that's how much he weighs. Is the idea, instead, that the existence of God is improbable with respect to our *total evidence . . .*? To show this, the atheologian would have to look into all the evidence *for* the existence of God . . . This is vastly messier and more problematic than a terse and elegant demonstration of a contradiction [as attempted by the failed logical problem of evil].[94]

Hence agnostic Graham Oppy concedes that 'If theists can reasonably suppose that they have lots of evidence which supports the claim that God exists, then they may reasonably believe that there is a solution to "the problem of evil", even if they do not know what that solution is.'[95]

Due to his cutting-edge contributions to the philosophy of religion and the theory of knowledge, Plantinga has been lauded as not only 'the best *Christian* philosopher of his time', but as 'the most important philosopher of any stripe'.[96] As John G. Stackhouse comments, due to the excellence of Plantinga's labours 'the Christian view of things simply has to be taken seriously by any questioner with the integrity to appreciate sound philosophy.'[97] Many philosophers have followed Plantinga's example, re-affirming and updating the case for God. Hence Craig writes of 'a resurgence of interest in natural theology – that branch of theology which seeks to offer cogent argument or reasons for God's existence apart from the resources of authoritative divine revelation.'[98]

The Intellectual Resurrection of Theism

On 8 April (Good Friday) 1966, *Time Magazine* ran a cover story by John T. Elson entitled 'Is God Dead?', about the 'death-of-God' movement in American theology. 'Even within Christianity,' it stated, 'now confidently renewing itself in spirit as well as form, a small band of radical theologians has seriously argued that the churches must accept the fact of God's death, and get along without him.'[99] Craig explains that 'According to the movement's protagonists, traditional theism was no longer tenable and had to be once and for all abandoned. Ironically, however, at the same time that theologians were writing God's obituary, a new generation of young philosophers was rediscovering His vitality.'[100] A few years later, *Time* carried a cover story asking 'Is God coming back to life?' Interest in the philosophy of religion grew to the point where, in 1980, *Time* ran a story on 'Modernizing the case for God', describing the contemporary movement among philosophers putting new life into the arguments for God.

> In a quiet revolution in thought and argument that hardly anybody could have foreseen only two decades ago, God is making a comeback. Most intriguingly, this is happening not amongst theologians or ordinary believers, but in the crisp intellectual circles of academic philosophers, where the consensus had long banished the Almighty from fruitful discourse.[101]

The shift documented by *Time* prompted Craig to write that 'when one recalls the bleak days of the "Death of God" movement in the sixties, it is not unfair to speak of a veritable resurrection of theism.'[102] Gary R. Habermas notes that 'Over the last few decades, it seems the table has turned on naturalists.'[103] Richard M. Gale reports a 'startling resurgence of theism within philosophy during the past thirty or so years'.[104] So pronounced is this renaissance that noted theologian Wolfhart Pannenberg confidently pronounces that 'Atheism as a theoretical position is in decline worldwide.'[105] Atheist philosopher Quentin Smith has highlighted the 'influx of talented theists'[106] into philosophy departments, saying that 'Perhaps one-quarter or one-third of philosophy professors are theists, with most being orthodox Christians.'[107] Smith laments that 'Academia has now lost its mainstream secularisation . . . If naturalism is the true world-view and a "Dark Age" means an age when the vast majority of philosophers (and scientists) do not know the true world-view, then we have to admit that we are living in a Dark Age.'[108]

The 2005 World Congress of the International Academy of Humanism took as their theme 'Towards a New Enlightenment', stating 'we are facing a new dark ages.' Scientist-turned-theologian Alister McGrath calls this 'a fascinating glimpse of the crisis of confidence . . . gripping atheism at the moment.'[109] Whether it bespeaks a new dark age or a new enlightenment, increasing numbers of philosophers and scientists are certainly deploying 'a tough-minded intellectualism in defence of . . . theism.'[110] As J.P. Moreland notes, 'there has been a noticeable increase in the number of intellectuals who embrace historic Christianity as a rational worldview.'[111] Roy Abraham Varghese talks of a 'resurgence of rational theism in science and philosophy . . .'[112] Indeed, as another scientist-turned-theologian, John Polkinghorne, comments, 'we are living today in a . . . period of intense activity in natural theology . . . The revival that has taken place has been more at the hands of the scientists than of the theologians.'[113]

While the theory of evolution has been thought by some to undermine belief in God (and has been both promoted and opposed on such ideological grounds), the scientific discovery of a cosmic beginning in the 'big bang' has replaced the ancient Greek idea of an eternal universe and confirmed theist's belief in a cosmic beginning. Astrophysicist Robert Jastrow writes that, for non-believing scientists 'the story ends like a bad dream';[114] for, having scaled the mountains of ignorance, 'he is greeted by a band of theologians who have been sitting there for centuries.'[115] Cosmologists have also discovered that life depends upon a 'finely-tuned' set of physical laws, a 'just right' combination many interpret as evidence that our universe was designed for life. Hence, as Michael J. Wilkins and J.P. Moreland observe, 'A significant and growing number of scientists, historians of science, and philosophers of science see more scientific evidence now for a personal creator and designer than was available fifty years ago.'[116]

Moreover, as John G. West reports, while theists have long noted legitimate interpretations of the Bible that don't conflict with evolution:[117]

> a growing number of scientists and philosophers of science have voiced scepticism of key parts of neo-Darwinian, including its central claim that natural selection and random mutation are sufficient to explain the intricate and highly-functional complexity we see throughout the natural world. Some of these scholars are proponents of what is known as 'intelligent design,' which proposes that 'certain features of the universe and of living things are best explained by an intelligent cause, not an undirected process such as natural selection.' [However] These criticisms made of neo-Darwinism extend well beyond [those] who subscribe to intelligent design.[118]

For example, in an article entitled 'Why Pigs Don't Have Wings', published in October 2007, leading atheist philosopher of mind Jerry Fodor criticised evolutionary psychology *and its underlying adaptationist assumptions*, noting:

> an appreciable number of perfectly reasonable biologists are coming to think that the theory of natural selection can no longer be taken for granted . . . Shake a stick at a Darwinist treatise and you're sure to find, usually in the first chapter, claims for the indispensability of adaptationism. Well, if adaptationism really is the only game in town, if the rest of biology really does presuppose it, we had better cleave to it warts and all. What is indispensable therefore cannot be dispensed with, as Wittgenstein might have said. The breaking news, however, is that serious alternatives to adaptationism have begun to emerge; ones that preserve the essential claim that phenotypes evolve, but depart to one degree or other from Darwin's theory that natural selection is the mechanism by which they do. There is now far more of this sort of thing around than I am able to survey . . . the classical Darwinist account of evolution as primarily driven by natural selection is in trouble on both conceptual and empirical grounds.[119]

In sum, the naturalistic-atheistic worldview has never been in such a precarious intellectual position. 'Many philosophers are today talking about the collapse of modern atheism', writes Terry L. Miethe, 'not necessarily that there are less atheists, but that there is less reason for being one . . . because of the philosophical, scientific, and ethical evidence for the existence of God.'[120] McGrath is right to observe that 'Atheism remains an important challenge to faith throughout the Western world . . .',[121] but he is also correct in continuing into the observation that 'many of its critics believe that the movement has lost its way and that its intellectual credentials and cultural appeal have dwindled in recent years.'[122] As Ralph McInerny notes, on the one hand, 'It's very rare that someone thinks he can really refute theism. So what you get are arguments against it but no one thinks of them as conclusive.'[123] William C. Davies likewise reports that 'Critics of theism (at least among philosophers) have all but given up thinking that God's existence can be disproved.'[124] On the other

hand, 'There are very many, and generally well-received, philosophical attempts to show the reasonableness of theism . . .'[125] As
James F. Sennett and Douglas Groothuis confirm, 'Natural theology is alive and well in contemporary philosophy.'[126] Hence
Norman L. Geisler writes of 'a *collapse* of the *intellectual grounds*
for holding an *athei*st position',[127] while Paul Copan and Paul K.
Moser report that theism 'flourishes and multiplies in the academic world.'[128]

A Change of Mind for Antony Flew

'it may well be that no one is as surprised as I am that my
exploration of the Divine has after all these years turned from
denial to discovery.'
– Antony Flew[129]

As Roy Abraham Varghese explains, 'within the last hundred
years, no mainstream philosopher has developed the kind of systematic, comprehensive, original, and influential exposition of
atheism that is to be found in Antony Flew's fifty years of atheological writings.'[130] It was thus a symbolic high water mark for the
intellectual resurrection of theism when Flew, 'an icon and champion for unbelievers for decades,' a scholar dubbed 'the world's
most influential philosophical atheist,'[132] announced in January
2004 that he had come to believe in a God because 'the case for an
Aristotelian God who has the characteristics of power and also
intelligence, is now much stronger than it ever was before.'[133] If
his newfound belief in a minimal form of theism upset people,
well 'that's too bad', said Flew. 'My whole life has been guided
by the principle of Plato's Socrates: Follow the evidence, wherever it leads.'[134] As Craig J. Hazen wrote, Flew's defection was big
news 'not only about his personal journey, but also about the persuasive power of the arguments modern theists have been using
to challenge atheistic naturalism.'[135] Jay W. Richards captures
something of the earth-shattering nature of Flew's change of
mind.

> For over fifty years the British philosopher Antony Flew was the
> English-speaking world's most intellectually serious public athe-
> ist. He first engaged Christian apologist C.S. Lewis at Oxford in

1950 and continued to pursue scholarly defences of atheism for over five decades. His basic argument was always the same: there just wasn't enough evidence to believe in God. Then, at age eighty-one, he changed his mind.[136]

Why did Flew change his mind? Flew explains his reasons at length in his 'last will and testament',[137] written with the help of Roy Abraham Varghese: *There Is a God* (Harper One, 2007). Unfortunately, prominent atheists (including Richard Dawkins and Roy Hattersley) responded to Flew's apostasy with *ad hominem*[138] assertions about his losing his marbles in his dotage,[139] or about his hedging his bets with respect to the afterlife. In *There Is A God*, Flew comments:

> When reports of my change of mind were spread by the media . . . some commentators were quick to claim that my advanced age had something to do with my 'conversion.' It has been said that fear concentrates the mind powerfully, and these critics had concluded that expectations of an impending entrance into the afterlife had triggered a deathbed conversion. Clearly these people were familiar with neither my writings on the non-existence of an afterlife nor with my current views on the topic . . . I do not think of myself 'surviving' death. For the record, then, I want to lay to rest all those rumours that have me placing Pascalian bets.[140]

Harper One deputy publisher Mark Tauber complained that a *New York Times Magazine* feature by Mark Oppenheimer 'generalized from Flew's aphasia to senility – which is far from accurate.'[141] Oppenheimer suggested that Varghese had (unwittingly) railroaded the aging Flew into expressing opinions that were not his own. Flew responded with a press release saying:

> My name is on the book and it represents exactly my opinions. I would not have a book issued in my name that I do not 100 percent agree with. I needed someone to do the actual writing because I'm 84 and that was Roy Varghese's role. The idea that someone manipulated me because I'm old is exactly wrong. I may be old but it is hard to manipulate me. This is my book and it represents my thinking.[142]

As Varghese wrote to the *New York Times Magazine*, 'the substantive portions of the book came from a combination of Tony's published and unpublished writings . . . as well as extensive correspondence and numerous interviews with him . . . The cute sub-titles and the enchanting anecdotes, I'm afraid, did not originate with Tony although he OKed them . . . Tony edited, corrected and approved at least ten versions of the manuscript.'[143] Tauber confirms that 'Varghese took Tony's thoughts and put them in publishable form. This is not an unusual practice.'[144]

On 12 March 2008 Flew (now aged 85) participated in a panel discussion on *There Is A God* with philosopher Gary R. Habermas and New Testament scholar N.T. Wright, at a conference held in Westminster Chapel. As an audience member I can attest that, while Flew did display a tendency to forget names, and to drift off subject when answering questions, he clearly did still know his stuff, and his own mind. Under what might be considered some quite leading questions, Flew refused to go further than acknowledging his openness to the *possibility* of Jesus' resurrection. He also told the (mainly Christian) audience in no uncertain terms that he thought life after death was impossible.

In a perfectly lucid interview just prior to the publication of *There is a God*, Flew explained his defection from atheism in his own words:

> With every passing year, the more that was discovered about the richness and inherent intelligence of life, the less it seemed likely that a chemical soup could magically generate the genetic code. The difference between life and non-life, it became apparent to me, was ontological and not chemical. The best confirmation of this radical gulf is Richard Dawkins' comical effort to argue in *The God Delusion* that the origin of life can be attributed to a 'lucky chance.' If that's the best argument you have, then the game is over . . . I would add that Dawkins is selective to the point of dishonesty when he cites the views of scientists on the philosophical implications of the scientific data.
>
> Two noted philosophers, one an agnostic (Anthony Kenny) and the other an atheist ([Thomas] Nagel), recently pointed out that Dawkins has failed to address three major issues that ground the rational case for God. As it happens, these are the very same

issues that had driven me to accept the existence of a God: the laws of nature, life with its teleological organization and the existence of the Universe.[145]

Conclusion

Whatever the cause, 'there's more interest in religion generally now than there was say 20 to 30 years ago in the Western world',[146] and the percentage of atheists worldwide has declined. As McGrath observes:

> The term 'postatheist' is now widely used to designate the collapse of atheism as a worldview in Eastern Europe and the resurgence of religious belief throughout many of those areas that had once been considered officially atheist. Yet it is now clear postatheism is not limited to the East; it is becoming a recognizable presence within Western culture. Atheism, once seen as Western culture's hot date with the future, is now seen as an embarrassing link with a largely discredited past.[147]

Michael Shermer muses, 'At the beginning of the twentieth century social scientists predicted that belief in God would decrease by the end of the century because of the secularization of society. In fact . . . the opposite has occurred . . . Not only is God not dead, as Nietzsche proclaimed, but he has never been more alive.'[148] A 2005 survey by *Free Inquiry* found that the marginalization of secularism was more pronounced in America than in Europe, and presciently concluded: 'the culture war for which battle lines are now being drawn may forge a new landscape for religion in American public life.'[149] Atheist philosopher Michael Martin's response to the survey anticipated 'that secularism will be on the defensive and even in a decline.'[150] Yet Martin held out the hope that this 'decline might well give birth to a resurgence of secularism', while warning that 'without continued effort on the part of dedicated secularists, this resurgence will not occur.'[151] Martin's hopes were about to be fulfilled . . .

Recommended Resources

William P. Alston, 'Religious Language and Verificationism', in Paul Copan and Paul K. Moser (eds.), *The Rationality of Theism* (London: Routledge, 2003).

James Kelly Clark (ed.), *Philosophers Who Believe: The Spiritual Journeys of 11 Leading Thinkers* (Downers Grove: IVP, 1993).

William Lane Craig and J.P. Moreland (eds.), *Naturalism: A Critical Analysis* (London: Routledge, 2001).

Antony Flew with Roy Abraham Varghese, *There is a God: How the World's Most Notorious Atheist Changed His Mind* (London: Harper Collins, 2007).

Alister McGrath, *The Twilight of Atheism: The Rise and Fall of Disbelief in the Modern World* (London: Rider, 2004).

Thomas V. Morris (ed.), *God and The Philosophers: The Reconciliation of Faith and Reason* (Oxford: Oxford University Press, 1994).

Roy Abraham Varghese (ed.), *The Intellectuals Speak Out about God* (Washington, DC: Regnery Gateway, 1984).

Online Papers

A.J. Ayer: Language, Truth, Logic and God (an excerpt from *Language, Truth and Logic*), www.stephenjaygould.org/ctrl/ayer_metaphysics.html.

Michael D. Beaty, 'God Among the Philosophers', www.religion-online.org/showarticle.asp?title=53.

James A. Beverly, 'Thinking Straighter: Why the world's most famous atheist now believes in God', www.christianity today .com/ct/2005/april/29.80.html.

William Cash. 'Did atheist philosopher see God when he "died"?', http://neardeath.home.comcast.net/religion/001_pages/02.html.

Paul Copan, 'God can't possibly exist given the evil and pain I see in the world!', www.bethinking.org/resource.php?ID=30&TopicID=3&CategoryID=3.

Kelly James Clark, foreword to *Philosophers Who Believe*, www.calvin.edu/academic/philosophy/writings/pwbintro.htm.

William Lane Craig, 'The Resurrection of Theism', www.leaderu .com/truth/3truth01.html.

William Lane Craig, 'The Problem of Evil', www.bethinking.org/resource.php?ID=60&TopicID=3&CategoryID=3.

William Lane Craig, 'God is Not Dead Yet,' www.christianitytoday.com/ct/2008/july/13.22.html.

Gary R. Habermas and Antony Flew, 'My Pilgrimage from Atheism to Theism: An Exclusive Interview with Former British Atheist Professor Antony Flew', www.biola.edu/antonyflew/flew-inter-view.pdf.

Antony Flew, 'Flew Speaks Out', www.bethinking.org/science-christianity/intermediate/flew-speaks-out-professor-antony-flew-reviews-the-god-delusion.htm.

Douglas Groothuis, 'The Great Debate', www.christianitytoday.com/bc/2008/004/12.39.html.

Gary R. Habermas, 'Antony Flew's Deism Revisited', www.epsociety.org/ library/articles.asp?pid=28.

Daniel Hill, 'What's New in Philosophy of Religion?', www.philosophynow.org/archive/articles/21hill.htm.

Alvin Plantinga, 'Spiritual Autobiography', www.calvin.edu/125th/wolterst/p_bio.pdf.

Quentin Smith, 'The Metaphilosophy of Naturalism', www.philoonline.org/library/smith_4_2.htm.

Benjamin Wiker, 'Exclusive Flew Interview', www.tothesource.org/10_30_2007/10_30_2007.htm.

Peter S. Williams, 'A Change of Mind for Antony Flew', www.arn.org/docs/williams/pw_antonyflew.htm.

Peter S. Williams, 'The Definitional Critique of Intelligent Design Theory – Lessons from the Demise of Logical Positivism', www.arn.org/docs/williams/pw_definitionalcritique.htm.

Peter S. Williams, 'Design and the Humean Touchstone', www.arn.org/docs/williams/pw_humeantouchstone.htm.

Peter S. Williams, 'Flew's Trenchant Response to The God Delusion', www.epsociety.org/blog/2008/07/antony-flews-trenchant-response-to.asp.

Audio

William Lane Craig, 'Furor Over Flew's *There Is A God*', www.reasonablefaith.org/site/News2?page=NewsArticle&id=5887.

William Lane Craig, 'Philosophy 01', www.rfmedia.org/RF_audio_video/RF_podcast/Philosophy_01.mp3.

William Lane Craig, 'Philosophy 02', www.rfmedia.org/RF_audio_video/RF_podcast/Philosophy_02.mp3.

William Lane Craig, 'Philosophy 03', www.rfmedia.org/RF_audio_video/RF_podcast/Philosophy_03.mp3.

William Lane Craig, 'Philosophy 04', www.rfmedia.org/RF_audio_video/RF_podcast/Philosophy_04.mp3.

William Lane Craig, 'Philosophy 05', www.rfmedia.org/RF_audio_video/RF_podcast/Philosophy_05.mp3.

Gannon Murphy, 'God and the Problem of Evil', http://maclaurin.org/mp3s/maclaurin_institute__copyright_20036.mp3.

Video

Douglas Geivett, 'Problems of Evil', http://hisdefense.org/LinkClick.aspx?link=http%3a%2f%2fhisdefense.org%2fvideo%2fGeivett+-+Problems+of+Evil.WMV&tabid=136&mid=954.

2

Long Live the New Atheism?

*'Never more than today has there been such evidence of vitality in
. . . the return to religious thinking, proof that God is not dead but
that he was merely and briefly dozing . . . The trend has escalated to
such an extent that we are now obliged to take up old defensive
positions.'*
– Michel Onfray[1]

As we saw in the previous chapter, theism has made impressive
advances since the mid-twentieth century. However, one would
hardly expect atheists to take this state of affairs lying down. As
Alister McGrath writes, 'Until recently, Western atheism had
waited patiently, believing that belief in God would simply die
out. But now, a whiff of panic is evident. Far from dying out,
belief in God has rebounded . . .'[2] Moreover, as Gavin Hyman
comments:

> although modernity has undoubtedly witnessed a turn from tra-
> dition-based religious commitment, this has not resulted in the
> widespread atheism that many had previously predicted. In fact,
> outright atheism remains a minority confession, and the modern
> Western world has witnessed the proliferation of alternative 'spir-
> itualities' of various kinds. Many, it seems, are dissatisfied with
> atheism as the 'final truth' of the human condition.[3]

The tone of the contemporary debate about theism clearly reflects
not only global events such as the 'War on Terror', but also 'the
extent to which American atheists have felt themselves beleagu-
rard.'[4] It is saddening to discover that 'A survey undertaken by

researchers at the University of Minnesota in 2006 identified atheists as America's most distrusted minority. . . '[5] Or to find the *American Sociological Review* reporting in 2006 that it is generally thought socially acceptable in America to say you are intolerant of atheists.[6] The status of American atheists as a 'distrusted minority' is understandably fertile ground for a range of more or less 'militant' attempts to assert an atheist identity within society. I have every sympathy with Daniel Dennett's plea that 'Whatever your theology, you can firmly object when you hear family or friends sneer at atheists or agnostics or other godless folk.'[7] Likewise, I stand shoulder to shoulder with Richard Dawkins in being appalled at the attitude displayed by many who profess the name of Christ. It is shameful that Dawkins can quote American writer Ann Coulter saying, 'I defy any of my co-religionists to tell me they do not laugh at the idea of Dawkins burning in hell.'[8] I for one do *not* laugh at the idea of Dawkins burning in hell (not that I think hell involves literal burning, and not that I'd presume to forecast Dawkins' eternal destination). Coulter should consider the following scriptures: James 3:9–10, 1 Peter 3:15–16 and Luke 5:27–36. Dawkins ends the first chapter of *The God Delusion* with a pledge: 'I shall not go out of my way to offend, but nor shall I don kid gloves to handle religion more gently that I would handle anything else.'[9] Critics should extend Dawkins *et al.* a comparable courtesy.

'We're Bright'

> *'efforts among atheists to promote fellowship by calling one another bright have not, it must be said, proven a great success. . . '*
> – David Berlinski[10]

In a July 2003 *New York Times* article entitled 'The Bright Stuff', Daniel Dennett wrote:

> The time has come for us brights to come out of the closet. . . A bright is a person with a naturalist as opposed to a supernaturalist world view . . . The term 'bright' is a recent coinage by two brights in Sacramento, Calif., who thought our social group – which has a history stretching back to the Enlightenment, if not

before – could stand an image-buffing and that a fresh name might help. Don't confuse the noun with the adjective: 'I'm a bright' is not a boast but a proud avowal of an inquisitive worldview.[11]

Naturalists are too diverse for inclusion into 'our social group'. The coinage of 'bright' is an attempt to give naturalists a measure of political unity and as such it underlines the lack of unity it seeks to address. 'Most brights don't play the "aggressive atheist" role', laments Dennett.

> We don't want to turn every conversation into a debate about religion, and we don't want to offend our friends and neighbors, and so we maintain a diplomatic silence. But the price is political impotence . . . If you're a bright, what can you do? First, you can be a powerful force in American political life if we simply identify ourselves.[12]

Dennett tries to use the supposedly all-encompassing terminology of 'brights' to politicize naturalists, but this attempt to unify highlights the difference between politicized, 'aggressive' and other, 'non-aggressive' atheists. Even atheists who *are* 'aggressive' don't necessarily welcome the 'bright' initiative. Christopher Hitchens notes that his own 'annoyance at Professor Dawkins and Daniel Dennett, for their cringe-making proposal that atheists should conceitedly nominate themselves to be called "brights," is part of a contentious argument.'[13]

One cannot fail to notice the specifically *American* context of this 'bright' political manoeuvre. 'In some parts of the US it takes courage to come out as an atheist,' writes atheist philosopher Richard Norman, 'But let's be honest – in Britain today, for most of us, it's a doddle.'[14] Conversely, as Rod Liddle reports:

> Asked about his faith during the BBC documentary *The Blair Years*, the former Prime Minister said this: 'You talk about it in our system and frankly people do think you're a nutter.' And he added that British voters imagined that leaders who were informed by religion 'would commune with the Man Upstairs and then come back and say I've been told the answer, and that's it.' The public wouldn't like that.[15]

Theologian Tina Beattie compares the role of religion in American and British politics, writing:

> Whereas a confession of atheism might still damage those seeking office in American public life, British politicians are viewed with suspicion if they give the impression of allowing their personal religious beliefs to inform their political decisions. Tony Blair was the most overtly Christian prime minister in modern times, but his then press secretary, Alistair Campbell, sought to deflect any reference to Blair's religion when he told a television interviewer, 'We don't do God.' . . . attempts by British atheists such as Dawkins to portray themselves as daring radicals in their embrace of atheism are a little far fetched. Atheism in Britain simply does not create the kind of controversy that it does in America.[16]

Dennett's rhetoric is vulnerable to the suspicion that he is attempting to restrict inquisitiveness to the 'bright' worldview (casting believers as unthinking tradition-followers); which undermines his protest about 'bright' being a noun. Dawkins makes the same protest:

> The noun bright was coined in March by Paul Geisert and Mynga Furtrell of Sacramento, California. In April, I heard them give a presentation on the new word in Florida, and they launched The-Brights.net soon after. The new meme was almost immediately given a boost by two enthusiastic articles in large-circulation newspapers. On June 21, I wrote 'The future looks bright' for *The Guardian* . . . And on July 12, the distinguished philosopher Daniel Dennett followed up with 'The bright stuff' for *The New York Times* op-ed page. So, the bright meme is launched. Will it spread . . . Or will it nose-dive into the sand? I'm hoping it will take of. . . despite the hostility of those who misunderstand the humble noun as an arrogant adjective.[17]

The very fact that Dennett and Dawkins have to make this point, about 'bright' being a 'humble noun', doesn't bode well for the long-term prospects of the brand.

Journalist Matt Purple's report on the 2007 'Crystal Clear Atheism' conference in Northern Virginia simultaneously underlines the failure of the 'bright' initiative to bring political unity to naturalists and undermines the claim that 'bright' is a 'humble noun'.

> Luminaries who spoke at the conference . . . included Oxford professor Richard Dawkins, author Sam Harris and journalist Christopher Hitchen . . . the convention . . . brought into focus a divide among atheists as to their identity as a movement and the nature of the enemy they faced . . . Dawkins portrayed a black-and-white intellectual battle between atheism and religion. He denounced the 'proposterous nonsense of religious customs' and compared religion to racists . . . By contrast, Harris's speech was a more tempered critique of the atheist movement itself. While Harris said he believes science must ultimately destroy religion, he also discussed spirituality and mysticism and called for a greater understanding of allegedly spiritual phenomena . . . While the audience gave Dawkins a standing ovation, Harris received only polite applause . . . Atheists are still a small minority in America . . . But they are a proudly elitist and self-certain minority. When asked what the main difference between believers and atheists was, Dawkins had a quick answer: 'Well, we're bright.'[18]

Do I detect an adjective?

Seditious Sam

Sam Harris' speech at the 2007 'Crystal Clear Atheism' conference[19] caused a rumpus among his fellow atheists because he advocated abandoning, not only the 'bright' brand, but the use of any and all terms (most especially 'atheist') that identify the worldview of those who dissent from all supernatural beliefs:

> In accepting a label, particularly the label of 'atheist,' it seems to me that we are consenting to be viewed as a cranky sub-culture . . . as a matter of strategy, we have walked into a trap . . . this whole notion of the 'new atheists' . . . has been used to keep our criticism of religion at arm's length, and has allowed people to dismiss our arguments without meeting the burden of actually answering them

. . . So, let me make my somewhat seditious proposal explicit: We should not call ourselves 'atheists.' We should not call ourselves 'secularists.' We should not call ourselves 'humanists,' or 'secular humanists,' or 'naturalists,' or 'sceptics,' or 'anti-theists,' or 'rationalists,' or 'freethinkers,' or 'brights.' We should not call ourselves anything. We should go under the radar – for the rest of our lives. And while there, we should be decent, responsible people who destroy bad ideas wherever we find them.[20]

Harris argued for a self-critical advocacy of 'reason' and 'intellectual honesty' that is opposed to religion in general *without ever explicitly opposing religion in general*, and which is against theism in particular *without ever admitting to being atheistic*.

We should do nothing more than advocate reason and intellectual honesty – and where this advocacy causes us to collide with religion, as it inevitably will, we should observe that the points of impact are always with specific religious beliefs – not with religion in general. There is no religion in general . . . the concept of atheism imposes upon us a false burden of remaining fixated on people's beliefs about God and remaining even-handed in our treatment of religion. But we shouldn't be fixated, and we shouldn't be even-handed . . . Christians often complain that atheists . . . balance every criticism of Muslim extremism with a mention of Christian extremism. The usual approach is to say that they have their jihadists, and we have people who kill abortion doctors. Our Christian neighbours . . . are right to be outraged by this pretence of even-handedness, because the truth is that Islam is quite a bit scarier and more culpable for needless human misery than Christianity has been for a very, very long time . . . I'm still the kind of person who writes articles with rather sweeping titles like 'Science must destroy religion' – but it seems to me that we should never lose sight of useful and important distinctions . . .[21]

Harris asked his audience to

consider what would happen if we simply used words like 'reason' and 'evidence.' . . . there are very few people, even among religious fundamentalists, who will happily admit to being enemies of reason. In fact, fundamentalists tend to think they are champions of reason and that they have very good reasons for believing in God. Nobody wants to believe things on bad evidence. The desire to know what is actually going on in the world is very difficult to argue with. In so far as we represent that desire, we become difficult to argue with. And this desire is not reducible to an interest group. It's not a club or an affiliation, and I think trying to make it one diminishes its power . . . It seems to me that intellectual honesty is now, and will always be, deeper and more durable, and more easily spread, than 'atheism.'[22]

Since the desire to champion reason 'is not reducible to an interest group', and thus does nothing to distinguish oneself from even religious fundamentalists (who 'think they are champions of reason and that they have very good reasons for believing in God'), it consequently does nothing to identify on which side of the worldview divide between naturalism and supernaturalism one stands. While Harris isn't denying that he stands on the naturalistic side, his fellow atheists don't merely want to make piecemeal attacks on specific supernatural beliefs, they want to advocate a *naturalistic* worldview. Ellen Johnson, President of American Atheists, responded:

Harris cannot see why we need a name for a group of people who are 'against' something, or who don't believe in something. Take racism he says. There isn't any term for people who are against racism. We give ourselves a name because we are proud of who we are. A group needs to be identified in some way. And we want to be a 'group.' We aren't just against something. We *are* something . . . Is Greenpeace a negative organization because they are against pollution? Sounds silly doesn't it? Yet we buy into this nonsense when it is said about us . . . While we remain hung up on arguments over defining ourselves the extremist right wing Theists in America are defining the socio-political agenda for America . . . Trying to distance ourselves from our Atheism is not the answer . . . To say we should not have a name is to not exist. For far too long there have been words in our society that were considered taboo. If you didn't say them, those things didn't exist. We cannot allow ourselves to be made invisible . . . American Atheists will never back down on wearing our name proudly . . . I invite Atheists to stand proud and use the name Atheist proudly . . .[23]

In an article (perhaps ironically) entitled 'Response to my Fellow Atheists', Harris complains that 'there is something cult-like about the culture of atheism. In fact, much of the criticism I have received of my speech is so utterly lacking in content that I can only interpret it as a product of offended atheist piety.'[24] He also re-affirms his 'under the radar' tactic:

Imagine President Bush announcing his veto of federal funding for embryonic stem-cell research . . . A reporte . . . can ask one of the following questions. Which would you choose to best strike a blow against religious ignorance in this country? *1. Mr. President, what rational basis is there to worry about the fate of three-day-old human embryos? These embryos do not have nerve cells, much less the nervous systems they would need to suffer their destruction on any level* . . . *2. Mr. President, as an atheist, let me ask what rational basis is there to worry about the fate of three-day-old human embryos? These embryos don't have nerve cells, much less the nervous systems they would need to suffer their destruction on any level* . . . Which question would you like to see asked on the evening news? To my mind, (1) is clearly better than (2). *Much* better. And yet, many atheists are behaving as though they prefer (2). They seem to believe that our goal, as advocates of reason, will be best served by our using the term 'atheist' without concern for its associations, thereby removing its stigma. They believe that announcing ourselves as a constituency in increasingly visible ways is the best strategy for success. Well, all I can say is that question (1) would probably have the support of 200 million Americans *today*. Question (2), while virtually identical in content, would likely alienate 180 million of these people . . . So pick your strategy.[25]

While assiduously failing to mention one's atheism may have benefits in some situations, Harris' tactic leaves his 'fellow atheists' empty-handed when it comes to discussing broader worldview issues. Being reserved about one's atheism for tactical reasons in *certain* circumstances isn't at all the same thing as foregoing any factual description of one's metaphysical views in *all* circumstances! Atheists can acknowledge the wisdom of the former suggestion (just as Christians debating public policy may leave aside arguments based upon revelation in favour of arguments based upon mutually accepted data) without thinking that the latter is a good idea (anymore than Christians think it acceptable to reject revelation). Moreover, to suggest that atheists hide their atheism as a mater of policy seems intellectually dishonest. This is not the way for atheists to improve their public image.

The 'New Atheists'

'There are two kinds of atheists, ordinary atheists who do not believe in God and passionate atheists who consider God to be their personal enemy.'
– Freeman Dyson[26]

The attempt to re-brand atheists as 'brights' was premature at best, and lives on mainly due to the life-support efforts of Dawkins and Dennett. Harris' attempt to marshal a naturalism that dare not speak its name appears still-born. Meanwhile, by focusing on substantive metaphysical, ethical and political issues, the secular resurgence hoped for by atheist philosopher Michael Martin blossomed in 2006–2007 with the publication of several high profile books by atheists addressed to the general public, including Dennett's *Breaking the Spell: Religion as a Natural Phenomenon*, Harris' *Letter to a Christian Nation* and Dawkins' *The God Delusion*. These dedicated secularists, and those following in their wake (e.g. Hitchens,[27] Grayling), seem determined to revitalize the stereotypical confrontation of 'science vs. religion' – stereotypical because it depends upon the false assertion that, as naturalist Tom Clark writes, 'The root conflict is rather between science and *faith*, two different ways of justifying beliefs about the world which lead to naturalism and supernaturalism, respectively.'[28]

Most fundamentally, as Albert Mohler observes, 'It is not so much that Dawkins is attempting to convince believers that they should no longer believe in God . . . Dawkins is attempting a very different cultural and political move. He wants to make *respect for* belief in God socially unacceptable.'[29] (Of course, it's hard to do the latter without doing the former.) Dawkins is the unofficial figure-head of this secular resurgence, and John Cornwell describes the socio-political dimension of his agenda well:

> Dawkins . . . has called upon the faithless, the waverers, and even firm religious believers to follow him into radical atheism not merely as a private conviction but as a public confession. Religion, he insists, is the principle source of the world's evil . . . At the same time he seeks a more just world for atheists. They must 'come out', he insists; profess courageously their convictions, or lack of them. Just as women, blacks, gays, and lesbians have demanded their human rights, he asks that atheists stand up and be counted. His slogan: 'Atheist Pride!'[30]

Like Dawkins, I'd rather live in a society where atheists felt that publicly confessing their atheism wasn't courageous. After all, a pre-requisite of debate on any subject is knowing what the other person thinks! However, it seems to me that Dawkins and I, as residents of the British Isles, already live in a society where this is the case. Indeed, if anything, it is the public profession of theism that raises eyebrows where we come from. So Dawkins has a point, but one that is somewhat overplayed.

While generally welcomed by atheists,[31] the 'New Atheist' approach (whether or not it owns the 'atheist' label) is nevertheless highly controversial.

> The growing militancy and stridency of recent atheist writers has been noted with interest by cultural commentators, and with concern by those who believe that its overstatements and serious misrepresentations of religion are compromising its intellectual credibility. This development is widely interpreted to point to the increasing defensiveness of the movement, especially in the face of the growing public influence and credibility of religion.[32]

As Michael Ruse complains, 'Since the turn of the millennium, a new militancy has arisen among religious sceptics . . . Whenever religious beliefs conflict with scientific facts or violate principles of political liberty, we must respond with appropriate aplomb. Nevertheless, we should be cautious about irrational exuberance.'[33] The in-house debate about whether or not to be 'aggressive' atheists – as opposed to the debate about *how best to be aggressive* (to re-brand with the 'brights', or not to re-brand; or to 'de-brand' with Harris?) – led atheist C.L. Hanson to draw the tongue-in-cheek distinction between 'mean' and 'nice' atheists.

> Mean atheists think that religion is ninety-nine parts pure stupidity mixed with one part lying, opportunistic con artists. And they want to tell that to religious people whenever they're asked to 'respect' someone's faith. The nice atheists, by contrast, believe that religion is more complicated than the stupidity-plus-con-artists model and/or that we should at least make an effort to get along with religious people. The fight between the two groups is this: When the mean atheists and the nice atheists get together, it's not so much that it annoys the mean atheists to be asked to play nice. It's more that they just want to be able to call the nice atheists names . . .[34]

Beyond Belief

> *'the world needs to wake up from its long nightmare of religious belief.'*
> – Steven Weinberg[35]

On 5 November 2006, what amounted to the first New Atheist conference, 'Beyond Belief: Science, Religion, Reason and Survival', was held at the Salk Institute for Biological Studies in California (with Dawkins, Dennett and Harris attending).[36] The spirit of New Atheism was encapsulated by the meeting's opening address, in which Nobel laureate Steven Weinberg offered the exultation that 'Anything that we scientists can do to weaken the hold of religion should be done and may in the end be our greatest contribution to civilization.'[37] According to the event's brochure:

> Just 40 years after a famous *Time* magazine cover asked 'Is God Dead?' the answer appears to be a resounding 'No!' According to a survey by the Pew Forum on Religion & Public Life in a recent issue of *Foreign Policy* magazine, 'God is Winning'. Religions are

increasingly a geopolitical force to be reckoned with. Fundamentalist movements – some violent in the extreme – are growing. Science and religion are at odds in the classrooms and courtrooms. And a return to religious values is widely touted as an antidote to the alleged decline in public morality. After two centuries, could this be twilight for the Enlightenment project and the beginning of a new age of unreason?[38]

This gathering addressed three questions: 'Should science do away with religion?', 'What would science put in religion's place?' and 'Can we be good without God?' The consensus view was naturally that science (narrowly defined as naturalistic explanations of natural phenomena) should do away with religion (defined in terms of a 'blind faith' unrecognizable to Christian orthodoxy), that science should replace religion (with science), and that we can be good without God (because of evolutionary group dynamics). In other words, as *New Scientist* put it, 'science can take on religion and win.'[39]

Commenting on the 'Beyond Belief' conference, anthropologist Melvin J. Konner lamented that 'With a few notable exceptions, the viewpoints have run the gamut from A to B. Should we bash religion with a crowbar or only with a baseball bat?'[40] Dawkins' 'take-no-prisoners approach (religious education is "brainwashing" and "child abuse") was condemned by . . . Konner, who said he had "not a flicker" of religious faith, as simplistic and uninformed.'[41] Konner castigated Harris and Dawkins: 'I think that you and Richard are remarkably apt mirror images of the extremists on the other side, and that you generate more fear and hatred of science.'[42] Neil deGrasse Tyson, director of the Hayden Planetarium, advocated a civil approach:

> Persuasion isn't always 'Here are the facts – you're an idiot or you are not,' he said. 'I worry that your methods' – he turned toward Dr. Dawkins – 'how articulately barbed you can be, end up simply being ineffective, when you have much more power of influence.' Dawkins replied that he 'gratefully accepted' the rebuke.[43]

As anthropologist Scott Atran complained, 'The arguments being put forward here are extraordinarily blind and simplistic . . . I just don't think scientists, when they step out of science, have any better insight than the ordinary schmuck on the street. It makes me embarrassed to be an atheist.'[44]

Enlightenment 2.0
Reporting on the 2007 'Beyond Belief' conference for *New Scientist*, Michael Reilly wrote that:

> one thing is clear: the edifice of 'new atheism' is burning. The first firebrand is lobbed into the audience by Edward Slingerland, an expert on ancient Chinese thought and human cognition at the University of British Columbia in Vancouver, Canada. 'Religion is not going away,' he announced. Even those of us who fancy our-selves rationalists and scientists, he said, rely on moral values – a set of distinctly unscientific beliefs. Where, for instance, does our conviction that human rights are universal come from? 'Humans' rights to me are as mysterious as the holy trinity,' he told the audi-ence at the Salk Institute for Biological Studies. 'You can't . . . cut someone open and show us their human rights,' he pointed out. 'It's not an empirical thing . . . It's a purely metaphysical entity.' This is a far cry from the first 'Beyond Belief' symposium a year ago, at which many militant non-believers . . . came together to hammer home the virtues of atheism . . . That gathering made much of the idea that humans can be moral without believing in God, and that science should do away with religion altogether. The mood at this follow-up conference was different . . . Even the title of this year's meeting, 'Beyond Belief II: Enlightenment 2.0', suggested the need for revision, reform and a little more toler-ance.[45]

Un-Pious Critics

'Ironically, some of the sternest critics of the New Atheists to date have been fellow atheists.'
– University of Cambridge, Investigating Atheism Website[46]

Many non-believers have distanced themselves from the antago-nistic rhetoric of the New Atheists as counter-productive, and as outstripping the substance of its intellectual foundations. Psychologist Jonathan Haidt objects that 'when I read the new atheist books, I see . . . battlefields strewn with the corpses of straw men.'[47] UCL philosopher Tim Crane writes that although he is an atheist,

> It seems to me that many of the claims made by the new atheists are simply not true, and that their view of the role of religion in world affairs is in many ways mistaken . . . going on in this way about religion is not a very sensible approach to tackling the problems of the world . . . it is surprisingly difficult . . . to change people's beliefs. But if there is one thing which should be obvious here, it is that the way to do it is (generally) not to tell them that they are stupid, irrational or hopelessly ignorant.[48]

Richard Norman complains, 'In the "religion" that Dawkins and Hitchens relentlessly attack I simply do not recognize the many good, sensitive, intelligent and sometimes wonderful religious people I know.'[49] Norman observes, 'By far the commonest criticism directed against the New Atheists is that they do over-generalize, and I think that the criticism is justified.'[50] He continues,

> The circularity of Hitchen's argument [is that] Religion poisons everything. What about the good things done in the name of religion? If they're really good, that just shows that they're not really religious. The same circular argument appears in Hitchens' discussion of the atrocities generated by secular creeds. He says of totalitarian societies that because their leaders are regarded as infallible, such states are theocracies and therefore essentially religious.[51]

Mary Ridell calls *God Is Not Great* 'an encyclical whose many qualities include no shred of tolerance or doubt'.[52] Even Daniel Dennett admits that Hitchens 'occasionally adopts a double standard'.[53] As Stephen Prothero (chair of Boston University's religion department) comments in *The Washington Post*:

> Hitchens claims that some of his best friends are believers. If so, he doesn't know much about his best friends . . . *God Is Not Great*

assumes a childish definition of religion and then criticizes religious people for believing such foolery. But it is Hitchens who is the naïf . . . the only people who believe that religion is about believing blindly in a God who blesses and curses on demand and sees science and reason as spawns of Satan are unlettered fundamentalists and their atheistic doppelgangers . . . Hitchens is a brilliant man, and there is no living journalist I more enjoy reading. But I have never encountered a book whose author is so fundamentally unacquainted with its subject. In the end, this maddeningly dogmatic book does little more than illustrate one of Hitchens's pet themes – the ability of dogma to put reason to sleep.[54]

Reviewing *Letter to a Christian Nation* for *The Telegraph*, Kenan Malik complains that Sam Harris, likewise, 'appears to take as literal a view of religion as the fundamentalists themselves'.[55] David Berlinski pays Harris the back-handed compliment that while '*Letter to a Christian Nation* is . . . devoid of any intellectual substance whatsoever, it is, at least, brisk, engaging, and short. To anyone having read Daniel Dennett's *Breaking the Spell: Religion as a Natural Phenomenon*, these will appear very considerable virtues.'[56]

Michael Shermer reveals:

I found myself wincing at Dawkins' references to religious people as 'faith-heads,' as being less intelligent, poor at reasoning, or even deluded, and to religious moderates as enablers of terrorism. I shudder because I have religious friends and colleagues who do not fit these descriptors, and I empathize at the pain such pejorative appellations cause them . . . I am not convinced by Dawkins's argument that without religion there would be 'no suicide bombers, no 9/11 [etc.]' . . . many of these events . . . were less religiously motivated than politically driven, or at the very least involved religion in the service of political hegemony.[57]

Dawkins recognizes that *The God Delusion* has received poor reviews, but puts this down to bias. 'I think that because the book has the word "God" in the title they get religious people to review it. So what do you expect?'[58] However, as Peter Steinfels writes, 'The criticism [of *The God Delusion*] is not primarily, it should be pointed out, from the pious, which would hardly be noteworthy, but from avowed atheists as well as scientists and philosophers writing in publications like *The New Republic* and *The New York Review of Books*, not known as cells in the vast God-fearing conspiracy.'[59] For example, atheist Thomas Nagel laments Dawkins' 'amateur' attempts at philosophy: 'Dawkins dismisses, with contemptuous flippancy the traditional . . . arguments for the existence of God offered by Aquinas and Anselm. I found these attempts at philosophy, along with those in a later chapter on religion and ethics, particularly weak . . . '[60] Agnostic scientist H. Allen Orr is scathing, writing:

> *The God Delusion* seems to me badly flawed. Though I once labelled Dawkins a professional atheist, I'm forced, after reading his new book, to conclude he's actually more an amateur . . . his book makes a far from convincing case. The most disappointing feature of *The God Delusion* is Dawkins's failure to engage religious thought in any serious way . . . One reason for the lack of extended argument in *The God Delusion* is clear: Dawkins doesn't seem very good at it.[61]

Orr is equally unimpressed by Dennett's *Breaking the Spell*.

> The existence of a God meme is no better established than the existence of God . . . To suppose that a kind of physics can demolish a kind of metaphysics is to commit what philosophers call a category mistake. Dennett is right to emphasize that his scientific analysis doesn't require us to prejudge religion's metaphysical claims, but that's only half the story. It doesn't let us *post*-judge them, either . . . Religious beliefs, including those abstract ones having little relation any particular tradition, may well be mistaken. But it seems clear that any such conclusion must come from someplace other than science.[62]

Adam Kirsch, writing in *The New York Sun*, agrees.

> Dennett falls prey to . . . the assumption that a human phenomenon can be fully explained by an explanation of its origins.

Drawing on recent, speculative work by evolutionary theorists, Mr. Dennett sketches a picture of how religion might have arisen as a naturally selected adaptation to the early human environment . . . But even if such Darwinian just-so stories were confirmed – and it is not immediately clear how they could be tested – it would make no difference to the fact of religious experience . . . the reality of religious experience cannot be abolished by explaining it as an adaptation to our prehistorical environment.[63]

A Rueful Response

'I think Dawkins is ignorant of just about every aspect of philosophy and theology and it shows.'
– Michael Ruse[64]

In February 2006 philosopher Michael Ruse had a notorious exchange of emails with Daniel Dennett, in which the former labelled the latter's book *Breaking the Spell* 'really bad and not worthy of you',[65] and in which he continues:

I think that you and Richard [Dawkins] are absolute disasters in the fight against intelligent design – we are losing this battle . . . what we need is not knee-jerk atheism but serious grappling with the issues – neither of you are willing to study Christianity seriously and to engage with the ideas – it is just plain silly and grotesquely immoral to claim that Christianity is simply a force for evil, as Richard claims – more than this, we are in a fight, and we need to make allies in the fight, not simply alienate everyone of good will.[65]

Astonishingly, Ruse publicly criticized Dawkins on the front cover of Alister and Joanna McGrath's book *The Dawkins Delusion*, stating *'The God Delusion* makes me embarrassed to be an atheist, and the McGraths show why.' Ruse continued the argument in an article for *Skeptical Inquirer* lamenting the fractured state of atheism in the face of 'creationism' (which, for Ruse, encompasses ID).

Those of us against creationism live in a house divided. One group is made up of the ardent, complete atheists. They want no truck with the enemy, which they are inclined to define as any person of religious inclination – from literalist (like a Southern Baptist) to deist (like a Unitarian) – and they think that anyone who thinks otherwise is foolish, wrong, and immoral. Prominent members of this group include Richard Dawkins [and] Daniel Dennett . . . The second group . . . contains those who have no religious belief but who think that one should collaborate with liberal Christians [by which Ruse means theistic evolutionists] against a shared enemy, and who are inclined to think that science and religion are compatible.[67]

Ruse acknowledged that in this debate:

The rhetoric is strong and nasty. I have accused Dennett of being a bully and someone who is pig ignorant of the issues. He has told me that I stand in danger (perhaps over the point of danger) of losing the respect of those whose respect I should crave . . . Dawkins likens me to Neville Chamberlain, the British Prime Minister who tried to appease Adolf Hitler.[68]

Ruse pragmatically replies that 'When Hitler [i.e. 'creationism'] attacked Russia [i.e. theistic evolution], England and America [atheists] gave aid to Stalin [i.e. Christians who accept evolution]. It was not that they particularly liked Stalin, but they worked on the principle that the enemy of my enemy is my friend.'[69] Ruse concluded with a plea for unity: 'Fundamentalism, creationism, intelligent design theory – these are the real threats. Please God – or non-God – let us quit fighting ourselves and get on with the real job that faces us.'[70] However, Ruse thinks it unlikely that this plea will be headed. 'The Dawkins-Dennett school allows for no compromise. Religion is false. Religion is dangerous. Religion must be fought in every way. There can be no working with the enemy. Those like me who work with religious people are like the appeasers before the Nazis. This was the message thumped out again and again at [the 2006 Beyond Belief conference].'[71]

Religion, Tolerance and the Public Square

'Tolerance is a rare and important virtue. It has its limits, but they are usually drawn too tightly and in the wrong places.'
– A.C. Grayling[72]

One of the philosophically weakest but most politically radical polemics to emerge from the New Atheist movement to date is A.C. Grayling's *Against All Gods* (Oberon Books, 2007). I agree with Grayling (Professor of Philosophy at Birbeck College, University of London) that 'all who have secure grounds for their views should not be afraid of robust challenge and criticism.'[73] Unfortunately, Grayling offers next to nothing by way of a robust engagement with the purported grounds either of religion or of his own naturalistic outlook. Of particular relevance to the debate about the New Atheism, Grayling is annoyed by

> apologists [who] charge the non-religious with being 'fundementalists' if they attack religion too robustly, without seeming to notice the irony of employing, as a term of abuse, a word which principally applies to the too-common tendencies of their own outlook. Can a view which is not a belief but a rejection of a certain kind of belief really be 'fundamentalist'? Of course not . . .[74]

However, Grayling himself points out that being non-religious, or more specifically being an 'atheist', is at best a partial description of a broader worldview: 'no atheist should call himself or herself one . . . A more appropriate term is "naturalist", denoting one who takes it that the universe is a natural realm . . .'[75] In popular usage 'atheist' is a synonym for 'naturalist', and while atheism in the strict sense may or may not be incapable of the fundamentalist qualification, naturalism ('atheism' *in its popular sense*) certainly *is* capable of the feat. Grayling seeks to prevent the 'fundamentalist' label being applied to his own position by equivocating over the meaning of 'atheism'.

Verbal manoeuvring aside, Grayling asserts, 'It is . . . time to put to rest . . . a phrase used by some religious people when talking of those who are plain-spoken about their disbelief in any religious claims: the phrase "fundamentalist atheist."'[76] The mere fact that 'fundamentalist' *qualifies* 'atheist' in this phrase should tip us off to the fact that it is *not* intended to describe those who are merely 'plain-spoken' about their atheism. However, Grayling thinks that 'fundamentalist' is necessarily a redundant qualifier where atheism is concerned, and he poses the following rhetorical question: 'What would a non-fundamentalist atheist be? Would he be someone who believed only somewhat that there are no supernatural entities in the universe . . .?'[77] Grayling's perplexity notwithstanding, the concept of an atheist with doubts seems to make at least as much sense as the concept of a 'Sunday Christian' to me. Nevertheless, a better answer to Grayling's question is that 'fundamentalist atheist' satisfies Gary Wolf's description of the New Atheists as non-believers who 'condemn not just belief in God but *respect* for belief in God'[78] and who think that 'Religion is not only wrong; it's evil.'[79] Grayling's *Against All Gods* is itself one of the most extreme salvos from the 'fundamentalist' atheist camp.

Grayling writes, 'Does Religion deserve respect? I argue that it deserves no more respect than any other viewpoint, and not as much as most . . . It is time to reverse the prevailing notion that religious commitment is intrinsically deserving of respect, and that it should be handled with kid gloves and protected by custom and in some cases law against criticism and ridicule.'[80] I agree that it is not religious commitment *per se* that deserves respect but rather *the person* with a religious commitment, and whose commitment (all things being equal) should therefore be at least *tolerated*. As Grayling writes, 'The point to make in opposition to the predictable response of religious believers [Grayling doesn't say what he takes that response to be] is that *human individuals merit respect first and foremost as human individuals.*'[81] Christianity agrees with Grayling here; there is no basis in Christian theology for valuing one person more highly than another, and certainly not on the basis of what they believe.

> Shared humanity [which the Christian views in terms of all people 'being made in the image of God'] is the ultimate basis of all person-to-person and group-to-group relationships, and views which premise differences between human beings as the basis of moral consideration, most especially those that involve claims to possession by one group of greater truth, holiness, or the like, start in absolutely the wrong place.[82]

Grayling's point may have bite against some religions, but is in basic agreement with Christianity. Grayling's position expresses a humanism with Christian roots in the Renaissance humanism (and ultimately, of course, in the Bible) of scholars such as Dutch theologian Desiderius Erasmus. However, Grayling asserts:

> It is time to demand of believers that they take their personal choices and preferences in these non-rational and too often dangerous matters into the private sphere, like their sexual proclivities. Everyone is free to believe what they want, providing they do not bother (or coerce, or kill) others . . . *it is time to demand and apply a right for the rest of us to non-interference by religious persons and organizations – a right to be free of proselytisation* and the efforts of self-selected minority groups to impose their own choice of morality and practice on those who do not share their outlook.[83]

Our democratic system could do a better job of representing the views of the population and deciding issues on the merit of relevant arguments. However, we do live in a democracy, so there is no question of religious minorities imposing their own choice of morality and practice on any majority who don't share their outlook (indeed, the opposite is often the case).[84]

Grayling may be right to complain about 'people of religious faith, who take themselves to have an unquestionable right to respect for the faith they adhere to, and a right to advance, if not indeed impose (because they claim to know the truth, remember) their views on others.'[85] He certainly has a right so to complain. However, it is not *my faith* that has a right to be respected, but *my person*. This right does not exclude dissent, or robust intellectual questioning. However, it does extend to the expectation that those who criticise my faith should be held to the same standards of civil academic discourse as should apply when the boot is, so to speak, on the other foot.

Grayling clearly takes himself to have a right to advance *his* views, precisely because *he* claims to know the truth. Complaining about religious believers engaging in the same behaviour, for the same reason, mires Grayling in a double standard. Ironically (and leaving aside Grayling's straw man assertion about religious beliefs being non-rational preferences), in the very process of advocating the view that 'Everyone is free to believe what they want, providing they do not bother (or coerce, or kill) others . . .',[86] Grayling is both a) *bothering* religious people – by writing a polemic against their beliefs (something I'm happy for him to do), and b) advocating coercing religious believers!

Grayling's position seems to be that people should be free to hold whatever beliefs they like, without fear of coercion, *just as long as they don't believe that their religious beliefs should accompany them into the public square*; in which case they should be coerced not to do so. Since Grayling's beliefs entail the coercion of others in the public square, then, *according to his own criteria*, he shouldn't be free to believe as he does. As Thomas Paine warned, 'He that would make his own liberty secure must guard even his enemy from oppression; for if he violates this duty he establishes a precedent that will reach to himself.'[87] Grayling has clearly drawn the limits of tolerance too tightly, and has fallen within his own definition of intolerance: 'an intolerant person . . . wishes others to live as he thinks they ought and . . . *seeks to impose his practices and beliefs upon them.*'[88]

If Grayling wants to be free to believe that people should be coerced to leave their religious beliefs out of the public square, he should accept that people are free to believe that he is wrong, and thus to believe that people should be free to bring their faith into the public square (what they shouldn't be free to do is to commit acts of terrorism, etc.). Grayling can't have it both ways without falling foul of an obvious double standard (and *ad hoc* quibbles about the distinction between religious and non-religious metaphysical beliefs should by no means be permitted to exonerate Grayling on a technicality here). Indeed, Grayling adopts a self-excepting rule when he pleads for 'a right to be free of proselytisation' – for what is his book but *an act of proselytisation?* It wouldn't do to be told that a secular humanist can't proselytise because they aren't religious. Questionable definitions can't excuse double standards. Surely everyone should have the right to invite and participate in public debate concerning worldview issues; and equally, everyone should have a right to decline debate concerning such issues. For example, Jehovah Witnesses and Secular Humanists alike should, I believe, have the right to knock at my door offering literature and discussion (not that the latter ever do). And I should have the right to invite them in, or to politely send them away, as I see fit.

Grayling says nothing about the rights of the religious not to be proselytised by the non-religious. His proposed rights are discriminatory. Let me be clear: *I don't want any such right*. I *want* atheists to write public polemics like *Against All Gods*; but it seems only fair to expect the right of public reply. Consistency would seem to require Grayling to be in favour of banning this book (in fairness to Grayling I am forced to doubt that he is consistent)!

Grayling finally affirms the need to 'return religious commitment to the private sphere . . .'[89] However, some religious beliefs are *essentially* public-minded. For example, Christianity is by its very nature both a missionary religion and a religion that takes serving others seriously. Such beliefs simply *cannot* be relegated to the private sphere. One cannot simply ban the public proclamation of the 'gospel' message, or public acts of Christian charity, without thereby effectively banning Christianity. If Grayling is really committed to excluding all religion from the public sphere, both 'demanding and applying' a 'right' of the non-religious to 'non-interference' and 'to be free of proselytisation,' he is thereby necessarily committed (whether or not this is his intention – and we can only hope that it is not) to *making Christianity illegal!*

Grayling says more about his 'behind closed doors' view of religion in his essay 'Answering Critics'. He begins by affirming a belief in 'pluralism and the tolerance that alone makes pluralism workable',[90] whilst sensibly noting that 'tolerance does not mean accepting that anything goes. For example, believing in tolerance does not oblige one to tolerate murder . . .'[91] Tolerating murder would certainly make pluralism unworkable, but does tolerating religion necessarily undermine pluralism in the same way? Grayling claims that tolerance does not oblige one to tolerate 'folly or superstitious and fanciful worldviews descended from the ignorance of the cave-man (which is what religion is).'[92] This compact example of well-poisoning and the genetic fallacy aside, one can only hope that Grayling isn't drawing a strict parallel between intolerance of murder on the one hand and religion on the other. After all, intolerance of murder rightly justifies active opposition that goes far beyond writing strongly worded essays! 'What the evidence of history and reason shows to be an evil in the world,' says Grayling, 'one must oppose: and where the evil is great, it must be opposed robustly. So those who believe in, and base their lives upon, the ancient fairy tales . . . cannot expect their absurdities to be handled with kid gloves, not least because almost all of them try to foist their outlook on others; and far too many of them . . . are prepared to coerce or even kill those who do not agree.'[93] Of course, where religion entails murder then intolerance of murder and intolerance of religion co-inside and must be paralleled one with another. But lesser parallels surely call for lesser opposition. I don't expect my religious beliefs to be handled with 'kid gloves', but does Grayling really mean to say that we should be *intolerant* of every belief we perceive as being 'folly', 'superstitious' and/or 'fanciful'? Aren't such beliefs precisely the sort of thing that we should *tolerate* in the proper sense of the term? For example, I personally consider metaphysical naturalism to be a 'fanciful' worldview, a philosophical 'folly' against which I argue robustly in the public square. Nevertheless, naturalism is a worldview that I tolerate. I don't want to prevent the likes of Grayling from advocating naturalism in the public square. I simply want to engage with his perspective from mine in public and on even terms. And what about religion that isn't prepared to 'coerce' or 'foist' its outlook upon others? Or does Grayling (in a double standard) automatically equate any and all proselytisation with coercive foisting? That really is to attack a straw man. Grayling concludes his answer to religious critics by defining the limits of his tolerance:

> Unlike the espousers of these absurdities, many of whom are avowedly intolerant of different beliefs or none, I am prepared to tolerate their existence, *if they practice their religion in quietness and do not impose themselves upon others*. Religion is like sex: it is mostly for the privacy of the closet (though public sex as entertainment is acceptable – far more so than religion), and when it takes aberrant forms or leaks into the open in disruptive ways it should be abated. But . . . I hold that what religious people think and do is ridiculous and too often dangerous, which makes combating it a duty.[94]

So there we have it, everything that all religious people think and do should be opposed (as always ridiculous and sometimes dangerous), whilst yet being tolerated (even if it is less acceptable than pornography), but only as long as religion is a) *confined to the private sphere* and b) *not imposed upon others*. And it would *seem* that to Grayling the concept of religion being imposed upon others encompasses any and all forms of proselytisation – even forms less coercive than his own writings. Once again, the implication is that any religion that isn't prepared to confine itself to private acts between already consenting adults behind closed doors should not even be tolerated in a pluralistic society!

Christopher Hitchens, on the face of things at least, doesn't want to go there: 'Religious faith is . . . ineradicable . . . For this reason I would not prohibit it even if I thought I could. Very generous of me, you may say. But will the religious grant me the same indulgence?'[95] Allowing people their right to freedom of religion isn't exactly 'generous', although it is a good thing; and *of course* the religious should grant Hitchens 'the same indulgence'. As Vox Day writes in answer to the same question, 'for the Christian there is only one answer: by all means! If God . . . does not see fit to force Christopher Hitchens to worship him, then how can I, or any other Christian, fail to do other than follow that divine example? Free will is at the heart of the Christian faith.'[96] None of which means that *debate* concerning the truth-claims of our respective worldviews should be taboo; and yet Hitchens (like Grayling) expresses a desire to be *left alone* by religious people: 'I will continue to do this without insisting on the polite reciprocal condition – which is that *they in their turn leave me alone.*'[97] I take it that being 'left alone' means to not be subject to proselytisation. However, the relevant reciprocal condition here is *not* that Hitchens be 'left alone', but that theists not attempt to *prohibit* his atheism. Indeed, Hitchens' desire to be 'left alone' is actually contradicted by his desire not to prohibit religion, for certain forms of religion are intrinsically evangelistic, and are thus incapable of 'leaving him alone'. Hitchens can't have it both ways. Moreover, like Grayling, Hitchens evinces a double standard on this point, for he doesn't leave religious people 'alone'. If he did, he wouldn't have published his book! And yet I'm glad Hitchens cares enough about the truth as he sees it to bother publishing his book. What a terrible world it would be if we simply left each other 'alone' because we didn't care enough about either truth, or other people, to enter into dialogue concerning our differing understandings of reality.

It is sad and ironic to see the New Atheists' justifiable opposition to the evils of authoritarian, 'fundamentalist' religion (an opposition I share) leading the liberal West closer to the secular fundamentalism of totalitarian atheist states such as Communist China. Far from it being time to leave each other alone, or to 'return religious commitment to the private sphere'[98] – an act of oppression that can only fuel the fires of religious fundamentalism – I suggest that now, more than ever, is the time to encourage debate and cooperation between people with different worldviews on the common ground of their shared humanity. As Richard Norman warns:

> Humanism is more than atheism, it is about putting humanist beliefs and values into practice and trying to make the world a better place. And that is impossible unless we're prepared to cooperate with others who share those values, including those for whom the values are inseparable from a religious commitment . . . We have problems enough in the world. The threats of climate change, global poverty, war and repression and intolerance can never be countered unless we are prepared to work together on the basis of a shared humanity. Simplistic generalizations about religion don't help.[99]

If Christians and secular humanists can't agree on that, then the future looks bleak.

A Vital Debate

> *'Civilization is constituted by reasoned conversation. Civilized humans converse with one another, argue with one another, offer evidence to one another. Barbarians club one another.'*
> – Michael Novak[100]

I agree with Dawkins that 'The question of whether there exists a supernatural creator, a God, is one of the most important that we have to answer.'[101] I also agree with Gary Wolf's conclusion:

The New Atheists have castigated fundamentalism and branded even the mildest religious liberals as enablers of a vengeful mob. Everybody who does not join them is an ally of the Taliban. But so far, their provocation has failed to take hold . . . I take this as good news. Even those of us who sympathize intellectually have good reasons to wish that the New Atheists continue to seem absurd. If we reject their polemics, if we continue to have respectful conversations even about things we find ridiculous, this doesn't necessarily mean we've lost our convictions or our sanity. It simply reflects our deepest, democratic values. Or, you might say, our bedrock faith: the faith that no matter how confident we are in our beliefs, there's always a chance we could turn out to be wrong.[102]

Writing in the *New York Times* Daniel Dennett asserts 'We don't believe in ghosts or elves or the Easter Bunny – or God.'[103] Dennett's use of the term 'we' – which apparently refers to what sociologist Peter Berger dubbed 'global faculty club culture'[104] – is prejudicial.[105] Some people *do* believe in elves.[106] Some children believe in the Easter Bunny. Many people believe in ghosts.[107] The majority of people believe in God. Of course, a head-count cannot settle questions about the truth, rationality, or desirability of these beliefs. Personally, I don't believe in elves, the Easter Bunny, or ghosts. However, I do 'believe in God, the Father almighty, creator of heaven and earth'. As a Christian theist I believe God exists, and I trust in him. Moreover, I think that this combination of belief and trust (faith) is (at least in my own case, and in the case of many people that I know) a good thing. That is, I think theism is true, and I also think theism can be both rational and desirable (even if it isn't always so). Dennett's prejudicial roll-call is designed to suggest that all faith, and therefore my faith, is false, irrational and undesirable. I beg to differ. In what follows I will take issue with the most prominent arguments of the most prominent contemporary apologists for atheism. And at each and every turn, I will demonstrate that the case against theism simply doesn't cut the philosophical mustard.

Recommended Resources

Websites

Beyond Belief 2006, http://beyondbelief2006.org/.
Beyond Belief 2007, http://thesciencenetwork.org/ Beyond Belief2/
Richard Dawkins Net, www.richarddawkins.net/.

Online Papers

Michael Brooks, 'This Week: Beyond Belief', *New Scientist*, 18 November 2006, www.newscientist.com/channel/opinion/mg19225780.142-beyond-belief-in-place-of-god.html. etc.
William Lane Craig, 'God Is Not Dead Yet', www.christianityto-day.com/ct/2008/july/13.22
Daniel Dennett, 'The Bright Stuff', *New York Times*, 12 July 2003, www.the-brights.net/vision/essays/dennett_nyt_article.html
George Johnson, 'A Free-for-All on Science and Religion', *The New York Times*, 23 November 2006,www.nytimes.com/2006/11/21/science/21belief.html?_r=2&oref=slogin&page-wanted=print
Peter Steinfels, 'Books on Atheism Are Raising Hackles in Unlikely Places', *New York Times*, 3 March 2007, www.nytimes.com/2007/03/03/books/03beliefs.html?_r=1&ref=us&oref=s login
Jay Tolson, 'The New Unbelievers', www.templeton-cambridge.org/fellows/tolson/publications/2006.11.05/the_new_unbe-lievers/
Peter S. Williams, 'A Christian Response to *Against All Gods*. Part One: Intellectual Respectability', www.bethinking.org/resource.php?ID=385
Peter S. Williams, 'A Christian Response to *Against All Gods*. Part Two: Ethical respectability', www.bethinking.org/ resource.php?ID=392
Gary Wolf, 'The Church of the Non-Believers', *Wired Magazine*, November 2006, www.wired.com/wired/archive/14.11/athe-ism_pr.html

Audio

William Lane Craig, 'God Is Not Dead Yet', www.rfmedia.org/RF_audio_video/RF_podcast/Christianity_Today_Article.mp3

William Lane Craig, 'The New Atheism: 1 of 2', www.rfmedia.org/RF_audio_video/RF_podcast/Reasonable_Faith_book_09.mp3

William Lane Craig, 'The New Atheism: 2 of 2', www.rfmedia.org/RF_audio_video/RF_podcast/The_New_Atheism.mp3

Richard Dawkins on Point of Enquiry, 'The God Delusion', http://cdn.libsyn.com/pointofinquiry/10-16-06.mp3

Richard Dawkins on Point of Enquiry, 'Science and the New Atheism', http://cdn.libsyn.com/pointofinquiry/POI_2007_12_7_Richard_Dawkins.mp3

Nigel Warburton and A. C. Grayling, 'Atheism', http://cdn.libsyn.com/philosophybites/GraylingA.MP3

Wired Interview with Gary Wolf, http://sonibyte.com/audio/raw/1569.mp3.

Humanist Network News #24, 'The New Atheists on Organized New Thought (with Sam Harris, Daniel Dennett, Richard Dawkins and Christopher Hitchens at the 2007 Atheist Alliance International 'Crystal Clear Atheism' Conference)', http://cdn.libsyn.com/ihs/024-HNN_10_24_2007.mp3

Video

'The Four Horseman (Hitchens, Dennett, Dawkins and Harris in Discussion)', http://media.richarddawkins.net/video/4h/4H_Hour1_web.mov and http://media.richarddawkins.net/video/4h/4H_Hour2_web.mov

3.

Is Faith the Root of All Evil?

'I do everything in my power to warn people against faith itself, not just against so-called "extremist" faith. The teachings of "moderate" religion, though not extremist in themselves, are an open invitation to extremism.'
– Richard Dawkins[1]

A.C. Grayling is keen to 'criticise religions . . . as institutional phenomena which . . . have done and continue to do much harm in the world, whatever good can be claimed for them besides'.[2] That's like criticising public transport because trains sometimes crash, while acknowledging that trains are safer than cars. Still, Grayling's general point remains. As Gerard J. Hughes writes, 'Religious beliefs can be very powerful, and the temptation to harness this power for ends which have nothing to do with religion is likely to remain strong. Where religion is thus abused, atheism will always have its principled defenders.'[3]

Dark Matters

'I don't get up out of a nice warm bed and go to church because I'm frightened of going to hell if I don't. I get up out of a sense of love and loyalty.'
– Russell Stannard[4]

BBC Radio 4's Bel Mooney asked author Philip Pullman why he is 'so vehemently anti organised religion'. He replied:

Simply from looking at history. A large proportion of what the Christian Church has done has been intolerant, cruel, fanatical, whichever part of the spectrum you look at, whether it's the Inquisition with the Catholics burning the heretics, or whether it's the other end of the spectrum – the Puritans in New England . . . hanging the witches . . . Wherever you look you see intolerance, cruelty, fanaticism, narrow-mindedness.[5]

The ensuing exchange was revealing.

Mooney: Well, historically there's no gainsaying that, but when I finished *The Amber Spyglass* one of the many things I thought was, Philip Pullman obviously hates the Church, but all the clerics I meet are decent, bearded chaps in the half-empty churches, doing good works and bringing comfort to pensioners. They're not burning witches.
Pullman: Not any more. They wouldn't get away with it now.
Mooney: But they wouldn't want to.
Pullman: No, not the nice gentle ones who have half empty churches. But the ones who have churches that are full – the evangelicals, the fundamentalists – are full of hell-fire and damnation and fury and vengeance on anyone who disagrees with them.[6]

Pullman's image of evangelical and fundamentalist clerics full of fury and thoughts of 'vengeance upon anyone who disagrees with them', who would be out burning witches if they could 'get away with it now' – is *at best* the result of selective data-picking. I have attended and visited many well populated evangelical churches, and have never noticed a desire to enact vengeance upon anyone with a different viewpoint; let alone a desire to have anyone hung, or burnt at the stake. Nor would it be true to say that any of these churches has been 'full of hell-fire and damnation'. Although hell and damnation do get mentioned (and there are a range of views on these subjects), the context is either a loving desire to tell non-Christians that the grace of God displayed in Christ's crucifixion means that they can and should avoid hell, or else thankfulness at being enabled to avoid hell by the same grace we seek to share with others.

As for 'burning witches', social scientist Philip J. Sampson observes, 'the number of witchcraft prosecutions has often been greatly exaggerated, and we now know that the Inquisition tended to moderate rather than incite them.'[7] According to historian Hugh Trevor-Roper: 'in general the established church was opposed to the persecution [of witches].'[8] On the other hand, 'atheists and skeptics like Thomas Hobbes and Jean Bodin advocated the killing of witches, the latter of whom wanted it done in the slowest possible fire.'[9] This can be understood as part of 'the drive to eliminate all traces of superstition from a society newly dedicated to asserting the power of reason over nature.'[10] But I propose to leave the lengthy business of discussing case studies to others, with a word of caution from Richard Norman: 'religion has inspired not only some of the worst but also some for the best human achievements . . . To present religion and its works in a wholly negative light would in my view be hopelessly unbalanced.'[11]

The Epistemological Evil of Faith

'faith rejoices in unreason'
– A.C. Grayling[12]

The New Atheists propose a cost-benefit analysis of whether religion in general 'provides net benefits to humankind'[13] as compared with atheism in general.[14] This ethical equivalent of a 'dance off' is something of a red herring, and not only because 'There is no religion in general.' Sam Harris argues that 'Even if atheism led straight to moral chaos, this would not suggest that the doctrine of Christianity is *true*.'[15] But, equally, even if Christianity led straight to moral chaos, this wouldn't suggest that the doctrine of atheism is *true*. It is illegitimate to place the cart of ethical consequences before horse of truth. Suppose one considers Christianity and concludes that it is true; in such a case it would surely be unreasonable to assess one's commitment purely by reference to its this-worldly consequences. Indeed, *if* Christianity is true, *then*, bearing eternity in mind, it's hard to think of anything that adds greater 'utility' to existence than a literally evangelical Christian! Hence, interesting as the proposed 'dance off' may be, I propose to focus on some deeper issues at play in the 'root of all evil' argument.

Harris assumes the utilitarian norm that the right thing to do is that which produces the greatest aggregate happiness: 'Questions of morality are questions about happiness and suffering . . . Religion allows people to imagine that their concerns are moral when they are not – that is, when they have nothing to do with suffering or its alleviation.'[16] Indeed, it is not only religion that allows people to imagine that their concerns are moral when they have nothing to do with the alleviation of suffering – any scepticism about utilitarianism allows *that*. Christianity is interested in the alleviation of suffering, but Christian ethics isn't consequentialist. Harris can't be allowed to rig the rules of the proposed 'dance-off' by simply *assuming* utilitarian ground-rules. Jonathan Haidt spots the tick here, in that:

> Harris gives us a standard liberal definition of morality . . . He then goes on to show that the Bible and the Koran, taken literally, are immoral books because they're not primarily about happiness and suffering, and in many places they advocate harming people. Reading Harris is like watching professional wrestling or the Harlem Globetrotters. It's great fun, with lots of acrobatics, but it must not be mistaken for an actual contest. If we want to stage a fair fight between religious and secular moralities, we can't eliminate one by definition before the match begins.[17]

Even supposing (for the sake of argument) that Christianity would fail to measure up by the utilitarian standard, such a failure could not be endowed with any definitive import unless utilitarianism captures the truth about morality – something even atheists aren't uniformly prepared to grant.[18] As Richard Norman argues, 'What utilitarianism fails to take on board . . . is that though some people's interests sometimes have to be sacrificed for the interests of others, there are limits. There are some things which, morally, you cannot do to people for the sake of a greater good . . . Human beings . . . are not simply constituents of one great heap of well-being.'[19] Even Daniel Dennett cautions that 'A human life worth living is not something that can be uncontroversially measured, and this is its glory.'[20]

I have labelled the 'root of all evil' argument after the documentary written and presented by Richard Dawkins, and broadcast in two parts by the UK's Channel 4 in January 2006.[21] In fairness to Dawkins, we should note that 'the title *The Root of All Evil?* was not his preferred choice . . . Channel 4 had insisted on it to create controversy. Dawkins has stated that the notion of anything being the root of *all* evil is ridiculous.'[22] Nevertheless, it is due to Dawkins' popularization of the theme that this imprecise label springs to mind, for according to Dawkins' documentary 'The time has come for people of reason to say: enough is enough. Religious faith discourages independent thought, it's divisive, and it's dangerous.'[23] The crucial point here is that Dawkins' comment about religion discouraging 'independent thought', and his attempt to contrast religious believers with 'people of reason', lies at the very heart of the 'root of all evil' argument. Hence Dawkins proclaims:

> Fundamentalist religion is hell-bent on ruining the scientific education of countless thousands . . . Non-fundamentalist, 'sensible' religion may not be doing that. *But it is making the world safe for fundamentalism by teaching . . . that unquestioned faith is a virtue . . .* if children were taught to question and think through their beliefs, instead of being taught the superior virtue of faith without question, it is a good bet that there would be no suicide bombers.[24]

Richard Norman observes that 'For Dawkins the problem is that all religious believers are committed to faith rather than reason . . . So for him the difference between the so-called moderate, sensible religious believers and the fundamentalists is a minor one . . . it's religion as such that is the problem.'[25] As Dawkins explains: 'I do everything in my power to warn people against faith itself, not just against so-called "extremist" faith. The teachings of "moderate" religion, though not extremist in themselves, are an open invitation to extremism.'[26]

Sam Harris likewise acknowledges that 'many people of faith make heroic sacrifices to relieve the suffering of other human beings,'[27] yet asks: 'is it necessary to believe anything on insufficient evidence in order to behave this way?'[28] It is the supposed endorsement by all religion, however 'moderate', of the essential irrationality of 'blind faith' that the New Atheists see as under-pinning the suffering caused by religion, and thus as the central issue in their ethical critique. Daniel Dennett concurs, saying that:

> religion [is] the greatest threat to rationality and scientific progress . . . religion . . . doesn't just disable, it honours the disability. People are revered for their capacity to live in a dream world, to shield their minds from factual knowledge and make the major decisions in their lives by consulting voices in their heads that they call forth by rituals designed to intoxicate them . . . This imperviousness to reason is, I think, the property that we should most fear in religion. Other institutions or traditions may encourage a certain amount of irrationality . . . but only religion demands it as a sacred duty.[29]

In other words, the 'root of all evil' argument is at root the argument that

1) Anything that stops people fulfilling their moral obligations – defined by the utilitarian principle that the good is 'that which produces the greatest happiness for the greatest number' – should be opposed;
2) Religious faith (unlike atheism) necessarily requires belief without evidence, and belief without evidence entails a failure to fulfil one's moral obligations (especially one's *intellectual* obligations);
3) Therefore, religion should be opposed.

(Note that the conclusion is not that all religion is *false*; this is an anti-*belief* argument, not an anti-*truth* argument.) The New Atheists desire to defend rationality against irrationality, and good against evil. In this, they are to be commended. However, both premises of the above 'root of all evil' argument are false. Consider the utilitarianism of the first premise.

> Contrary to what utilitarianism implies, some acts just appear to be intrinsically right or wrong (torturing babies for fun), some rules seem to be intrinsically right or wrong (punishing only guilty people), some areas of life seem to be intrinsically trivial

(what to eat for breakfast) or supererogatory (giving half your income to the poor). From the moral point of view, some motives (morally) should be blamed or praised for what they are intrinsically and not because such acts of praise or blame produce utility, and humans seem to have intrinsic value and rights, which ground what is just and unjust treatment regarding them . . . utilitarianism fails to explain adequately these features of the moral life.[30]

Leaving aside problems with utilitarianism (the first premise could be re-stated without relying on utilitarianism), the deeper problem here (and one worth sustained attention, because it underlies several New Atheist arguments), evinced by the second premise, is that the *New Atheists misunderstand both faith and reason.*

Misunderstanding Faith and Reason

'if you want a concession, I've always said that naturalism is an act of faith . . .'
– Michael Ruse[31]

Dawkins criticizes faith for requiring 'blind trust, in the absence of evidence, even in the teeth of evidence.'[32] This is ironic given the role played by blind trust in Dawkins' own beliefs.[33] For example, responding to the question, 'What do you believe is true even though you cannot prove it?', Dawkins said:

> Darwinism is the explanation of life on *this* planet, but I believe [*without proof*] that all life, all intelligence, all creativity and all 'design' anywhere in the universe, is the direct or indirect product of Darwinian natural selection. It follows that design comes late in the universe, after a period of Darwinian evolution. Design cannot precede evolution and therefore cannot underlie the universe.[35]

Even Dawkins' assertion that 'Darwinism is the explanation of life on *this* planet' is a matter of 'faith', as he admitted in a 2005 interview: 'There cannot have been intermediate stages [in the

evolutionary climb up Mount Improbable] that were not benefi-
cial . . . There's got to be a series of advantages all the way . . . If
you can't think of one, then that's your problem, not natural
selection's problem. Natural selection – well, *I suppose that is a sort
of matter of faith on my part . . .*'[36] Dawkins' criticism of faith
exhibits a double standard. The question is whether theists can
transcend this double standard so that they aren't merely arguing
that 'you're just as bad as we are'!

Harris complains that 'While believing strongly, without evidence, is considered a mark of madness or stupidity in any other
area of our lives, faith in God still holds immense prestige in our
society.'[37] The odd thing about this complaint is that Harris
inevitably believes many things 'strongly, without evidence' that
he couldn't have any evidence for, but which it would nonetheless be rightly considered a mark of madness or stupidity if he
didn't believe! For example, Harris believes that the world did *not*
spring into existence five minutes ago, complete with false memories, tree rings that never grew, etc. Neither do I. But this common sense hypothesis is by definition compatible with all the
available empirical evidence, and so our (surely 'strong') belief to
the contrary is necessarily something we believe 'without evidence'.

'In an open letter to his daughter Juliet, Dawkins advises her to
only accept beliefs supported by evidence: 'Have you ever won-
dered how we know the things that we know?',[38] asks Dawkins.
The answer, he says (and he does seem to mean *the* answer), is
'evidence'.[39] Dawkins advises, 'next time somebody tells you that
something is true, why not say to them: "What kind of evidence
is there for that?" And if they can't give you a good answer, I
hope you'll think very carefully before you believe a word they
say.'[40] Dawkins' assertion that *all* beliefs must be justified on the
basis of other beliefs before they count as rational entails an infinite regress of justifications that can never be accumulated. It is
clearly *not* the case that *all* beliefs have to be justified with evidence before they count as rational.

It's not just the New Atheists who misunderstand the nature of
reason. Carl Sagan embraces the idea that 'superstition is . . .
merely belief without evidence'.[41] But if 'belief without evidence'
is 'superstition', then we are all superstitious. Every argument

rests on logical principles that brook no support (on pain of begging the question), and every empirically grounded statement depends upon the assumed reliability of perceptual practices that are impossible to justify without circularity. Nevertheless, Sagan quotes Bertrand Russell with approval: 'it is undesirable to believe a proposition when there is no ground whatever for supposing it true.'[42] In responding to the question 'What grounds would you have for believing that proposition?',[43] Sagan flounders: 'That's a very good question that leads to an infinite regress . . . if you wish to have the statement justified in internal logic – that is, a self-consistent closed system – obviously it cannot, because it leads to an infinite regress. But as I was saying, it seems to me that the approach of sceptical scrutiny commends itself to our attention because it has worked so well in the past.'[44] Sagan thus admits his theory of knowledge is incoherent, but attempts to justify it with an inference from pragmatic results (once again the cart is put before the horse)!

Thankfully, the proposition that 'it is undesirable to accept any belief formed without proper regard for relevant epistemic duties' is both logically consistent and more pragmatically useful if one's goal is the truth, rather than simply the best naturalistic explanation presently available. Evidence is important, but it is *not* the be-all and end-all of rationality. Indeed, one cannot coherently celebrate the virtues of evidence-based reasoning *unless* one also celebrates the virtues of *rationally appropriate belief without evidence!* It would be better to say that superstition is *belief without proper regard for relevant intellectual duties.*

On the one hand, then, Christians can and should question, not the assumption that faith should be *rational* (of course it should), but the assumption that faith is irrational *unless based upon evidence.* Christians can and should argue that 'believing . . . without evidence' is an occasional rational *necessity*; and that it is, moreover, at least rationally *permissible* in many cases, *including that of belief in God* (more on this later). On the other hand, Christians can and should deny that faith requires belief 'in the face of evidence and against reason', or that it *requires* belief 'without evidence'. Above all, Christians should argue that Christian faith is compatible with a proper regard for relevant intellectual duties.

Understanding Reason

> *'We know the truth not only by means of the reason but also by means of the heart. It is through the heart that we know the first principles.'*
> – Pascal[45]

All argument (including those of the New Atheists) rests upon trust in the truth of certain basic principles. While these principles cannot be called into question without being assumed (any attempt to doubt them is self-contradictory), neither can they be justified in any way that doesn't assume their truth (any attempt to justify these basic principles is question begging). One cannot doubt that 'nothing can both be and not be in the same way at the same time' (the law of non-contradiction) without assuming that one's doubt is the case in contrast to its not being the case. However, one cannot give any justification for this principle that doesn't depend upon the very principle in question. Commitment to the laws of reason is an act of fundamental trust. All proof ultimately requires trust in something which cannot itself be 'proved', but which must be assumed. Such an ultimate assumption is an indispensably 'basic' belief.

Beliefs within the 'game' of reason may be supported or discredited to one degree or another, but we cannot turn the rules of reason upon themselves anymore than we can pick ourselves off the ground by our own shoelaces. As Roy Abraham Varghese argues:

> it is a fact of universal and immediate experience that human beings are not only capable of knowing but that they are indeed endowed with a knowledge-base encompassing essential and ultimate principles of reality. It is this knowledge-base that underlies all thought and rationality and every exercise of the human mind . . . How do we know that these affirmations are true and how can we demonstrate their truth? Well, we know them to be true because that is what our minds tell us – instinctively, immediately – but we cannot demonstrate them to be true because all demonstrations would presuppose their truth . . . Nevertheless, we know that these affirmations are true affirmations and if any interlocutor wishes to deny them the burden of proof lies with the interlocutor . . . In

making such affirmations, we are remaining true to self-evident facts while those who deny them are flying in the face of these facts . . . At its most fundamental level, rationality can be experienced and exercised but not demonstrated.[46]

Back to Basics

The system of a person's beliefs and their relations one to another is their 'noetic structure'. As a matter of necessity, some beliefs in a person's noetic structure are not supported by any other beliefs. To think that this is not the case is either to posit an infinite regress of beliefs, or to deny that circular argumentation is fallacious. Such unsupported, independent beliefs – which are by definition held 'without evidence' – are called 'basic beliefs'. Basic beliefs are 'beliefs that one holds but not on the basis of other beliefs that one holds.'[47] Basic beliefs form the foundation of one's noetic structure, because while basic beliefs are not held on the basis of other beliefs, they can provide the basis for other beliefs ('non-basic' or 'mediate' beliefs that one holds on the basis of other beliefs): 'Some of our beliefs are basic, beliefs not believed on the basis of other beliefs we hold, and some beliefs are non-basic, beliefs that are acquired and maintained by the evidential support of other beliefs.'[48] In the case of non-basic beliefs, one holds them on the basis of considering the relationship between other more or less basic beliefs one holds (a belief is more or less basic depending upon the number of other beliefs it is based upon, and the overall strength of the epistemic relationships involved in its adoption). In the case of basic beliefs, 'one simply finds oneself believing them in certain circumstances, and one does not believe them simply on the basis of other beliefs that one holds.'[49]

Examples of basic beliefs include perceptual beliefs: 'one simply *finds oneself believing* the sky is blue when one is in the *appropriate circumstances*: one is outside, one looks at the sky, and the sky is blue.'[50] We find ourselves with perceptual beliefs not because we have *argued* our way to a conclusion, but because our cognitive faculties simply *give us* that belief. Memories are basic beliefs. I *remember* drinking coffee with friends yesterday. I don't argue my way to this conclusion using evidence. Indeed, despite the fact that my memory has proven unreliable in the past, there is no need for me to obtain independent evidence as to whether or not I drank coffee with friends yesterday for my belief that I did to be rational (i.e. to be a belief I am within my intellectual rights to hold). The generally accurate nature of my memory is itself a basic belief (indeed, its something I know through memory!). Many moral beliefs are also basic: 'Somewhere in one's moral reasoning one reaches a set of beliefs that are bearers of intrinsic value; they are not valued as a means to some other end or for some extrinsic reason. At this level one reaches one's basic moral beliefs.'[51] Other basic beliefs include 'elementary *truths of logic* . . . certain *mathematical beliefs*. And there are certain framework or fundamental beliefs such as *belief in an external world, belief in the self,* etc. These are foundational beliefs that we typically reason from and not to . . .'[52]

The existence of *some* basic beliefs in our noetic structure is unavoidable, in that:

> it is *impossible* that the only beliefs we have the right to be certain about are the ones that we have proven . . . if everything needed to be proven, then the premises of *every* proof would also need to be proven. But if you need to prove the premises of every proof, you would then need a proof for your proof . . . and so on – forever. Thus it makes no sense to demand that everything be proven because an infinite regress of proofs is impossible. So when the premises of an argument are themselves in need of proof, the series of arguments needed to prove its premises must eventually end with an argument whose premises are all 'basic' . . . the rules for drawing inferences correctly, the truths of logic and mathematics [i.e. 'indispensably basic beliefs'], cannot themselves have proofs because they are the very rules we must use in order to prove anything . . . So proofs need belief in unproven rules as well as *premises* that we can know without proof . . .[53]

Of course, unless a belief is *indispensably* basic (i.e. self-contradictory to doubt), the mere fact that you believe something in a basic way shouldn't be taken as guaranteeing that your belief is *properly* basic, or 'warranted' (i.e. that one is within one's intellectual rights to hold the belief in question). Just as properly non-basic beliefs are beliefs that one is within one's intellectual rights to hold *on the basis of the relationship between other beliefs that one has an intellectual right to hold*, so a properly basic belief is a basic belief that one is within one's intellectual rights to hold *without its being held in a properly non-basic manner*. However, a belief can be both properly basic *and* properly non-basic: if one's belief is warranted and the warrant of one's belief includes, but is not exhausted by, properly non-basic reasons for belief. I *remember* drinking coffee with friends yesterday. I can also *infer* that I must have had coffee with friends from evidence (evidence that is itself composed of properly basic beliefs, such as the visual *perception* of mugs in my sink, or there being less coffee in house than I *remember*). Hence the total warrant attributable to my belief that I had coffee with friends yesterday has a *plural* origin, being composed of basic *and* non-basic warrant. The same can apply to belief in God.[54]

To accept beliefs plucked out of the air at random would obviously involve overstepping one's intellectual rights. We can *infer* that random belief formation is an unreliable method of belief formation; but the obvious nature of this claim about our intellectual rights makes it a good candidate for being a properly basic moral belief. On the other hand, the class of properly basic beliefs clearly extends further than the indispensably basic laws of reason beloved by the archetypal rationalist, or the indubitable data of sense impressions beloved by the archetypal empiricist.

The Crumbling of Classical Foundationalism

Both the 'rationalist' and the 'empiricist' subscribe to the epistemological theory called 'classical foundationalism' (CF). Many challenges to Christian faith presuppose the CF theory of rationality. According to CF in its broadest form, the only properly basic beliefs

> are propositions which are either evident to the senses, self-evident, or what philosophers call incorrigible. Beliefs that are evident to the senses are reports of immediate [empirical] experience – such as that there is a piece of paper before me . . . Beliefs that are self-evident are those which upon understanding them one sees them to be true – such as that 2 + 2 = 4, all bachelors are unmarried males, and the whole is equal to the sum of its parts. And

> finally, beliefs that are incorrigible are propositions about which one cannot be wrong. These are usually reports of one's own immediate subjective states . . .[54]

Since God's existence isn't evident to our empirical senses, self-evident or incorrigible, CF entails that belief in God isn't properly basic, and hence that if belief in God is to be warranted it must be as a properly non-basic belief. 'Belief in God therefore stands, says the classical foundationalist, in need of argument or evidence to be held rationally.'[56]

Many theists have accepted CF, believing that there are good arguments available to support a properly non-basic belief in God. I agree with the latter claim. However, as Nicholas Wolterstorff reports, 'On all fronts foundationalism is in bad shape. It seems to me that there is nothing to do but give it up for mortally ill . . .'[57] Without rejecting the claim that there are good grounds for properly non-basic belief in God, it can be argued that CF is insufficiently generous in its demarcation of properly basic beliefs, and that belief in God can be properly basic. CF holds that a belief is rational if and only if it is both

1) Self-evident, evident to the empirical senses, or incorrigible;
2) inferable from beliefs demarcated by criterion 1.

However, what is the status of CF *according to CF?* Does CF count as a properly basic belief *according to its own criteria?* No. CF itself is neither self-evident, nor evident to the empirical senses, nor incorrigible. Neither does CF appear to be inferable (or deducible) from any beliefs that CF would class as properly basic. CF is as self-contradictory as 'logical positivism'. As James Kelly Clark argues:

> no one has yet produced a good argument for CF from a set of beliefs warranted by the classical foundationalist criteria. In fact, it is difficult to see how one could possible infer CF from a set of beliefs such as that I am appeared to greenly, that there is a tree before me, and the whole is equal to the sum of its parts. Thus CF cannot be justified by its own criterion. CF is, therefore, *self-referentially inconsistent.*[58]

The 'principle of credulity' states that one ought to take things to be the way they seem to one to be unless one has sufficient reason to think otherwise. After all, if one adopts the opposite principle, resolving never to trust appearances unless given sufficient reason to trust them, one can never trust the appearance of a good reason to trust appearances, and one is stuck in complete scepticism! Hence, if a basic belief seems to one to be within one's intellectual rights to accept, then, by the principle of credulity, one is *prima facie* justified in accepting that it *is* warranted. Looking out of the window I find myself believing that I see a tree. I don't reason my way to this belief, and I don't need to reason my way to this belief in order for it to be rational. Since I have no sufficient reason to think that my cognitive apparatus is malfunctioning (I haven't just received a blow to the head, I haven't been presented with overwhelming reason to think that trees don't exist, etc.), and since there's nothing about my apparent environmental situation that obviously fails to cohere with my seeing a tree, my belief that I see a tree seems perfectly appropriate, and should be extended the status of a properly basic belief. Likewise, theistic belief grounded in religious experience carries the *prima facie* warrant of a properly basic belief. Hence, Alan G. Padgett concludes, 'belief in God can be and often is perfectly legitimate and proper without any philosophical arguments. In other words, Christian faith does not depend upon the practice of philosophy (specifically natural theology) but rather upon more direct, immediate, and spiritual sources of the knowledge of God.'[59] Properly basic belief in God may well be supportable by evidence, but evidence isn't *required* to make belief in God warranted. Nevertheless, properly basic belief in God is not a matter of 'blind faith'; it is not the result of 'picking a belief out of the air', it must remain sensitive to the need to defend belief from intellectual challenges, and it is compatible with a robust acceptance of natural theology.

Understanding Faith

> '*In the Christian sense, faith means courageous trust in an object one has good reason to see as credible.*'
> – David Marshall[60]

According to Daniel Dennett, 'canonical religious beliefs . . . have to be "taken on faith" and are not subject to (scientific, historical) confirmation.'[61] Dawkins defines faith as 'blind trust, in the absence of evidence, even in the teeth of evidence.'[62] As we have seen, there isn't anything wrong with belief 'in the absence of evidence' *if* it has the *prima facie* warrant due to a properly basic belief. Dawkins is right to object to holding beliefs 'in the teeth of evidence' (assuming that the counter-evidence is sufficiently strong). However, Dawkins is wrong to think that 'faith' *means* counter-factual belief. As Richard Norman cautions: 'faith means different things to different religious believers, and from the fact that they claim to have faith you can't infer that they are all irrationalists who believe things on "blind faith" without any evidence . . .'[63] Alister McGrath comments that Dawkins'

> arbitrary and idiosyncratic definition simply does not stand up to serious investigation. In fact, it is itself an excellent example of a belief tenaciously held and defended 'in the absence of evidence, even in the teeth of evidence' . . . [T]he classic Christian tradition has always valued rationality, and does not hold that faith involves the complete abandonment of reason or believing in the teeth of evidence. Indeed, the Christian tradition is so consistent on this matter that it is difficult to understand where Dawkins has got the idea of faith as 'blind trust' from.[64]

Julian Baggini defines faith as 'belief in what there is a lack of strong evidence to believe in. Indeed, sometimes it is belief in something that is contrary to the available evidence . . .'[65] According to A.C. Grayling 'Faith is a commitment to belief contrary to evidence and reason . . .'[66] Astonishingly, both philosophers represent the New Testament story of doubting Thomas (John 20:24–31) as endorsing 'the principle that it is good to believe what you have no evidence to believe'.[67] However, Jesus commends people who believe *without having to see for themselves*, not those who 'believe without evidence',[68] as Grayling erroneously claims. Before Jesus offered himself for empirical examination, Thomas was hardly being asked to believe without evidence! Moreover, the reason John (an eye-witness)[69] gives for recounting these events is that they are *evidence* for the truth of the gospel: 'Jesus did many other miraculous signs in the presence of his disciples, which are not recorded in this book. But these are written that you may believe that Jesus is the Christ, the Son of God, and that by believing you may have life in his name' (John 20:30–31). As Roger Steer notes:

> There was no expectation that the sceptical disciple should exercise blind trust in the absence of evidence . . . of course, generations of people since then have been invited to exercise faith without the privilege of sight granted to Thomas, but the point is that through the centuries followers of Christ have never been required to take a step – or make a leap – which is blind or irrational.[70]

J.P. Moreland correctly defines biblical faith as 'a trust in and commitment to what we have reason to believe is true'.[71] C.S. Lewis said that faith is 'the art of holding onto things your reason has once accepted, in spite of your changing moods.' For moods change whatever view your reason takes. As Lewis wrote:

> Now that I am a Christian I do have moods in which the whole thing looks very improbable: but when I was an atheist I had moods in which Christianity looked terribly probable . . . unless you teach your moods 'where to get off,' you can never be a sound Christian or even a sound atheist, but just a creature dithering to and fro, with its beliefs really dependent on the weather and the state of its digestion.[73]

Michael J. Langford distinguishes between 'blind' and 'heroic' faith: 'In the former case, one is resisting the onslaught of reason; in the latter, the onslaught of weariness or pain or temptation.'[74] Christian faith should be heroic, *but not blind*. As Tom Price observes, 'when the New Testament talks about faith positively it *only* uses words derived from the Greek root [*pistis*] which means "to be persuaded."[75] Faith and reason are not competitors, and 'the modern view of faith as something unrelated or even hostile to reason is a departure from traditional Christianity and not a genuine expression of it.'[76] Consider what the Bible says about evidence and reason.

- The cosmos is created by a rational God who made humans in his own 'image' (Genesis 1:27).
- God says to humans: 'let us *reason* together' (Isaiah 1:18).
- Samuel stood before Israel and said: 'I am going to confront you with *evidence* before the Lord' (1 Samuel 12:7).
- According to Jesus, the greatest commandment includes the requirement to 'love the Lord your God . . . *with all your mind*' (Matthew 22:37).
- Jesus said: 'at least *believe on the evidence* of the miracles' (John 14:11).
- When John the Baptist questioned if Jesus' was the messiah, Jesus *appealed to the evidence of his works* (cf. Matthew 11:4–6).
- Paul wrote of 'defending and confirming the gospel' (Philippians 1:7).
- Paul *'reasoned . . . explaining and proving'* (Acts 17:2–3).
- 'Every Sabbath [Paul] *reasoned* in the synagogue, trying to *persuade* Jews and Greeks . . . Paul entered the synagogue and spoke boldly there for three months, *arguing persuasively* about the kingdom of God. But some of them became obstinate; they refused to believe and publicly maligned the Way. So Paul left them. He took the disciples with him and had *discussions* daily in the lecture hall of Tyrannus.' (Acts 18:4, 19:8–9).
- Paul urges Christians to: '*stop thinking like children*. In regard to evil be infants, but *in your thinking be adults.*' (1 Corinthians 14:20).
- Paul advises Christians: 'Choose your words carefully and be ready to give answers to anyone who asks questions.' (Colossians 4:6).
- Christians are commanded: 'always be prepared to *give an answer* to everyone who asks you to give the *reason* for the hope that you have . . . with gentleness and respect' (1 Peter 3:15).

The Greek translated as 'reason' in 1 Peter 3:15 is *'apologia'* – from which we get the word 'apologetics', which can be defined as 'the art of giving a reasoned defence for Christian truth claims'. Apologetics is part of 'spiritual warfare' wherein Christians are called upon to '*demolish arguments* and every pretension that sets itself up against the *knowledge* of God . . .' (2 Corinthians 10:5). Spiritual warfare 'is against unbelief, not unbelievers [its goal] is not victory but truth. Both sides win'.[77]

In sum, as Christian philosopher Richard L. Purtill affirms, 'any claim that Christian belief should be without evidence or contrary to evidence is against the whole tenor of the New Testament.'[78] The biblical attitude to rationality is compatible with the view that a wide range of beliefs are properly basic, and that a belief's *being* properly basic counts (*ceteris paribus*) as a *reason* to believe it. However, the Bible is clearly against 'belief contrary to evidence and reason . . .'[79] As Paul says: 'Test everything. Hold on to the good' (1 Thessalonians 5:21). The Bible is unequivocally in favour of believers fulfilling their intellectual duties; it just doesn't formulate those duties in the self-defeating, narrow terms promulgated by Harris, Dawkins, Sagan, *et al.!*

The Catholic Church declares that 'God . . . can, by the natural light of human reason, be known with certainty from the works of creation.'[80] This statement has generally been understood as endorsing natural theology, which John Polkinghorne defines as 'the attempt to learn something of God from the exercise of reason and the inspection of the world – in other words, from reflection on general experience . . .'[81] Like scriptural passages such as Psalm 19 and Romans 1:18–20, this pronouncement could be read as affirming that God can be *perceived* (in a properly basic manner) through contemplating creation, rather the *proved* (in a properly non-basic manner). Nevertheless, such scriptural and theological assertions at least lay a foundation upon which natural theology may build, for, as Norman L. Geilser writes, 'It should not seem strange to those who believe in God's manifestation in His creation (Rom. 1:19–29; Ps. 19:1) that it is possible to arrive at knowledge of God by inference from these manifestations.'[82] Geisler and Corduan conclude:

> The relationship between an individual's total beliefs and the force of evidence [for God] is a complex one. There can be no doubt that we do hold many beliefs, even religious ones, apart from direct

rational evidence. Thomas Aquinas himself pointed out that it is a good thing that we do not have to have rational proofs for belief in God. Otherwise very few people would believe that he exists, since most of us would be prevented from believing by limitations of intellect and disposition . . . Nonetheless, to say that rational proof does not play as maximal a role as maybe Rene Descartes thought is far from allowing it no role at all . . . Theists have not usually come to believe that there is a God because they think this is the most unreasonable view they could hold.[83]

Colossians 2:8 warns Christians against being taken 'captive by philosophy and empty deceit according to human tradition . . . and not according to Christ', but this 'is not a prohibition against philosophy as such, but against false philosophy . . . In fact, Paul is warning against a specific false philosophy, a kind of incipient Gnosticism . . . the definite article "this" in [the] Greek indicates a particular philosophy.'[84] After all, Paul himself engages in philosophical argumentation (e.g. Acts 17). As C.S. Lewis wrote, 'Good philosophy must exist, if for no other reason, because bad philosophy needs to be answered.'[85] The New Atheists are unfortunately captivated by long-discredited misunderstandings of both faith and reason, misunderstandings that constitute 'an empty deceit according to human tradition'.

Dawkins, Child Abuse and the Atheist's Problem with Evil

'Morally . . . the new atheists cheat at every turn. They believe in doing "right," but never ground it in anything.'
– John Mark Reynolds[86]

Dawkins opines that 'Odious as the physical abuse of children by priests undoubtedly is, I suspect that it may do them less lasting damage than the mental abuse of having been brought up Catholic in the first place.'[87] Since the state has a duty to rescue children from their physical abusers, is the un-stated implication of Dawkins' statement here that the state has a duty to rescue children from their spiritual abusers as well? Dawkins was himself victim of a Latin Master who 'fondled' him: 'a disagreeable sensation for a nineteen-year-old, a mixture of embarrassment and skin-crawling revulsion.'[88] However, says Dawkins, this 'was certainly not in the same league as being led to believe that I, or someone I knew, might go to everlasting fire.'[89] Dawkins has in his sights the fact that the Catholic Church has traditionally taught that unbelievers (even, in some cases, protestant Christians) will spend eternity in a literally fiery hell: 'the *mental* abuse constituted by an unsubstantiated threat of violence and terrible pain, if sincerely *believed* by the child, could easily be more damaging than the physical actuality of sexual abuse. An extreme threat of violence and pain is precisely what the doctrine of hell is.'[90] For Dawkins, 'The threat of eternal hell is an extreme example of mental abuse, just as violent sodomy is an extreme example of physical abuse.'[91]

Like an anti drink-driving advert showing the intrinsic consequences of drink driving, the doctrine of hell should not be understood as a *threat*, but as a *warning* about the intrinsic consequences of rejecting God. Warning children not to stick their fingers into electricity sockets doesn't constitute child abuse; neither does warning children about the consequences of rejecting Jesus (according to Jesus himself). However, the warning about electricity sockets could be given in lurid detail, and might *thereby* constitute abuse. Likewise, the doctrine of hell can be dwelt upon in a lurid and theologically un-nuanced manner, and might *thereby* constitute abuse. Dawkins is right to point out the dangers of unnecessarily traumatizing children about the harsh truths of reality. Christians should always speak the truth as they see it, but they should speak the truth in love (cf. Ephesians 4:15).

Dawkins recognizes that many Christians question the literal content of the so-called 'traditional' doctrine of hell: 'it will be said that the Catholic Church no longer preaches hellfire in its full horror. That depends on how upmarket is your area and how progressive your priest. But eternal punishment certainly was the normal doctrine dished out to congregations, including terrified children, back in the time when many of the priests now facing expulsion or prosecution committed their physical abuses.'[92]

Yet with the 'traditional' doctrine in his sights, Dawkins laments, 'there is no doubt at all that many children sincerely believe it, often continuing right through to adulthood and old age, until death finally releases them.'[93] Concessions about *how* the doctrine is taught, and even *what* doctrine is taught aside, Dawkins' critique crucially assumes that the doctrine of hell is false. Once again a consequentialist ethic is illegitimately elevated over the fundamental question of truth. There is room for dispute among Christians over the content of the doctrine of hell, but little room for doubt over the basic doctrine that there is a real flipside to the possibility of heaven. Granted, if there is no hell then teaching its existence *in an insensitive manner* might result in unnecessary mental anguish. But if hell is real . . .

On the other hand, doesn't Dawkins' criticism cut both ways? Dawkins' atheism results in its fair share of mental anguish, as he acknowledges:

> A foreign publisher of my first book confessed the he could not sleep for three nights after reading it, so troubled was he by what he saw as its cold, bleak message. Others have asked me how I can bear to get up in the mornings. A teacher from a distant country wrote to me reproachfully that a pupil had come to him in tears after reading the same book, because it had persuaded her that life was empty and purposeless. He advised her not to show the book to any of her friends, for fear of contaminating them with the same nihilistic pessimism.[94]

On Dawkins' worldview there is no hell to fear, but there is no heaven to desire either – everything begins and ends in nothingness. In *Unweaving the Rainbow* Dawkins quotes Peter Atkins: 'We are children of chaos, and the deep structure of change is decay. At root, there is only corruption, and the unstemmable tide of chaos. Gone is purpose; all that is left is direction. This is the bleakness we have to accept as we peer deeply and dispassionately into the heart of the Universe.'[95] It is of course because Dawkins believes that these ideas are true that he doesn't consider them mental child abuse, but rather 'a very proper purging of saccharine false purpose [and a] laudable tough-mindedness in the debunking of cosmic sentimentality'.[96] Dawkins doesn't note that Atkins' assertions are metaphysical rather than scientific. He simply asserts that questions about the ultimate nature of reality are irrelevant to questions about personal meaning. 'Presumably there is indeed no purpose in the ultimate fate of the cosmos, but do any of us really tie our life's hopes to the ultimate fate of the cosmos anyway?'[97] In fact, many people *do* tie their life's hopes to the ultimate fate of the cosmos (cf. Revelation 21), and Dawkins' assertion is flawed because questions about the ultimate nature of reality are crucially relevant to questions about meaning.

Dawkins claims that he 'can show that from a Darwinian point of view there is more Darwinian advantage to a male in being promiscuous and a female being faithful, without saying that I therefore think human males are justified in being promiscuous and cheating on their wives. There is no logical connection between what is and what ought . . .'[98] However, Dawkins' world-view provides no grounds for saying that someone who takes the opposite point of view is objectively wrong. After all, 'There is no logical connection between what is and what ought' – it's all just a matter of choice:

> If somebody used my views to justify a completely self-centred lifestyle, which involved trampling all over other people in any way they chose . . . I think I would be fairly hard put to it to argue on purely intellectual grounds . . . I couldn't, ultimately, argue intellectually against somebody who did something I found obnoxious. I think I could finally only say, 'Well, in this society you can't get away with it' and call the police.[99]

In other words, 'might equals right'! A naturalistic worldview doesn't *justify* 'a completely self-centred lifestyle'; but then *it doesn't justify any lifestyle*. The choice between lifestyles, *including the choice between abusing children and trying to prevent abuse*, is *on Dawkins' own assumptions* nothing but a non-rational manifestation of a Nietzschean 'will to power'. For Dawkins, moral assertions are not factual assertions about what is the case that are either true or false, but merely subjective assertions that are not objectively true or false: 'there is a non-overlapping and exhaustive distinction between ideas that are false or true about the real world (factual matters, in the broad sense) and ideas about what we ought to do – normative or moral ideas, for which the words "true" and "false" have no meaning.'[100]

Dawkins asserts that: 'The universe that we observe has precisely the properties we should expect if there is, at bottom, no design, no purpose, *no evil, no good*, nothing but pitiless indifference.'[101] Hence Dawkins' ends up *explaining away* morality rather than explaining it – because his explanation requires us to translate talk about things being objectively right or wrong into talk about certain members of our species having the subjective *feeling* that something is 'right' or 'wrong' because they happen to have evolved that way through a process of *unintended* evolution. Dawkins claims to have 'seen through' morality in precisely the same way in which his explanation of religion – that it is *nothing but* an activity that happens to aid group survival (interesting that he doesn't explain science like this!) – 'sees through' religion. As John F. Haught comments:

> Dawkins declares that the biblical God is a monster; Harris that God is evil; Hitchens, the God is not great. But without some fixed sense of rightness, how can one distinguish what is monstrous, evil, or 'not great' from its opposite? In order to make such value judgements, one must assume, as the hard-core atheists [like Neitzsche or the early Sartre] are honest enough to acknowledge, that there exists somewhere . . . a realm of rightness that does not owe its existence completely to human invention, Darwinian selection, or social construction. If we allow the hard-core atheists into our discussion we can draw this conclusion: If absolute values exist, then God exists. But if God does not exist, then neither do absolute values . . . Belief in God . . . is not necessary in order for people to be highly moral beings. We can agree with our soft-core atheists on this point. But the real question, which comes not from me but from the hard-core atheists, is: Can you rationally justify your unconditional adherence to timeless values without implicitly invoking the existence of God? The hard-core atheists say 'no'.[102]

Evolution might account for our having certain moral *feelings* about actions, but it can't objectively *prescribe* that we objectively ought to pay attention to those feelings because they correspond to an objective moral ideal (where, in a naturalistic metaphysics, can one fit such a thing as an objective moral ideal?). Nor can it *obligate* us to pay attention to them, because only persons can prescribe or obligate behaviour, whilst a wholly naturalistic evolutionary history is impersonal. As agnostic philosopher Anthony O'Hear says of Dawkins, 'this particular Darwinian is quite unable to explain why we have an obligation to act against our "selfish" genes.'[103]

When Dawkins says that religion is 'the root of all evil' what he *means* by 'evil' is really 'things that a blind material process contingently caused me to dislike'. According to Dawkins (in a moment of 'hard-core' atheistic realism) there is, objectively speaking, 'no evil, no good . . .'[104] Dawkins says he realizes this is 'very weak . . . But I still think it's a separate issue from beliefs in cosmic truths.'[105] It is a separate issue, in the sense that *truths about an amoral reality can never discredit Dawkins' choice to condemn child abuse*; but it is far from being a separate issue in the sense that *truths about an amoral reality can never endorse Dawkins' choice to condemn child abuse*. As Richard L. Purtill says of purported moral arguments for atheism, 'If morality impelled us to take such a view, integrity might make us choose it. But if the view is true, morality has no force.'[106]

We must distinguish behaviours that do and do not cohere with a person's worldview.

> To avoid being too simplistic we must look to the essential teaching of what a religion is. We should look at its abuses, but we should also look at its core principles. Is taking up the sword in the name of Jesus to promote Christianity consistent with what Jesus affirmed? We could ask the same of Islam or Hinduism. Do the core beliefs of the religion actually advocate violent means as a way of dealing with others?[107]

Theists can say that those who do evil in the name of God are being inconsistent; but can the atheist maintain that the inquisition or the crusades are inconsistent with their worldview of an amoral universe? Obviously not, because *no action can fail to cohere with an amoral metaphysical framework*. As Ravi Zacharias explains, 'The denuding of people, in every sense of the word, that took place in concentration camps, brought about the logical outworking of the demise of God and the extermination of moral law . . . Disregarding the sanctity of life, and its resultant corollary of estimating the value of life by its quality, proved some of the Third Reich's metaphysical moorings.'[108] According to Auschwitz survivor and psychiatrist Victor Frankl, 'The gas chambers of Auschwitz were the ultimate consequence of the theory that man is nothing but the product of heredity and environment – or, as the Nazis liked to say, "of blood and soil". I am absolutely convinced that the gas chambers of Auschwitz . . . were ultimately prepared . . . in lecture halls of nihilistic scientists and philosophers.'[109] Hitler's pronouncement is preserved at Auschwitz: 'I freed Germany from the stupid and degrading fallacies of conscience and morality . . . we will train young people before whom the world will tremble. I want young people capable of violence – imperious, relentless and cruel.'[110] That was *his* subjective choice. Fascist Benito Mussolini explicitly grounded his dictatorship in moral relativism, writing that:

> If relativism signifies contempt for fixed categories and men who claim to be bearers of an objective, immortal truth . . . then there is nothing more relativistic than fascist attitudes and activity . . . From the fact that all ideologies are mere fictions, the modern relativist infers that everybody has the right to create for himself his own ideology and to attempt to enforce it with all the energy of which he is capable.[111]

I'm not saying that Dawkins *endorses* such behaviour. I am arguing that *Dawkins' worldview cannot coherently endorse moral opposition to such behaviour, whether evinced by atheists or theists.*

Conclusion

> *'it is just plain silly and grotesquely immoral to claim that Christianity is simply a force for evil, as Richard claims . . .'*
> – Michael Ruse[112]

Hell is the flip side to heaven (if heaven is freely accepted, it can be freely rejected), and both testify that life is not only meaningful, but serious. Christians should ponder how (and what) they teach about hell, especially to children. However, atheists should ponder Dawkins' acknowledgment that naturalism undermines the condemnation of anything (including child-abuse) as objectively evil. As Chapman Cohen – the third president of the National Secular Society – wrote, 'the real value of any theory depends ultimately upon its truth. The argument from consequences is only valid if it can be shown that these are in obvious conflict with facts.'[113] But for Dawkins *et al.*, moral values are not facts. Hence, aside from the fact that Dawkins' specific charge of 'mental child abuse' has nothing to do with theism *per se* (it only applies to Christians with a particular doctrine and a particularly bad way of communicating it), his objection is self-contradictory because it depends upon a notion of moral value that, as Dawkins himself argues, his naturalistic worldview cannot entertain.

Recommended Resources

David Aikman, *The Delusion of Disbelief: Why the New Atheism Is a Threat to Your Life, Liberty, and Pursuit of Happiness* (Tyndale House: SaltRiver, 2008).

Francis J. Beckwith and Gregory Koukl, *Relativism: Feet Firmly Planted in Mid-Air* (Grand Rapids, MI: Baker, 1998).

Theodore J. Chamberlain and Christopher A. Hall, *Realized Religion – Research on the Relationship between Religion and Health* (Philadelphia, PA: Templeton Foundation Press, 2000).

James Kelly Clark, *Return to Reason* (Grand Rapids, MI: Eerdmans, 1998).

Paul Copan, *How Do You Know You're Not Wrong?* (Grand Rapids, MI: Baker, 2005).

Paul Copan, *That's Just Your Interpretation* (Grand Rapids, MI: Baker, 2001).

William Lane Craig and Paul M. Gould, *The Two Tasks of the Christian Scholar: Redeeming the Soul, Redeeming the Mind* (Wheaton, IL: Crossway, 2007).

Tobias Jones, *Utopian Dreams: In Search of a Good Life* (London: Faber and Faber, 2007).

C.S. Lewis, *The Problem of Pain* (London: Fount, 2002).

J.P. Moreland, *Love Your God With All Your Mind* (Colorado Springs, CO: NavPress, 1997).

J.P. Moreland and Mark Matlock, *Smart Faith: Loving God With All Your Mind* (Colorado Springs, CO: Think, 2005).

J.P. Moreland and William Lane Craig, *Foundations of a Christian Worldview* (Downers Grove, IL: IVP, 2003).

Alvin Plantinga, *Warranted Christian Belief* (Oxford: Oxford University Press, 2003), www.ccel.org/ccel/plantinga/warranted.html.

Robert Spencer, *Religion of Peace? Why Christianity Is And Islam Isn't* (Washington, DC: Regnery, 2007).

Lee Strobel, *The Case for Faith: A Journalist Investigates the Toughest Objections to Christianity* (Grand Rapids, MI: Zondervan, 2000).

Keith Ward, *Is Religion Dangerous?* (Oxford: Lion, 2006).

Richard Weikart, *From Darwin To Hitler: Evolutionary Ethics, Eugenics, and Racism in Germany* (New York: Palgrave, 2004).

John G. West, *Darwin Day in America: How Our Politics and Culture Have Been Dehumanized in the Name of Science* (Washington DC: ISI, 2007).

John G. West, *Darwin's Conservatives: The Misguided Quest* (Washington, DC: Centre for Science & Culture, 2006).

Benjamin Wiker, *Moral Darwinism: How We Became Hedonists* (Downers Grove, IL: IVP, 2002).

Ravi Zacharias, *Can Man Live Without God?* (Dallas, TX: Word, 1995).

On-Line Papers

Kelly James Clark, 'Without Evidence or Argument: A Defense of Reformed Epistemology', www.calvin.edu/academic/philosophy/virtual_library/articles/clark_kelly_j/without_evidence_or_argument.pdf.

Paul Copan, 'The Moral Argument for God's Existence', www.4truth.net/site/apps/nl/content3.asp?c=hiKXLbPNLrF&b=778665&ct=1264233.

Paul Copan, 'Is Yahweh a Moral Monster? The New Atheists and Old Testament Ethics', http://epsociety.org/library/articles.asp?pid=45.

William Lane Craig, 'The Indispensability of Theological Meta-Ethical Foundations for Morality', www.leaderu.com/offices/billcraig/docs/meta-eth.html.

Dave Crofts, 'The Root of all Evil? Parts 1 and 2', www.christchurchcentral.co.uk/culture/rootofallevil1_1.htm; www.christchurchcentral.co.uk/culture/rootofallevil2_1.html.

Dinesh D'Souza, 'Was Hitler a Christian?', www.catholiceducation.org/articles/facts/fm0110.htm.

Gary R. Habermas, 'Atheism and Evil: A Fatal Dilemma', www.garyhabermas.com/books/why_believe/whybelieve.htm.

Logan Paul Gage, 'Staying Power: Does Religion Poison Everything?', www.discovery.org/scripts/viewDB/index.php?command=view&id=4393&program=CSC%20-%20Views%20and%20News.

Gregory Koukl, 'Intuition: A Special Way of Knowing', www.bethinking.org/resource.php?ID=26&TopicID=4 & CategoryID=6.

Peter May, 'Life After God? – The Ethics of Peter Singer', www.bethinking.org/resource.php?ID=302.

Alvin Plantinga, 'Theism, Atheism, and Rationality', www.leaderu.com/truth/3truth02.html.

Alvin Plantinga, 'Intellectual Sophistication and Basic Belief in God', www.leaderu.com/truth/3truth03.html.

Tom Price, 'Religion Causes Wars', www.bethinking.org/resource.php?ID=227&TopicID=4&CategoryID=6.

Roger Scruton, 'Dawkins is Wrong About God', http://catholiceducation.org/articles/science/sc0078.html.

Peter S. Williams, 'Review: Utopian Dreams', www.damaris.org/content/content.php?type=5&id=541.

Audio

William Lane Craig, 'Who Really Cares?', www.reasonable-faith.org/site/News2?page=NewsArticle&id=5887.

Richard Dawkins and John Lennox discuss *The God Delusion*, http://richarddawkins.net/audio/dawkins-lennox_part1.mov http://richarddawkins.net/audio/dawkins-lennox_part2.mov http://richarddawkins.net/audio/dawkins-lennox_part3.mov.

Daniel Dennett and David Cook, 'Discussing Religion', http://archive.wgnradio.com:8080/ramgen/wgnam/shows/ex720/Audio/religion060215mr.rm.

Keith Ward, 'Is Religion Dangerous?', http://richarddawkins.net.nyud.net:8080/audio/5live_mayo_ward.mp3.

Peter S. Williams, 'Doubting Thomas and the New Atheists.' www.damaris.org/cm/podcasts/category/peterswilliams.

Peter S. Williams, 'God and Purpose', www.damaris.org/cm/podcasts/category/peterswilliams.

Video

William Lane Crag, 'Can the world have objective values without God?', www.leestrobel.com/videos/Creator/strobelT1211.htm.

Dinesh D'Souza and Michael Shermer, 'Is Christianity Good For the World? Part One – Speeches', http://video.google.com/videoplay?docid=-9349347387360252848&hl=en.

Dinesh D'Souza and Michael Shermer, 'Is Christianity Good For the World? Part Two: Dialogue'.

Gregory Koukl, 'Faith', http://abetterhope.blogspot.com/2007/11/greg-koukl-what-is-faith.html.

Dinesh D'Souza and Michael Shermer, 'Is Christianity Good for the World?' Part 2, http://video.google.com/videosearch?q=Dinesh+D%E2%80%99Souza+and+Michael+Shermer%2C+%E2%80%98Is+Christianity+Good+for+the+World%3F%E2%80%99#.

J.P. Moreland, 'Right and Wrong as a Key to the Meaning of the Universe', http://webcast.ucsd.edu:8080/ramgen/UCSD_TV/8008.rm.

4

Is Religion Nothing Buttery Short of a Sandwich?

'everybody has their own pet theory of where religion comes from and why all human cultures have it.'
– Richard Dawkins[1]

Many atheists try to *explain away* belief in God as the result of 'nothing but' this or that natural cause. Elizabeth Burns and Stephen Law suggest that this 'religion is nothing but . . .' challenge 'would be effective if it could be shown that alleged experiences of God were caused by something other than God'.[2] It would be more accurate to say that the challenge would then be *partially* effective, in that it would undermine belief in God wholly based upon religious experience. However, Burns and Law point out, 'if God is omnipresent and the sustainer of all causal processes, *whatever* brings about an experience of God will, ultimately, be caused by God. It could only be shown that these alleged experiences were not caused by God if it could be shown that God does not exist.'[3] Hence, even if every case of theistic belief could plausibly be explained in terms of some naturalistic theory or other, that still wouldn't exclude positive answers to the questions 'Does God exist?' and 'Is belief in God warranted?'

Plantinga's Alternative Account of Warrant

Alvin Plantinga offers an alternative to the classical foundation-alist way of distinguishing between: a) beliefs which a person is within their epistemic rights to accept without an appeal to reasons and/or evidence, and b) beliefs that lack such 'warrant'. Since a *less generous* account of warrant than that offered by classical foundationalism would necessarily be self-defeating, Plantinga offers a *more generous* account of warrant. CF had the defect of excluding cases of clearly justifiable basic beliefs. For example, while I am surely justified in holding my belief that I had coffee with friends yesterday, this belief isn't self-evident, evident from the senses or incorrigible. Hence, according to CF, it is not a properly basic belief. The classical foundationalist would say that this is so much the worse for my belief that I had coffee with friends yesterday. Like Plantinga, I am inclined to say that this is so much the worse for the CF account of rationality. Coffee with friends beats classical foundationalism.

Plantinga's more generous account of warrant permits my coffee-with-friends belief, grounded in my apparent memory of the event, to count as properly basic. This is to its advantage. The same account of warrant also permits my belief in God, grounded in my apparent religious experience, to count as properly basic. This belief (like my coffee drinking belief) may well be supportable by evidence (the empty mugs are still in my washing-up bowl, and the Thomistic cosmological argument explains why they persist in existence), but according to Plantinga's account of warrant, evidence is not necessarily *required* to make belief in God rational, as is suggested by CF.

Plantinga observes that for many people God's existence is a basic belief, and proposes that

> there is a kind of faculty or cognitive mechanism, what Calvin calls a *sensus divinitatis* or sense of divinity, which in a wide variety of circumstances produces in us beliefs about God . . . The *sensus divinitatis* is a disposition or set of dispositions to form theistic beliefs in various circumstances . . . The deliverances of the *sensus divinitatis* are not . . . inferences from the circumstances that trigger its operation. It isn't that one beholds the night sky, notes that it is grand, and concludes that there must be such a person as God . . . It is rather that, upon the perception of the night sky . . . these beliefs just arise within us. They are *occasioned* by the circumstances; they are not conclusions drawn from them . . . In this

regard, the *sensus divinitatis* resembles perception, memory, and *a priori* belief.[4]

Basic belief in God looks like other basic beliefs that are properly basic, and it is therefore reasonable for theists to think of their basic belief in God in terms of a God-given cognitive mechanism which confers *proper basicality*, or warrant. The difference between theists and atheists concerning the suggestion that theistic belief is produced by some cognitive mechanism or other is not, therefore, about whether or not any such mechanism exists. Rather, the dispute is about whether such a mechanism is or is not a God-given cognitive mechanism (properly functioning and aimed at truth in an appropriate environment), a mechanism that therefore issues in warranted belief. In other words, the theist disputes the naturalistic 'nothing but'. Theists can see belief in God as properly basic because they can see it as the result of properly functioning cognitive faculties, given to humans by God with the truth-directed intent that they can know him in a properly basic manner, working in an appropriate environment (*Christian* theists consider the work of the Holy Spirit in the believer's mind to be a source of warranted Christian belief): 'if theistic belief is *true*, then . . . the natural thing to think is that the cognitive processes that *do* produce belief in God are aimed by their designer at producing that belief. But then the belief in question will be produced by cognitive faculties functioning properly according to a design plan successfully aimed at truth: it will therefore have warrant.'[5]

By the principle of credulity, beliefs that appear to be properly basic should be accepted as being true *until and unless there is sufficient reason to doubt them*. Unless they are indispensable or incorrigible, properly basic beliefs are defeasible claims, at least in principle. Challenges against apparently properly basic beliefs are of two sorts: *de facto or anti-truth* objections that the belief in question is *false*; and *de jure* or *anti-belief* objections that (despite appearances) the belief in question is *not properly basic*. A *de jure* objection is the objection that a belief 'doesn't originate in the proper function of cognitive faculties successfully aimed at producing true beliefs'.[6] Hence a *de jure* objection to theism is a claim or argument to the effect that *irrespective of its truth-value*, theism is at any rate unjustifiable, or rationally unjustified, or irrational, or not intellectually respectable, or contrary to sound morality, or without sufficient evidence, or in some other way rationally unacceptable, not up to snuff from an intellectual point of view . . . the basic idea is that belief of this sort is not produced by properly functioning truth-aimed cognitive faculties or processes. It is not produced by belief-producing processes that are free of dysfunction and whose purpose is to furnish us with true belief. And this means that the presumption of the reliability of properly functioning cognitive faculties does not apply . . .[7]

However, as Plantinga notes, 'What you properly take to be [warranted] depends on what kind of beings you think human beings are, and what sort of beliefs you think their noetic faculties will produce when they are functioning properly . . .'[8] This being so, 'the dispute as to whether theistic belief is . . . (warranted) can't be settled just be attending to epistemological considerations.'[9] But this is just what *de jure* arguments try to do.

You may think humankind is created by God in the image of God . . . with a natural tendency to see God's hand in the world about us . . . Then of course you will not think of belief in God as in the typical case a manifestation of any kind of intellectual defect. Nor will you think it is a manifestation of a belief-producing power or mechanism that is not aimed at truth . . . On the other hand . . . you may think there is no God . . . Then perhaps you will be inclined to accept the sort of view according to which belief in God is an illusion of some sort, properly traced to wishful thinking or some other cognitive mechanism not aimed at truth . . . (Freud) or to a sort of disease or dysfunction on the part of the individual or society (Marx). And this dependence of the question of warrant . . . on the truth or falsehood of theism leads to a very interesting conclusion. If the *warrant* enjoyed by belief in God is related in this way to the *truth* of that belief, then the question whether theistic belief has *warrant* is not after all independent of the question whether theistic belief is *true*.[10]

In other words, *de jure* objections to theism are *question-begging*, and 'a successful atheological objection will have to be to the

truth of theism, not to its rationality, or justification, or intellectual respectability.'[11] Before atheologians can discredit a basic
belief in God with reference to this or that *process* of belief-formation, they must first prove that God does not exist, because 'if
Christian belief is true then it is highly probable that it is
warranted.'[12] The atheologian can't attack theism simply by referencing a process of belief formation, because any process they
mention could be a process intended by God:

> To show that there are natural processes that produce religious
> belief does nothing, so far, to discredit it; perhaps God designed us
> in such a way that it is by virtue of those processes that we come
> to have knowledge of him. Suppose it could be demonstrated that
> a certain kind of complex neural stimulation could produce theis-
> tic belief. This would have no tendency to discredit religious belief
> – just as memory is not discredited by the fact that one can pro-
> duce memory beliefs by stimulating the right part of the brain.
> Clearly, it is possible both that there is an explanation in terms of
> natural processes of religious beliefs (perhaps a brain physiologi-
> cal account of what happens when someone holds religious
> beliefs), and that these beliefs have a perfectly respectable epis-
> temic status . . .[13]

If one wants to argue that belief in God is *not* warranted one must
do so *indirectly*, sidestepping the question of warrant *per se* and
offering objections to *the existence of God* rather than to *the appro-
priateness of belief in God*. Plantinga applies this insight to Freud's
critique of theism as wish-fulfillment:

> Even if it were established that wish-fulfillment *is* the source of
> theistic belief, that wouldn't be enough to establish that the latter
> had no warrant. It must also be established that wish-fulfillment *in
> this particular manifestation* is not aimed at true belief . . . Perhaps
> this is how God has arranged for us to come to know him. If so,
> then the particular bit of the cognitive design plan governing the
> formation of theistic belief is indeed aimed at true belief, even if
> the belief in question arises from wish-fulfillment . . . how would
> Freud . . . establish that the mechanism whereby human beings
> come to believe in God [as a basic belief] is *not* aimed at the truth?

> This is really the crux of the matter. Freud . . . simply takes it for
> granted that there is no God and that theistic belief is false; he then
> casts about for some kind of explanation of this widespread phe-
> nomenon of mistaken belief. He hits on wish-fulfillment and
> apparently assumes it is obvious that this mechanism . . . is not
> aimed at the production of true belief – so that such belief lacks
> warrant . . . this is a safe assumption if in fact theism *is* false. But
> then Freud's . . . criticism really depends on his atheism: it isn't an
> independent criticism at all.[14]

The atheist can't know that a cognitive mechanism leading to a
basic belief in God is unreliable without first knowing that God
doesn't exist, so they can't show that belief in God is unwarranted simply by identifying a relevant cognitive mechanism and
asserting that it is unreliable. To show that the mechanism is
unreliable they would have to show that the mechanism isn't
intended by God, and to do *that* they must disprove God's existence on independent grounds (and to do *that* they must do more
than complain about the supposed lack of evidence supporting
theism).

The fact that theistic belief grounded in appropriate experiences counts as properly basic means that, contrary to the
assumptions of classical foundationalism, theism can be rational
without evidential support: 'if theistic and Christian beliefs are
properly basic with respect to warrant, they do not stand or fall
on the strength of evidence. . . .'[15] Non-theists may of course
attempt to use naturalistic theories to account for theism *if they
believe they have already disproved theism*, but they cannot use such
theories to attack theism, for 'There is no sensible challenge to the
rationality or rational justification or warrant of Christian belief
that is not also a challenge to its *truth*. That is, there is no *de jure*
challenge that is independent of a *de facto* challenge.'[16] Plantinga
points out that 'This fact by itself invalidates an enormous
amount of recent and contemporary atheology; for much of that
atheology is devoted to *de jure* complaints . . .'[17]

Plantinga's account of warrant rebuts *de jure* objections to theistic belief. It also provides theists with grounds for resisting *de
facto* objections, at least of a certain epistemic weight. This is
because there are cases where a properly basic belief can itself

have more epistemic weight than a *de facto* challenge it faces. Suppose you are tried for murder but that you believe, in a properly basic manner (e.g. based on memory that you were elsewhere at the time, albeit without witnesses) that you didn't commit the crime. Suppose the evidence presented in court points to your guilt. You wouldn't *necessarily* be obliged to believe yourself guilty! That would depend upon the strength of the evidence for your guilt compared to the inherent strength of your properly basic belief in your innocence. A properly basic belief in your innocence might override a great deal of evidence pointing to your guilt, even if there is some level of evidence that would force you to acquiesce (like a *Cluedo* player forced to deduce that their own character is the murderer). In the same way, religious experience can be sufficiently compelling in and of itself to soak up at least some *de facto* objections brought against it.

Plantinga's account of warranted theistic belief is not an argument for God's existence, but for taking theist belief formed in appropriate circumstances as being warranted until proven otherwise, and thus as being wholly immune to *de jure* objections and partially immune to *de facto* objections.

'Belief in God is nothing but . . .'

> *'The final decisive edge enjoyed by scientific naturalism will come from its capacity to explain traditional religion . . . as a wholly material phenomenon.'*
> – Edward O. Wilson[18]

Failure to provide a plausible naturalistic explanation for theistic belief would be a mark against a naturalistic worldview, but the ability to provide such an explanation would not be a mark against theism. One simply cannot justify the 'nothing buttery' of such a claim without begging the question. As Kai Nielson admits, 'naturalistic explanations [of theistic belief] will become of paramount interest only when the critique of theism has been thought to have done its work.'[19] Richard Dawkins notes that he structured *The God Delusion* so as to treat the search for an evolutionary explanation of religion *as a quest that arises from the conclusion that God does not exist*: 'The non-existence of God is the main conclusion of the first half of my book. The second half is devoted to questions that arise from it. Why, if religion is false, do so many people believe in it?'[20]

Theists needn't grant the existence of a plausible naturalistic explanation of religious belief in the first place. As William P. Alston writes, 'The first thing to consider is whether mystical experience *can* be given an adequate explanation in terms of purely natural causes. If we consider the actual attempts to do this . . . we must judge them to be highly speculative and, at best, sketchily supported by the evidence . . .'[21] Even if we were in possession of a naturalistic explanation of mystical experience:

> The case of sense perception shows us that the object perceived need not be among the *proximate* causes of experience. Those causes are all within the subject's brain, which is not itself perceived. What we sensorily perceive is located further back along the causal chain leading to the experience. Hence even if the proximate causes of mystical experience are all within the natural world, the possibility remains that God figures further back among the causes of the experience in such a way as to be perceived in having that experience.[22]

Breaking Dennett's Spell

'They will see me as just another liberal professor trying to cajole them out of some of their convictions, and they are dead right about that – that's what I am, and that's exactly what I am trying to do.'
– Daniel Dennett[23]

Theistic believers claim both that theism is true and that theistic religion exists primarily because God wants people to believe in him. In response, Daniel Dennett tries to tell a coherent, plausible and wholly naturalistic story that incorporates theistic religious belief. His story is that early humans evolved the capacity to see things in goal-directed terms, and that they generalized the application of this capacity, treating anything that frustrated or frightened them as the intention of an agent. From here, beliefs about deities 'evolved'. This 'just so story' story contradicts all claims about historical revelation, but Dennett skirts around this issue by asserting that 'historical arguments . . . simply cannot be introduced into serious investigation, since they are manifestly question begging.'[24] In this, Dennett is mistaken. Historical arguments for revelation need not be question-begging. Arguments for revelation may proceed on the basis of an open-minded agnosticism; or they may be deployed merely to justify the move from a general philosophical theism to a specific religious tradition. Indeed, it is the assumption of naturalism that begs the question against historical arguments for revelation. It is actually Dennett who argues in a circle here, by writing of 'the scientific method, with its assumption of no miracles',[25] as if he can avoid studying historical revelation claims by definitional fiat. Moreover, Dennett embraces a self-defeating *scientistic* epistemology, asking if there is 'any good reason – and *scientific* reason, we might say, for believing in God'.[26]

John Gray comments that 'When Dennett delivers on the promise of the book – a naturalistic explanation of religion – the result is embarrassingly naive.'[27] Atheist Jeremy Stangroom complains:

> Dennett's argument is certainly interesting, but there are significant problems with it. Particularly, it suffers from one of the standard difficulties of the evolutionary approach, namely [that] there is . . . no obvious way to determine whether its conjectures are true. Dennett . . . openly admits that much of what he suggests might turn out to be false. However, the problem runs deeper than this: it is not so much that his specific ideas might be false, it is that it is not clear how one would determine whether they are or not.[28]

Dennett admits that his naturalistic story might be wrong, writing that he tries

> to tell *the best current version* of the story science can tell about how religions have come to be what they are. I am not at all claiming that this is what science has already established about religion. The main point of this book is to insist that we *don't* yet know – but we can discover – the answers to these important

questions . . . Probably some features of the story I tell will prove in due course to be mistaken. Maybe many of them are wrong . . . My description of the evolution of various features of religion . . . is definitely 'just a theory' – or, rather, a family of proto-theories, in need of further development . . . If somebody wants to put a sticker in this book, saying that it presents a theory, not a fact, I would happily concur. *Caution!* It should say. *Assuming that these propositions are true without further research could lead to calamitous results.*[29]

Note Dennett's faith in the *discoverability* of a true naturalistic explanation for theistic religion: 'The main point of this book is to insist that we *don't* yet know – but we can discover – the answers to these important questions.'[30] Dennett doesn't completely ignore his share of the burden of proof here, since he does review some theistic arguments in a half-hearted attempt to undermine natural theology. However, even to succeed in undermining natural theology is not the same thing as establishing the naturalistic worldview Dennett assumes throughout. Dennett acknowledges that the existence of a naturalistic story that includes theistic religion doesn't show that theism is false, since even to succeed in providing a plausible naturalistic explanation of a belief is not to call into question the warrant of that belief. For example, 'divination, which appears just about everywhere in human culture . . . could be understood as a natural phenomenon . . . *whether or not it is actually a source of reliable information* . . .'[31] The same goes, as Dennett acknowledges, for theism: 'it could be true that God exists . . . and yet *still* religion itself . . . is a perfectly natural phenomenon.'[33]

By Dennett's own admission, then, *everything hinges upon how he cashes in his promissory note to deal directly with the question of whether or not God exists.* How disappointing that when, 'at long last', Dennett turns 'to the promised consideration of arguments for the existence of God,' we find a mere eleven-paragraph, six-page 'bird's-eye view of the domain of inquiry, expressing my own verdicts but not the reasoning that has gone into them . . .'[33] Dennett the naturalist has about as much interest in rebutting natural theology as a naturist has in preserving their modesty with a fig-leaf.

> Philosophers have spent two millennia and more concocting and criticizing arguments for the existence of God . . . and arguments against the existence of God . . . Many of us brights have devoted considerable time and energy at some point in our lives to looking at the arguments for and against the existence of God, and many brights continue to pursue these issues, hacking away vigorously at the arguments of believers as if they were trying to refute a rival scientific theory. But not I. I decided some time ago that diminishing returns had set in on the arguments for God's existence, and I doubt that any breakthroughs are in the offing, from either side.[34]

Aside from its horticultural rhetoric, and hints that Dennett hasn't kept up to date with this vibrant field of inquiry, the most interesting thing about Dennett's jaundiced view of natural theology is his last three words, which one might think undermine his easy reliance upon the assumption of naturalism. However, Dennett keeps his focus exclusively on one side of the balance, skimming over straw man versions of the argument from historical revelation, as well as the ontological and cosmological arguments. The design argument is barely discussed. Other major theistic arguments simply aren't mentioned. In short, *by his own admission, Dennett's scanty treatment of the crucial point at issue falls far short of justifying the naturalistic assumption underlying the rest of his book.* As Keith Ward cautions:

> Dennett's requirement that a scientific study of religion should treat it as a 'purely natural' phenomenon . . . sets out with the assumption that all religious beliefs (all the ones about non-natural or non-physical realities like God) are false [and] amounts to treating all religious believers as deluded or perhaps even mentally challenged. Most contemporary anthropologists think that beginning with such a strong prejudice is not the right way to undertake a properly scientific enquiry.[35]

Dennett effectively begs the question against theism for the majority of his book, before conspicuously failing to deliver on the all-important question of God's existence.

Dennett's argument exhibits the same faulty structure as Dawkins' argument for evolution. Dawkins admits that natural things look designed, but asserts that evolution can explain away this apparent design. Dawkins acknowledges that he can't show *which* circuitous path life took up 'Mount Improbable' (and hence can't prove *that* life took such a path). Nevertheless, he asserts, 'graded ramps can be found the other side and the peak eventually scaled'.[36] How does Dawkins know that these ramps can be found *in advance of showing what they are*? Because their existence is required by his favoured theory; their existence is a philosophical deduction rather than a scientific observation or inference: 'Without stirring from our chair, we can see that it must be so,'[37] Dawkins explains, 'because nothing except gradual accumulation could, in principle, do the job . . .'[38] That is, the job of explaining apparent design *without reference to actual design* (for of course actual design *can* explain the existence of apparent design)! Dawkins' argument is question begging: there must be a graded ramp because the alternative (design) is ruled out *a priori*. As Dennett comments, 'This is a purely theory-driven explanation, argued a-priori from the assumption that natural selection tells the true story – some true story or other – about every curious feature of the biosphere . . . it assumes that Darwinism is basically on the right track.'[39]

How disappointing, then, to find Dennett arguing in an analogous circle: naturalism requires (what it currently lacks) a plausible naturalistic explanation for religion. Dennett asserts that a true account can be provided in principle, and he outlines one candidate for such an account. Dennett acknowledges that he hasn't got all the details worked out yet, but he deduces that there must be a naturalistic explanation, because the existence of such an explanation is required by his favoured theory. Dennett's argument is plainly question begging: there must be a naturalistic explanation for religion because the alternative (sound metaphysical thinking and/or divine revelation and/or divinely designed properly basic belief) is ruled out *a priori*! As John F. Haught observes, 'Dennett's belief that science can provide an adequate understanding of religion is obviously not a scientifically proven or even provable claim. It is a dogma, a declaration of faith . . . almost everything Dennett writes about religion is based on his own belief in scientific naturalism . . .'[40]

The best that can be said for *Breaking the Spell*, then, is that it is a subtle yet flawed attempt to fill in an acknowledged explanatory gap in the naturalistic worldview, an attempt that does at least as much to draw attention to the explanatory failure in question as it does to remedy it. Denis Alexander is rightly unimpressed, commenting that

> scientists coming to the book expecting to find rigorous science will go away disappointed . . . [*Breaking the Spell*] is not really a scientific study of religion at all, but the author's attempt to justify his own belief that religious beliefs represent 'nothing but' utilitarian functions . . . a problem, of course, with all such psychological explanations for the acquisition of beliefs is that they inevitably act as two-edged swords, and in the process all types of belief of whatever hue are sucked into the same philosophical black hole.[41]

Could be True, Might be True, Self-Defeating if True

'Criticisms of religion based on accounts of psychological origin hold little sway among professional philosophers.'
– John O'Leary-Hawthorn[42]

It isn't too difficult to concoct hypotheses that, *if true*, might result in people believing all sorts of things (including theism and atheism) irrespective of the truth-value of those beliefs. Descartes' thought experiment about an evil demon systematically deceiving us, Schopenhauer's suggestion that humans are in the impersonal grip of the 'will to life' and Darwin's suggestion that our cognitive apparatus is the product of a blind watchmaker concerned only with survival, all qualify. But the mere fact that a theory, *if true*, can explain why theists believe in God *on the assumption that theism is false*, does nothing to establish either the truth of the theory of belief-formation concerned, or the truth of atheism.

While it's easy to concoct hypotheses that, *if true*, might result in people believing all sorts of things (including theism and atheism) irrespective of the truth-value of those beliefs, it's hard to construct such hypotheses *so that that the hypotheses don't undermine themselves.* C.E.M. Joad considers the suggestion that religion is nothing but a matter of wish-fulfillment, arguing that

> If it is in fact the case that our thoughts are not free but are dictated by our wishes, and that reasoning is, therefore, mere rationalizing, then the conclusion applies also to the reasoning of psycho-analysis . . . Since, therefore, it seems to follow that, if psychoanalysis is correct in what it asserts about reason, it is meaningless to ask whether psycho-analysis is true, there is no reason to suppose that it is correct in what it asserts about religion.[43]

Alister McGrath, considering Dawkins' concept of theistic belief as a 'meme',[44] the supposed cultural analogue of a gene, writes that

> Dawkins' answer lies in the ability of the God-meme to replicate itself in the human mind . . . The problem with this approach is immediately obvious. If all ideas are memes, or the effects of memes, Dawkins is left in the decidedly uncomfortable position of having to accept that his own ideas must also be recognized as the effects of memes. Scientific ideas would then become yet another example of memes replicating within the human mind. This would not suit Dawkins' purpose at all, and he excludes the notion [in] a case of special pleading . . .[45]

The 'explaining away' approach to religion suffers from a *tu quoque* problem explored by C.S. Lewis in *The Prilgrim's Regress*.

> 'Argument,' said Master Parrot, 'is the attempted rationalization of the arguer's desires.' 'Very good,' replied the jailor . . . 'Now: what is the proper answer to an argument proving the existence of the Landlord?' 'The proper answer is, "You say that because you are a [believer]" . . . ' 'Good. Now just one more. What is the answer to an argument turning on the belief that two and two make four?' 'The answer is, "You say that because you are a mathematician".'[46]

A double standard backs the argument that religious belief is 'nothing but' the product of whatever belief-production mechanism is favoured by the atheist, whereas non-religious beliefs (such as the atheist's belief that religious beliefs are nothing but this or that) are assumed to be the product of critical faculties aimed at truth. As Lewis observes:

> The Spirit of the Age wishes to allow argument and not to allow argument . . . If anyone argues with them they say that he is ration-alizing his own desires, and therefore need not be answered. But if anyone listens to them they will argue themselves to show that their own doctrines are true . . . You must ask them whether any reasoning is valid or not. If they say no, then their own doctrines, being reached by reasoning, fall to the ground. If they say yes, then they will have to examine your arguments and refute them on their merits: for if some reasoning is valid, for all they know, your bit of reasoning may be one of the valid bits.[47]

Love Me, Fear Me, Ignore Me

In the June 2006 edition of BBC's *Focus Magazine*, Dennett hypothesized that 'Religions have evolved in order to protect themselves. What we see today are the hardiest specimens, which in order to survive have had to change. The ones that have pros-pered have created an aura around themselves and inspire love in their followers. When you really love someone, you respond dramatically to any sensed threat – nobody gets to even ask ques-tions about my beloved.' However, the core doctrinal beliefs, attendant attitudes, and consequent actions of Christian spiritu-ality have remained unchanged since its inception. Perhaps this has to do with the religion being anchored in the eye-witness testimony of certain first-century folk coming to terms with expe-riences centered upon a Jew from Nazareth.[48] Dennett's evolu-tionary explanation of religion ignores the ineluctably *historical* nature of religions like Judaism and Christianity, illegitimately assuming that no purported revelation can be genuinely histori-cal. Moreover, the first followers of the notorious Jew from Nazareth asked him lots of questions (they sometimes contra-dicted him, and one famously refused to believe eye-witness testimony unless they could have the same experience). Ever since those first-century days, people have asked tough questions about Jesus. Some questioners become followers as a result. Some followers are professional questioners (theologians, philosophers, scientists, lawyers, journalists, etc.). Christianity subverts Dennett's description of religion to such an extent that it constitutes a straw man.

In the same article Dennett tries to psychoanalyze the 'resurgence of religion in some countries', arguing that 'The main reason is that the high-tech world intimidates people, so they cast about for a sense of their own power in the world.' One often hears atheists claim that people invented belief in God because the natural world intimidated them and they needed to secure a sense of power over the world (although one might have thought that early man was bright enough to notice that sacrificing all that food and wine to the gods didn't reliably procure the desired outcomes). Yet Dennett thinks that the technology humans have invented to give them power over the natural world so intimidates them (but not him for some reason) that they re-invent belief in God! In other words, unless immunized by atheism (which is excused naturalistic explanation and chalked up to the superior intellectual freedom of the atheist), humans believe in God because they lack power, and because they have power. Can Dennett have it both ways? Perhaps there is some golden mean of power over the world that would give those poor unfortunate believers psychological permission to be atheists. Perhaps atheists should instigate a campaign to take us back, not to 'year zero', but to the 1950s, or the 1850s, or the 1750s! From where does Dennett get his sociological data? Religious people may be morally opposed to doing certain things with technology (e.g. screening embryos for BRCA1, BRCA2 and HNPCC genes so we can destroy those with a propensity to contract a treatable cancer in later life),[49] but this hardly counts as being 'intimidated by technology'. The Christian who opposes eugenics[50] may very well be the person who designed your laptop.

The Psycho-Historical Critique

As Dennett writes, 'Much has been written over the centuries about the historic processes by which polytheisms turned into monotheism . . .'[51] Supposedly, primitive ideas (caused by some sort of childish subconscious response to fear, frustration or what have you) gradually develop through animism and polytheism into monotheism, which, while more enlightened and less superstitious than the beliefs from which it 'evolved', is nonetheless 'nothing more than' the product of historical happenstance. According to Freud, primitive man lived a life filled with of fears of things like the forces of natural disasters, wild animals and illness, which he personified in the hope of getting into a relationship with them wherein he could somehow appease their wrath and sway them to his benefit. He made idols, built temples, prayed to his man-made gods and offered them animal sacrifices. This story does not fully explain the religious impulse, for if man unconsciously personified things in order to alleviate fear, why did he personify un-fearful things like trees (the Greek dryads) and wine (the Greek Bacchus)? Nevertheless, thereafter (or so the story goes), as religion developed, the number of posited supernatural forces dwindled to one in order to fulfill man's subconscious wish for an intimate relationship with a projection of the father figure: God (of course, the fact that humans wish something to be true does not necessarily mean that it isn't true. The fact that I desire sleep does not prove that I am an insomniac). Keith Ward laments:

> Despite the fact that there is virtually no extant evidence for what the origins of religion were . . . this has not stopped scholars making definitive claims about what really happened. This is an instance in which claims to certainty are in inverse proportion to the amount of evidence available . . . In his definitive work, *Theories of Primitive Religion*, the Oxford anthropologist Evans-Pritchard has established the uselessness of all this fantasizing, which is based on unreliable, uncritical or non-existent evidence.[52]

Ward argues for the possibility of an alternative interpretation, saying, 'There is little reason to think that prehistoric religion was founded solely in fear and ignorance . . . Why should it not have been founded on a primal intuition that the cosmos expresses, in its forms and rhythms, an underlying spiritual power, or complex of powers, in which human beings can share?'[53] The only answer forthcoming from Dennett *et al.* is grounded in the prior assumption of naturalism. Nevertheless, as Steven Lovell reports, 'a broadly Freudian critique seems, in the minds of many, to be a genuine obstacle and objection to accepting a religious world-view. This fact is remarkable in itself since Freudian psychology holds little weight among contemporary academics.'[54] Lovell notes several problems with the Freudian approach. For example, 'it is simply untrue that everyone who believes in God wishes that he should exist, for some have wished precisely the opposite.'[55] Moreover, Freudian arguments can easily be constructed *against atheism* ('The Oedipus complex, which Freud saw as the root of religious belief, provides a much more natural explanation of atheistic than theistic commitment') *and agnosticism* ('we could . . . diagnose agnosticism as resulting from the fear of commitment . . . the desire for acceptance among our peers, or the desire to appear tolerant of religion while still avoiding the costs of being a committed believer').[56] This procedure yields 'an inconsistent set; it cannot be true that theism, agnosticism, and atheism are all unjustified (unwarranted). The combination of these three Freudian arguments should lead us to a new kind of agnosticism: agnosticism about the genuine value of Freudian style arguments.'[57] Lovell warns that Freudian arguments

> can be constructed against pretty much anything. They can even be constructed against Freudian arguments. If a Freudian explanation is possible for any belief we have, and if such arguments undermine our reasons for holding those beliefs then a serious question arises: can the Freudian approach avoid undermining itself? The answer to this question must be in the negative . . . the kind of Freudian dismissal we have been considering is self-defeating . . .[58]

James Frazer popularized the notion that the first stage in the supposed 'evolution' of religion was animism, followed by pantheism, polytheism, and finally monotheism. However, subsequent anthropological studies 'have turned this scenario on its head . . .'[59] According to Ward, 'that the earliest form of religious belief was animism [is] pure speculation without any evidence at all.'[60] Today theories like those of Freud and Frazer are generally 'recognized as inadmissible.'[61] David C. Downing reports that

'Frazier's uneven and methodologically flawed work has been largely set aside by later generations of anthropologists . . .'[62] Tina Beattie assures us that 'today no serious scholar would cite Frazer as an authoritative source on religions . . .'[63] McGrath concurs that 'Freud's account of the historical origins of religion is now generally regarded as totally unreliable . . . Professional anthropologists and sociologists of religion have generally passed over his historical accounts of the origins of religion, regarding them as amateurish conjectures not worth taking seriously.'[64]

The Psychology of Belief & Disbelief

'If God proved he existed, I still wouldn't believe in him . . . I don't believe in God, not because I can't but because I don't want to.'
– Martin Rowson[65]

Michel Onfray asserts that 'the neurosis that impels men to forge gods results from the usual workings of the psyche and the subconscious';[66] but he also asserts that 'the genealogy of atheism seems just as simple as that of belief.'[67] But if both belief and disbelief can be given a 'genealogy', the provision of genealogies surely has nothing to say about the truth or falsity of the God hypothesis. Indeed, J.P. Moreland argues that 'If one is going to give an account of religious belief or antibelief in terms of some theory of projection, then it would seem that atheism is a more likely candidate for projection than theism . . . If one were going to project a god to meet one's needs, a being much tamer, much more human, much more manageable would be a better candidate.'[68] As Christopher Hitchens asks, 'who wishes that there was a permanent, unalterable celestial despotism that subjected us to continual surveillance and could convict us of thought-crime, and who regarded us as its private property even after we died?'[69] Thomas Nagel candidly writes:

> I want atheism to be true and am made uneasy by the fact that some of the most intelligent and well-informed people I know are religious believers. It isn't just that I don't believe in God and, naturally, hope that I'm right in my belief. It's that I hope there is no God! I don't want there to be a God; I don't want the universe to be like that. My guess is that this cosmic authority problem is not

a rare condition and that it is responsible for much of the scientism and reductionism of our time.[70]

The idea that people are theists for reasons to do with comfort cuts both ways.[71] Psychologist Paul C. Vitz argues that 'in the Freudian framework, atheism is an illusion caused by the Oedipal desire to kill the father and replace him with oneself.'[72] C.S. Lewis acknowledged that 'The materialist conception would not have seemed so immensely probable to me if it had not favoured at least one of my wishes.'[73] Concerning his past agnosticism, Francis Collins admits that 'As a young man growing up in a world full of temptations, it was convenient to ignore the need to be answerable to any higher spiritual authority.'[74] As Aldous Huxley confessed, 'I had motives [primarily erotic] for not wanting the world to have meaning, consequently assumed that it had none, and was able without any difficulty to find satisfying reasons for this assumption. Most ignorance is vincible ignorance. We don't know because we don't want to know.'[75] The sordid sex lives of prominent twentieth-century atheists Jean-Paul Sartre and Simone de Beauvoir are notorious. A recent newspaper article recounts:

> Jean-Paul Sartre and Simone de Beauvoir were perhaps the most influential couple of the 20th century . . . a fascinating new book paints this supposedly high-minded duo as serial seducers bent on their own gratification and as *a couple who used their apparently lofty philosophy as a spring-board to excuse their multiple liaisons*, often with under-age teenagers who were broken by the experience . . . Sartre . . . liked to sleep with virgins, after which he rapidly lost interest . . . Today [de Beauvoir] would be behind bars for her sexual activities with her young pupils, but in those days she got away with it. Tragically, the lives of these girls . . . were permanently blighted. One took to self-harming, another committed suicide.[76]

Fellow existentialist Albert Camus 'joined in most of the couple's sex games. Camus slept with all their impressionable young girls'.[77] British atheist Bertrand Russell had (sometimes simultaneous) affairs with several women.[78] Would it be too cynical to highlight, in this context, Hitchens' complaint (reminiscent of Russell) that religion is 'the cause of dangerous sexual repression',[79] or Dawkins' secular 'commandment' to 'Enjoy your own sex life (so long as it damages nobody else) and leave others to enjoy theirs in private . . .'?[80]

According to Freud 'Psycho-analysis has made us familiar with the intimate connection between the father-complex and belief in God: it has shown us that a personal God is, psychologically speaking, nothing other than an exulted father, and it brings us evidence every day of how young people lose their religious beliefs as soon as their father's authority breaks down.'[81] This analysis prompts us to wonder about Freud's relationship with *his* father. In point of fact, Freud didn't respect his father, who failed to stand up for himself against anti-Semitic abuse. Benjamin Beit-Hallahmi, profiling atheists in *The Cambridge Companion to Atheism*, writes:

> Findings regarding those who come from religious homes and then give up religion show that they have had more distant relations with their parents . . . Avoidant adults are somewhat uncomfortable being close to others . . . in a study of 400 adults in the United States, those having an avoidant attachment style were most likely to identify themselves as either atheist or agnostic . . . Vetter and Green (1932–33) surveyed 350 members of the American Association for the Advancement of Atheism, 325 of whom were men. Among those who became atheists before age twenty, half lost one or both parents before that age.[82]

Vitz proposes a 'Theory of Defective Father', whereby a defective father may contribute to a person's rejection of God. Defective fathers may be 'weak, cowardly, and unworthy of respect . . . physically, sexually or psychologically abusive [or] absent through death or by abandoning or leaving the family.'[83] When Feuerbach was thirteen, his father abandoned the family to live with another woman. Marx didn't respect his father, who converted from Judaism to Christianity to make life easier for himself. Simone de Beauvoir's father cheated on his wife, sleeping with his friend's wives and frequenting the bordello. According to Vitz, 'Many children . . . interpret the death of their father as a kind of betrayal or an act of desertion. In this respect it is remarkable that the pattern of a dead father is so common in the lives of many prominent atheists.'[84] Nietzsche was four when his father died. Likewise, Bertrand Russell's father died when he was four years old. Camus lost his father as a one-year-old. Satre's father died a mere fifteen months after his son's birth. Sartre hated his stepfather, calling him 'a shit [*un con*]'.[85] One can see how those disposed to explain-away Christopher Hitchens' antitheism (for example) might proceed. Having noted how keen Hitchens is to protect sexual freedom (nudge, nudge), one might observe that not only does the phrase 'avoidant attachment style' seem to suit him (wink, wink), but that he has 'distant relations' with his relations. 'Hitchens' father was . . . personally reserved. His mother was more outgoing but committed suicide in an Athens hotel room. For their son Christopher, "family life pretty much ended then".'[86]

However, in contemplating such a psychological approach, 'I am not talking as the Lord would, but as a fool' (2 Corinthians 11:17). For all this shows is that theists can play the *ad homenim* game as well as atheists, if they so wish. But as C.S. Lewis complained, 'you must show that a man is wrong before you start explaining why he is wrong. The modern method is to assume without discussion that he is wrong and then distract his attention from this (the only real issue) by busily explaining how he became so silly.'[87]

Persinger's Magnetic Personality

> *'An exceptionally convincing line of research is that of Michael Persinger . . .'*
> – Philip A. Stahl[88]

Michael A. Persinger, a neuroscientist at Laurentain University in Canada, claims to be able to induce religious experiences in people using magnetic fields. As *New Scientist* reported:

> Persinger has been using a technique called transcranial magnetic stimulation to induce all sorts of surreal experiences in ordinary people . . . Through trial and error and a bit of educated guesswork,

he's found that a weak magnetic field – 1 microtesla, which is roughly that generated by a computer monitor – rotating anti-clockwise in a complex pattern about the temporal lobes will cause four out of five people to feel a spectral presence in the room with them. What people make of that presence depends on their own biases and beliefs. If a loved one has recently died, they may feel that person has returned to see them. Religious types often ident-ify the presence as God.[89]

Persinger featured in a BBC *Horizon* science documentary enti-tled 'God on the Brain' in 2003, in which Dawkins tried out Persinger's equipment with no noticeable effect.[90] Taking Persinger's results as given, there are several points that can be made. First, one cannot conclude from Persinger's results that 'brains plus magnetic fields equals a naturalistic explanation for theism'. At best, one can say that brains plus magnetic fields *plus a pre-existing belief in God* can *sometimes* result in experiences that people who already believe in God identify as an experience of the divine. Persinger's results don't explain the origin of belief in God, because they show that what people make of the feeling of presence induced by his apparatus *depends upon their prior beliefs*. Second, one cannot slide from discovering a physical mechanism resulting in an experience to the conclusion that such experiences are unreliable or misleading. Andrew Newberg, a neuroscientist at the University of Pennsylvania in Philadelphia, comments that

> if you're a religious person, it makes sense that the brain can do this, because if there is a God, it makes sense to design the brain so that we can have some sort of interaction. And we can't say that's wrong, either. The problem is that all of our experiences are equal, in that they are all in the brain. Our experience of reality, our expe-rience of science, our mystical experiences are all in the brain.[91]

Third, if low-level magnetic fields, like those generated by com-puters and hairdryers, are the cause of mystical experience, why don't more people report such experiences in the office or the hair salon? Persinger counters that the effect is produced by the pre-cise frequency and duration of the signals (and presumably by the precise, complex, rotating, anticlockwise pattern used in his experiments). However, the more specified the conditions under which Persinger's magnetic fields will produce mystic experiences, the less plausible their applicability as an explanation for mystical experiences 'in the wild' becomes. Where would early man have found magnetic fields of the right strength and frequency capable of zipping around his head anticlockwise? As Bob Holmes concludes, 'For whatever reason – natural or supernatural – our big, powerful brains clearly allow a novel sort of experience that we can call religion. But it's difficult to say much more than that.'[92]

However, we shouldn't take Persinger's results as a given.[93] As Joe Nickell reports:

> In late 2004 . . . a joint study by scientists from two Swedish universities called into question much of Persinger's research. The scientists attempted to replicate Persinger's findings using the identical magnetic-field apparatus . . . The researchers found no evidence that paranormal or religious experiences were caused by the electromagnetic stimulation . . . The researchers concluded that 'suggestibility may account for previously reported effects.'[94]

Clearly, the origin of belief in God cannot be explained by a theory requiring the *prior suggestion* that God exists and can be experienced. Moreover, not everyone who believes in God, or who thinks they have experienced God, is a psychologically 'pliant' personality.

To argue that 'naturalistic mechanism M produces belief in (or experience of) subject S, therefore belief in (or experience of) S is *nothing* but the functioning of M' is to engage in a self-defeating, reductive *non sequiter*. Mechanism M, the functioning of which accounts for S, is itself posited as a result of an experience of a subject (S^1) that is itself the result of some 'mechanism' (M^1); which means that, by the above argument, mechanism M (upon which the dismissal of belief depended) should itself be dismissed as illusory! The fact that, under laboratory conditions, imbibing too much alcohol and receiving a blow to the head results in some subjects seeing double is not sufficient grounds for positing the non-existence of identical twins!

Not in Our Genes

'Once reason is admitted as a characteristic of human nature . . . it can be shown to do the work imputed to phantom genes in almost any examples that sociobiologists want to bring up.'
– Stephen Jay Gould[95]

While there is no such thing as 'a gene for religiosity', let alone a gene for mystical experience, there are probably genetic *influences* upon personality factors that affect, but don't determine, a person's general responsiveness to spiritual matters in a very general sense of the term. Dean Hamer, director of the Gene Structure Unit at the National Cancer Institute in America, caused something of a stir in 2004 with the publication of his book *The God Gene: How Faith is Hardwired into our Genes*. Hamer claims to have pinpointed a gene (called VMAT2) which effects the flow of brain chemicals – associated with a range of emotions, such as anxiety, joy, and sadness – which are correlated with 'the deep meditative states of Zen practitioners and the prayerful repose of Catholic nuns.'[96] Hamer does not take this purported discovery to have any negative consequences for theism, claiming that 'Religious believers can point to the existence of a god gene as one more sign of the creator's ingenuity – a clever way to help humans acknowledge and embrace the divine.'[97]

Dennett positively references Hamer's work in *Breaking the Spell*. Hamer rated his test subjects using a questionnaire designed to measure their capacity for 'self-transcendence', which he describes as a person's ability to reach out beyond themselves, to see the world as a unity and to have 'spiritual feelings that are independent of traditional religiousness'.[98] The self-transcendence scale used by Hamer avoids questions about orthodox religious doctrines or practice. People who dislike organized religion can score high on the self-transcendence scale, which even counts a liking for such 'transcendent' activities as music and painting. Hence, as Albert Mohler observes, Hamer's study 'doesn't actually have anything directly to do with believing in God . . .'[99] Hamer acknowledges that the title of his book is a misnomer, in that there are probably hundreds of genes involved in the human propensity for transcendence. As Francis

Collins writes, Hamer's title 'was wildly overstated'.[100] Moreover, Hamer notes that 'Just because something is "genetically influenced" doesn't mean it's strictly hard-wired. People who practice meditation actually improve their scores. So even though there's a genetic proclivity, it certainly can be altered by people's actions and behaviors.'[101] According to Hamer, 'Our genes can predispose us to believe. But they can't tell us what to believe in.'[102]

However, we needn't take Hamer's results at face value, even when careful scientific caveats replace his tabloid title. As Dean Zimmer commented:

> The field of behavioral genetics is littered with failed links between particular genes and personality traits. Those alleged associations at first seem very strong. But as other researchers tried to replicate them, they faded away into statistical noise. In 1993, for example, a scientist reported a genetic link to male homosexuality in a region of the X chromosome. The report brought a huge media fanfare, but other scientists who tried to replicate the study failed. The scientist's name was Dean Hamer. Given the fate of Hamer's so-called gay gene, it is strange to see him so impatient to trumpet the discovery of his God gene.[103]

Zimmer argues that *the God gene* should be called 'A gene that accounts for less than one percent of the variants found in scores on psychological questionnaires designed to measure a factor called self-transcendence, which can signify everything from belonging to the green party to believing in ESP, according to one unpublished, unreplicated study.'[104] Other scientists have argued that 'Hamer's conclusions are simplistic and speculative, relying too much on anecdotal evidence and too little on testing of the VMAT2 gene to determine other possible connections to behavior.'[105] Francis Collins comments, 'As none of his data has been peer reviewed or published in the scientific literature, most experts have greeted the book with considerable skepticism . . .'[106]

Twins

Thomas J. Bouchard Jr. directed a famous study of twins reared apart. Looking at five different measures of religiosity, researchers found that the correlations between identical twins were typically double those for fraternal twins, 'suggesting that genetic factors play a significant role in the expression of this trait'.[107] How significant a role? While admitting that their findings 'indicate that individual differences in religious attitudes, interests and values arise from both genetic and environmental attitudes . . . genetic factors account for approximately 50 percent of the observed variance on our measures'.[108] Laura Koenig likewise led a study of 169 identical twin brothers and 104 fraternal twin brothers from Minnesota and showed that genetic factors could account for *almost half* the variability seen in the twin population's religiosity.[109] Of course, such genetic factors don't determine whether one ends up a Christian or a Buddhist (nothing, in other words, to determine whether one believes in God); rather, 'religious interest and commitment to certain practices . . . partly reflect genetically based personality traits such as traditionalism and conformance to authority.'[110] As Michael Shermer writes,

> 50 percent heritability of religious tendencies may sound like a lot, but that still leaves the other half . . . Virtually all studies implemented over the past century have found strong environmental factors in religiosity, including everything from family to class to culture. In other words, even with a genetic component to religiosity we still must examine other variables.[111]

Naturalist David Stove rejects any suggestion that 'humans are the helpless puppets of their genes':

> 'Our *stars* rule us,' says the astrologer. 'Man is what he eats,' says Feuerbach. 'We are what our infantile sexual experiences made us,' says the Freudian. 'The individual counts for nothing, his class situation for everything,' says the Marxist . . . There is simply no end of this kind of stuff. What is wrong with all such theories is this: That they deny, at least by implication, that human intentions, decisions, and efforts are among the causal agencies which are at work in the world. This denial is so obviously false that no rational person, who paused to consider it coolly and in itself, would ever entertain it for one minute . . . The falsity of all these theories of human helplessness is so very obvious, in fact, that the

puppetry theorists themselves cannot help admitting it, and thus are never able to adhere consistently to their puppetry theories . . . In this inevitable and tiresomely familiar way, Dawkins contradicts *his* puppetry theory. Thus, for example, writing in the full flood of conviction of human helplessness, he says that 'we are . . . robot-vehicles blindly programmed to preserve the selfish molecule known as genes,' etc. But at the same time, of course, he knows as well as the rest of us do, that there are often other causes at work, in us or around us, which are perfectly capable of counteracting genetic influences. In fact, he sometimes says so himself, and he even says that 'we have the power to *defy* the selfish genes of our birth.'[112]

Likewise, Francis Collins writes:

it is not impossible to imagine that certain personality types, themselves based upon weakly inherited factors, may be more prone to accept the possibility of God than others . . . There is an inescapable component of heritability to many human behavioral traits. For virtually none of them is heredity ever close to predictive. Environment, particularly childhood experiences, and the prominent role of individual free choices have a profound effect on us . . . Yes, we have all been dealt a particular set of cards . . . But how we play the hand is up to us.[113]

Evolutionary explanations fail to explain anything 'religious' beyond a propensity to openness towards a range of 'self-transcendent' activities that must themselves be given *independent* explanations. As Dawkins admits, 'Even though conventional Darwinian selection of genes might have favored psychological predispositions that produce religion as a by-product, it is unlikely to have shaped the details.'[114] But *belief in God is just such a detail*! In giving an independent explanation to this 'detail', one cannot legitimately follow Dennett in discounting either the role of rational human thinking about the world (i.e. philosophical thinking), or the role of purported historical revelation vouchsafed by genuine religious experience and/or publicly verifiable miraculous events.

Conclusion

In the *Cambridge Companion to Atheism* Phil Zuckerman observes that 'In recent years, a new attempt at explaining religious belief has emerged. Its central tenet is that belief in God is biologically determined, neurologically based, or genetically inborn . . . [However] Between 500 million and 750 million humans currently do not believe in God. Such figures render any suggestion that theism is innate or neurologically based manifestly untenable.'[115] At the very least, as John Hick concludes, 'a verdict of "not proven" is indicated concerning the attempt to establish a purely natural explanation of religion'.[116] Moreover, as Mel Thompson comments, 'If a sociologist argues that religion exists in order to hold society together, or a psychologist holds that religious belief is connected with guilt, that does not mean that what is believed is necessarily false. My reason for believing something is not the same as the truth of what I believe.'[117] In other words, the 'religion is nothing but . . .' objection is a prime example of the genetic fallacy.[118]

Recommended Resources

Richard Bauckham, *Jesus and the Eyewitnesses: The Gospels as Eyewitness Testimony* (Grand Rapids, MI: Eerdmans, 2006).

Mario Beauregard and Denyse O'Leary, *The Spiritual Brain: A Neuroscientist's Case for the Existence of the Soul* (New York: HarperOne, 2007).

James Kelly Clark, *Return to Reason* (Grand Rapids, MI: Eerdmans, 1998).

Paul Copan and Paul K. Moser (eds.), *The Rationality of Theism* (Routledge, 2003).

William Lane Craig and J.P. Moreland (eds.), *Naturalism: A Critical Analysis* (London/New York: Routledge, 2001).

R. Douglass Geivett and Gary R. Haberman, *In Defence of Miracles: A Comprehensive Case for God's Action in History* (IVP, Leicester: Apollos, 1997).

Colin J. Humphreys, *The Miracles of the Exodus* (London: Continuum, 2003).

Carole Seymour-Jones, *A Dangerous Liaison: A Revelatory New Biography of Simone De Beauvoir and Jean-Paul Sartre* (London: Century, 2008).

K.A. Kitchen, *On the Reliability of the Old Testament* (Grand Rapids, MI: Eerdmans, 2006).

J.P. Moreland and William Lane Craig, *Philosophical Foundations for a Christian Worldview* (Downers Grove, IL: IVP, 2003).

Armand M. Nicholi, Jr., *The Question of God: C.S. Lewis and Sigmund Freud Debate God, Love, Sex, And The Meaning of Life* (London/New York: Free Press, 2002).

Alvin Plantinga, *Warranted Christian Belief* (Oxford University Press: Oxford, 2003), www.ccel.org/ccel/plantinga/warranted.html.

Randall Price, *The Stones Cry Out: What Archaeology Reveals About the Truth of the Bible* (Eugene, OR: Harvest House, 1997).

Richard Swinburne, *Was Jesus God?* (Oxford University: Oxford, 2008).

Michael J. Wilkins and J.P. Moreland (eds.), *Jesus Under Fire – Modern Scholarship Reinvents the Historical Jesus* (Milton Keynes: Paternoster, 1996).

Paul C. Vitz, *Faith of the Fatherless: The Psychology of Atheism* (Dallas, TX: Spence, 1999).

On-Line Papers

Kelly James Clark, 'Without Evidence or Argument: A Defense of Reformed Epistemology', www.calvin.edu/academic/philosophy/virtual_library/articles/clark_kelly_j/without_evidence_or_argument.pdf.

John Cornwell, 'Religion as a Natural Phenomenon', www.timesonline.co.uk/tol/news/uk/science/article730931.ece.

Daniel Dennett vs. Alister McGrath, 'Breaking the Spell: Religion as a Global Phenomenon', www.thersa.org/acrobat/dennett_130306.pdf.

John Gray, 'Myths of Meaning: Breaking the Spell & Six Impossible Things Before Breakfast', www.newstatesman.com/200603200044.

David B. Hart, 'Daniel Dennett Hunts the Snark', www.firstthings.com/article.php3?id_article=5394.

Peter van Inwagen, 'Is It Wrong, Everywhere, Always, and for Anyone, to Believe?', www.faithquest.com/home.cfm?main=docs/philosophers/vaninwagen/clifford.cfm.

Adam Kirsch, 'If Men Are From Mars, What's God', www.nysun.com/article/27182.

Gregory Koukl, 'Intuition: A Special Way of Knowing', www.bethinking.org/resource.php?ID=26&TopicID=4&CategoryID=6.

Gregory Koukl, 'Is God Just an Idea?', www.str.org/site/News2?page=NewsArticle&id=6067.

Art Lindlsey, 'C.S. Lewis on Freud and Marx', www.cslewisinstitute.org/pages/resources/publications/knowingDoing/2002/LewisFreudMarx.pdf.

Steven Lovell, 'All in the Mind?', www.csl-philosophy.co.uk/.

Duncan McMillan, 'Origins of Belief [Lewis Wolpert's *Six Impossible Things Before Breakfast*]', www.union.ic.ac.uk/media/iscience/article_template_typ.php?articleid=108 .

Albert Mohler, 'The God Gene: Bad Science Meets Bad Theology', www.beliefnet.com/story/154story_15458.htm.

Michael Murray, 'God and Neuro-Science', www.reasonable-faith.org/site/PageServer?pagename=q_and_a.

H. Allan Orr, 'The God Project', www.newyorker.com/archive/2006/04/03/060403crbo_books?currentPage=1.

Alvin Plantinga, 'Theism, Atheism, and Rationality', www.leaderu.com/truth/3truth02.html.

Alvin Plantinga, 'Intellectual Sophistication and Basic Belief in God', www.leaderu.com/truth/3truth03.html.

Glenys Roberts, 'Dangerous liaisons and sex with teens: The story of Sartre and de Beauvoir as never told before', www.dailymail.co.uk/pages/live/femail/article.html?in_article_id=559137&in_page_id=1879.

Paul C. Vitz, 'The Psychology of Atheism', www.origins.org/truth/1truth12.html.

Leon Wieseltier, 'The God Genome', www.nytimes.com/2006/02/19/books/review/19wieseltier.html.

Peter S. Williams, 'God on the Brain', www.damaris.org/content/content.php?type=5&id=33.

Chris Winchester, 'Breaking the Spell: Religion as a Natural Phenomenon', www.reasons.org/resources/apologetics/other_papers/breaking_the_spell.shtml.

Audio

Susan Blackmore vs. Alister McGrath, 'Is Belief in God a Dangerous Delusion?', http://richarddawkins.net/article,2395,Sue-Blackmore-debates-Alister-McGrath,Bristol-University.

Daniel Dennett on Point of Enquiry, 'Breaking the Spell', http://cdn.libsyn.com/pointofinquiry/3-3-06.mp3.

Daniel Dennett & David Cook, 'Discussing Religion', http://archive.wgnradio.com:8080/ramgen/wgnam/shows/ex720/Audio/religion060215mr.rm.

Alvin Plantinga, 'Evolution vs. Atheism', www.sbts.edu/mp3/Norton/20071025plantinga.mp3.

Alvin Plantinga, 'Evolutionary Anti-Naturalism Argument', www.hisdefense.org/LinkClick.aspx?link=Audio%2fPlantinga+-+Evolutionary+Arguments+against+Naturalism.ram&tabid=136&mid=939.

Michael Sudduth, 'Epistemic Objections to Religious Belief', http://radioapologia.com/archives/Epistemic_Objections_to_Religious_Belief_by_Dr_Michael_Sudduth.mp3.

Peter S. Williams, 'All in the Mind?', www.damaris.org/cm/podcasts/category/peterswilliams.

5

Does Science Explain Everything?

'All attempts to reconcile faith with science . . . are consigned to failure and ridicule . . .'
– Christopher Hitchens[1]

Displaying a breath-taking degree of question-begging intellectual arrogance, French New Atheist Michel Onfray asserts that there is an *a priori* association between atheism, intelligence, rationality, and science on the one hand, and between monotheism and a pathological disdain for all three virtues on the other.

> Monotheism loathes intelligence . . . Intelligence . . . produces rational, convincing explanations based on reasoning; it rejects every manufactured fiction. With its help, we spurn myths and fairy tales. We need no posthumous paradise, no salvation or redemption of the soul, no all-knowing, all-seeing God. Properly and rationally directed, intelligence, a priori atheist, wards off all magical thinking . . . Monotheism does not really like the rational work of scientists . . . they cherish nights of the mind propitious for the nurturing of their fables . . . Monotheisms have no love for intelligence, books, knowledge, science.[2]

Clearly, then, we could not expect anyone who is intelligent and who has an adequate working knowledge of science to write a book using rational argumentation to defend belief in God. As Benjamin A. Plotinsky suspects, 'Onfray's . . . guiding principle is not science or knowledge or reason, but rather indiscriminate – and often un-researched and irrational – opposition to religion.'[3]

Several cautionary notes should be issued to those who are fond of the oft-heard 'science explains everything' objection to religion. First, Daniel Dennett's *Breaking the Spell* calls attention to the fact that science has *not*, yet, explained everything: 'I am not at all claiming that this is what science has already established . . . The main point of this book is to insist that we *don't* yet know . . . the answers to these important questions . . . Probably some features of the story I tell will prove in due course to be mistaken. Maybe many of them are wrong . . .'[4] As Anthony Kenny comments, 'The atheist conclusion, at least as expounded by most vociferous atheists in our day, is that there isn't anything left to explain once science has done its best, and that doesn't seem to be true.'[5] Second, to adopt the faith that science *will* explain, or is *in principle capable of explaining*, everything, is to paint oneself into an epistemological corner. To restrict one's intellectual horizons to the scientifically knowable, such that searching for 'any good reason' equals searching for 'any *scientific* reason',[6] is self-contradictory. The 'science explains everything' objection is built upon too narrow a conception of rationality. Third, the quixotic definition of science as 'the search for exclusively natural explanations' secures a merely linguistic victory, analogous to Nelson declaring that he sees no ships because he is holding the telescope to his eye-patch.

'Science' as Rhetorical Trump Card

Nineteenth-century thinker Ludwig Feuerbach promoted atheism by claiming that he had 'modern science' on his side and that he was advocating 'the science of reality in its truth and totality.'[7] Hitler thought that 'The dogma of Christianity gets worn away before the advances of science.'[8] In the same vein, Rudolf Bultmann notoriously remarked that 'it is impossible to use electric light and the wireless and to avail ourselves of modern medical and surgical discoveries, and at the same time to believe in the New Testament world of spirits and miracles.'[9] Of course, a great many people manage this 'impossible' feat. What Bultmann meant was clearly something along the lines of 'belief in the supernatural is an intellectually unsustainable position for well-educated adults in a scientific age'. For many atheists, 'intellectually sustainable' and 'scientific' (defined so that it excludes any explanation incompatible with naturalism) are more or less synonymous. Hence the appeal to 'science' is often nothing but a rhetorically powerful way to assert that theism is, as Antony O'Hear says, 'intellectually unsustainable'.[10] However, this is just an assertion; and as Nigel Warburton warns, 'Confident assertion is no substitute for argument . . .'[11]

In contrast with O'Hear, John Gray pays contemporary religious scholars the following compliment: 'One cannot engage in dialogue with religious thinkers in Britain today without quickly discovering that they are, on the whole, more intelligent, better educated and strikingly more freethinking than unbelievers (as evangelical atheists still incongruously describe themselves).'[12] According to Gray, accusations of intellectual unstustainability (which may be cast in the language of science) say more about the accuser than the accused:

> Karl Marx and John Stuart Mill were adamant that religion would die out with the advance of science. That has not come about, and there is not the remotest prospect of it happening in the foreseeable future. Yet the idea that religion can be eradicated from human life remains an article of faith among humanists. As secular ideology is dumped throughout the world, they are left disorientated and gawping. It is this painful cognitive dissonance, I believe, that accounts for the particular rancour and intolerance of many secular thinkers. Unable to account for the irrepressible vitality of religion, they can react only with puritanical horror and stigmatize it as irrational.[13]

Stripped of its rhetorical packaging, the charge of irrationality – which is basically what the 'science explains everything' objection amounts to – is little more than atheologians asserting that theists are thick because they disagree with them.

Kai Nielsen states that 'for someone living in the twentieth century with a good philosophical and scientific education, who thinks carefully about the matter . . . it is irrational to believe in God . . . *if* people do have a good scientific and philosophical education . . . they should come to see that it is irrational to believe in

God.'[14] However, there are many contemporaries with a good philosophical and scientific education, who think carefully about the matter, and who do not think it is irrational to believe in God. A.J. Ayer was 'puzzled by the fact that philosophers whom he respected intellectually, such as Michael Dummett, had religious beliefs', but at least he 'had to admit that this was the case'.[15] As Plantinga writes:

> Very many well-educated people (including even some theologians) understand science and history in a way that is entirely compatible both with the possibility and with the actuality of miracles. Many physicists and engineers, for example, understand 'electrical light and the wireless' vastly better than Bultmann or his contemporary followers, but nonetheless hold precisely those New Testament beliefs Bultmann thinks incompatible with using electric lights and radios . . . there are any number of . . . contemporary intellectuals very well acquainted with science who don't feel any problem at all in pursuing science and also believing in miracles, angels, Christ's resurrection, the lot.[16]

Although aspects of the 'science vs. religion' objection are sometimes presented as anti-truth objections to theism, it is far more usual to meet it in the anti-belief mode of a feeling that there is some kind of an intellectual problem with accepting modern science and believing in God (in certain circles this is 'not the done thing'). A lack of specificity in this sort of objection often indicates that what is really going on is some hand waving in the direction of what Cambridge University historian of science Jim Endersby calls 'the mythical clash between science and religion'.[17] Exactly which traditional religious convictions fail to stand up under the scrutiny of precisely which scientific theories? Atheists often fail to say. There is no argument here, only rhetoric.

'Science', 'Christian Theology', and the Relationship between Them

> *'the conflict between science and religion is unavoidable.'*
> – Sam Harris[18]

Science tries to understand the truth about material reality. Scientific methods are well suited to this quest. However, scientists aren't infallible. For one thing, scientists have different philosophical beliefs – disagreements about reality that cannot be settled on scientific grounds alone – which affect how they think about science and its theories. For example, some scientists believe in metaphysical naturalism. Others do not. This philosophical disagreement cannot be settled on scientific grounds alone, but it affects how different scientists think about a lot of subjects. Furthermore, however careful scientists are, they can get things wrong. Science makes progress, often by modifying or discarding previously well-regarded theories as inadequate or plain wrong. Scientists should always remember that it is reality that calls the shots, not science (and that reality cannot simply be defined as being naturalistic).

Christian theology is a quest to understand all truth (including the truth about material reality) in terms of a Christian worldview. The word theology comes from two Greek terms, *theos* (god) and *logos* ('word' or 'reason'). Theology is literally 'reasoning about god' or 'discourse about god'. As universities developed in the twelfth and thirteenth centuries a name had to be found for the systematic study of the Christian faith at university level. Under the influence of writers such as Peter Abelard, the Latin word *theologia* came to mean 'the discipline of sacred learning', embracing all Christian doctrine, rather than just doctrine about God. Hence Alister McGrath defines Christian theology as: 'an attempt to make sense of the foundational resources of Christianity [e.g. revelation, reason, tradition and experience] in the light of what each age regards as first-rate methods.'[19]

Aquinas referred to theology as the 'queen of the sciences' (for Aquinas 'science' –*scientia* in Latin – simply meant 'knowledge'). Theology is the highest level of theoretical engagement with reality of which human beings are capable. This is because theology relies upon and subsumes all of the other theoretical academic disciplines (philosophy, science, history, etc.) into an overarching worldview: 'The working assumption [of the medieval university] was that all diverse particulars of knowledge discovered and analyzed in the specialized academic disciplines, found their coherence in God. It was the unifying power of theology that elevated her to the queen of sciences, being assisted by her handmaiden philosophy.'[20]

Theologian David Ford argues that 'the best centres of theology . . . recognize that, if God is really related to the whole of reality, then they need to engage with not only what usually comes under religious studies, but also with many other disciplines [including] the natural sciences . . .'[21] Theology requires dialogue with the other academic disciplines, including science, in order to fulfil its mission as the queen of sciences. Hence Christian theology is committed to a high view of science: 'Modern science arose within the bosom of Christian theism; it is a shining example of the powers of reason with which God has created us; it is a spectacular display of the image of God in us human beings. So Christians are committed to taking science and the deliverances of contemporary science with the utmost seriousness.'[22]

When theologians seek to integrate an understanding of material reality into their theology, they talk of the 'two books of God', the Bible and nature. If both 'books' come from God, it makes sense to think that they don't contradict each other and that they even throw light on each other. However, theologians are just as fallible as scientists. Theologians have different philosophical commitments, disagreements that cannot be settled on scriptural or scientific grounds alone, which affect how they think about theology. Moreover, however careful theologians are, they can get things wrong. Theology makes progress, often by modifying or discarding previously well regarded theories as inadequate or plain wrong (few if any contemporary theologians would defend a theory of the atonement in quite the same terms as did Anselm). Theologians must remember that it is reality that calls the shots, not them.

It shouldn't be surprising that these fallible human quests, science and theology, sometimes conflict. Such conflict doesn't necessarily mean that science disproves theology, any more than it means that theology disproves science. Conflict can result from the fallibility of science, of theology, or of both, rather than from any contradiction between the 'two books of God'. According to Michael Ruse:

> Most people think that science and religion are, and necessarily must be, in conflict. In fact, this 'warfare' metaphor, so beloved of nineteenth-century rationalists, has only a tenuous application to reality. For most of the history of Christianity, it was the Church that was the home of science . . . the arrival of evolution, particularly in the form of Charles Darwin's *Origin of the Species*, put this tolerance to severe test. But without denying that there were strong opinions on both sides, the truth seems to be that much of the supposed controversy was a function of the imagination of non-believers (especially Thomas Henry Huxley and his friends), who were determined to slay theological dragons whether they existed or not.[23]

As Alister McGrath reports, 'The idea that science and religion are in perpetual conflict is no longer taken seriously by any major historian of science.'[24]

Such conflict as there is between theology and science is often the product of philosophical disagreements between certain scientists and certain theologians. For example, discussing the 1662 *Book of Common Prayer*, in which God is a being 'thought of as wielding absolute power', Humanist Anthony Freeman objects that 'We no longer live in a world where such an idea has any place.'[25] According to Freeman, 'That world was already becoming obsolete in 1662, with the scientific discoveries of Sir Isaac Newton and others. More recent developments in science and philosophy have removed us from it entirely.'[26] Freeman's point seems to be that once we discover a law of nature, it is no longer possible to suppose that God might cause an event that cannot be described in terms of that law. Indeed, the purported problem here is not so much one caused by the discovery of particular physical laws, but by the general concept of there being physical laws *per se*: 'you can square the idea of a creator God with the well-regulated world of science, but how can you make sense of prayers in which you ask God to intervene and do things now? It can't be done . . .'[27] Freeman gives no justification for his philosophical assertion concerning the incompatibility of science and belief in miracles (an assertion, ironically enough, with which Newton would not have agreed). As William Lane Craig argues:

> The law of gravity states what will happen under idealized conditions with no natural or supernatural factors intervening. Catching the apple doesn't overturn the law of gravity or require the formulation of a new law. It's merely the intervention of a person with free will who overrides the natural causes operative in that particular circumstances. And that, essentially, is what God does when he causes a miracle to occur.[28]

To use natural laws to argue against theism is question begging.

Space is Dark and Large, and We are Small by Comparison . . .

'we should not think there's anything special about us. We used to think we were the centre of the Universe and now we know we're not.'
– Richard Dawkins[29]

As *The Hitch Hiker's Guide to the Galaxy* says, 'Space . . . is big. Really big. You just won't believe how vastly hugely mind-bogglingly big it is. I mean you may think it's a long way down the road to the chemist, but that's just peanuts to space.'[30] The small size and non-centrality of the Earth in the universe are scientific discoveries atheists love to reference as if they *obviously* undermined the rationality of belief in human significance, and thereby the belief in God (although it isn't obvious why reason to doubt the significance of humans is automatically reason to doubt the rationality of theism *per se*). Steven Weinberg majored on this theme at the 2006 'Beyond Belief' conference, where he said:

> Science has historically downgraded human beings from a central role in creation . . . As we learn more and more about the

universe, science sees less and less sign of any special role for human beings either in the laws of nature themselves or in the history of the universe of the sort that's imagined by traditional religion. First, there's the discovery that the earth is not at the centre of the solar system; then the solar system is not at the centre of creation, it's just one of many in our galaxy; our galaxy is not unique . . . the universe has billions of galaxies extending in every direction . . .[31]

The wittiest reply to the doubt that God could be interested in 'little-old us' came from Pascal, who wrote, 'If you want to say that man is too feeble to deserve communication with God, you have to be very elevated to be the judge of that.'[32]

In *The Varieties of Scientific Experience: A Personal View of the Search for God* (posthumously published in 2006) the late Carl Sagan makes a sustained argument along these lines. Beginning with the observation that most of the cosmos is dark, he equates darkness with nothingness: 'I stress that the universe is mainly made of nothing, that something is the exception. Nothing is the rule.'[33] Of course, even a *dark* something is a dark *something* (e.g. the space-time continuum itself). Looking at the Solar System, Sagan announces that 'there are four large bodies other than the Sun',[34] and pronounces, 'the rest is debris'.[35] Unfortunately, 'debris' carries connotations of insignificance that aren't necessarily accurate. Suppose ten chunks of rock had fallen off a cliff (perhaps due to natural weathering), of which five were much larger than the rest; and suppose that one of the smaller rocks were sculpted into a bust of Carl Sagan. Would it be accurate to describe the sculpted rock as a 'piece of debris'?[36] Obviously, the answer is yes (in one sense) and no (in another). Likewise, whether or not the Earth is 'debris' depends on factors besides its size or the origin of the material of which it is made.[37]

Sagan says 'the world that we live on is a tiny and insignificant part of a vast collection of worlds.'[38] Earth may be tiny relative to Saturn and Jupiter, but unless significance is proportional to size, there is no indication of the Earth's insignificance in this fact. And significance isn't proportional to size. Cars are bigger than humans, but humans are surely more significant. Indeed, some humans are larger than others, but that doesn't make them more significant. Sagan's implicit argument is 'size-ist'. C.S. Lewis pointed out that although our scientific model of creation may have changed, 'The insignificance (by cosmic standards) of the Earth became as much a common-place to the medieval, as to the modern, thinker; it was part of the moralists' stock-in-trade, used, as Cicero uses it, to mortify human ambition.'[39] In the twelfth century Moses Maimonides wrote that 'if man examines the universe as he understands it, he knows how small a part of it he is . . . mankind and certainly all other species of living things are naught in comparison with all of continuing existence.'[40]

In point of fact, Earth is larger than the average sized thing in the cosmos (and people are in the average size band, between the microscopic and the macroscopic levels). And while Earth is one world in 'a vast collection of worlds',[41] and our Sun is 'one of a vast multitude',[42] neither are at all 'average'. We now know that when Sagan states that 'the average star is in no major way different from the Sun'[43] he is wrong. As Benjamin Wiker reports, 'Our sun is not a typical star but is one of the 9 percent most massive stars in our galaxy, and is also very stable. Further, the sun hits the Goldilocks mean for life – neither too hot (like a blue or white star) nor too cold (like a red star) – and its peak emission is right at the visible part of the electromagnetic spectrum – the very, very thin band where not only vision is possible but also photosynthesis.'[44] But even if Sagan didn't have the facts wrong, is an average student with average looks, average grades and average interests thereby *insignificant*? There is no inherent relationship between metaphysical significance and mathematical mediocrity.

The Copernican Myth

The picture of the cosmos developed by the ancient Greeks (principally Aristotle and Ptolemy) had Earth in the middle being circled by a series of nested, concentric spheres containing the planets and the stars. At first this model was a good fit with the available evidence. Over the years various observations were made that didn't fit this model, but which could be made to fit by adding circles within circles (called 'epicycles') in order to obtain ever more complex and accurate movements from the heavenly bodies. Eventually, astronomers like Copernicus (1473–1543) argued that the old model was needlessly complicated, and that it was simpler to suppose that the Earth and the other planets were orbiting the Sun. This shift, from a model with Earth at the centre to one with the Sun at the centre, is known as 'the Copernican revolution'.

Sagan affirms that our failure to inhabit 'the centre of the galaxy, where things are clearly important,'[45] has a negative implication for theism (although quite what the implication is meant to be is never spelt out). According to Sagan, Earth is 'somewhere out in the galactic boondocks, the extreme suburbs, where the action isn't. We are situated in a very unremarkable, unprepossessing location in this great Milky Way Galaxy.'[46] The implicit argument seems to be something like this: the belief that humans are significant is a corollary of theism that is, somehow, falsified by the observation that we don't live in the centre of the cosmos. This 'somehow' can be cashed out as the principle that significance is related to location (that the 'centre of the galaxy' is 'where things are clearly important') and that our failure to inhabit this central location therefore implies our lack of meta-physical significance, and thereby entails that theism is false. Sagan presents us with a lovely turn of phrase, but a terrible, deeply problematic argument.

As far as we know we *are* the only 'action' in the cosmos, at least as far as intelligent life goes; and hence, by definition, the 'action' is wherever we are. We are not in the centre of the Galaxy. Therefore, the action is *not* in the centre of the galaxy. It's *here*! All the evidence is *against* the principle that significance is related to the centrality of one's location in space. Then again, it should be obvious that the link between location and significance presupposed by Sagan's argument is non-existent. Is someone in the middle of a room necessarily more important than someone at the edge? The value of a thing is not determined by its spatial position. As Keith Ward writes, 'It does not follow that, just because we are not physically at the centre of the universe, we are not central to God's plans.'[47]

Michel Onfray asserts that the church rejected heliocentrism because 'Creation by a perfect God could take place only in the centre, the zone of perfection . . . To exist on the periphery would be a mark of inconceivable imperfection . . .'[48] However, in the pre-Copernican scheme of things, the centre of the universe was the dumping ground at the bottom, rather than the nerve-centre at the heart of the universe. Onfray, Sagan, *et al.* are wrong to think of the Ptolemaic view regarding Earth as a universal high point that Copernicus reduced to lowly insignificance. As Robert C. Koons argues:

> It is sometimes thought that our displacement from the centre of the universe by Copernicus somehow contradicted at least Christian theism. But this seems to be based on the erroneous assumption that everything believed by ancient Christians was taken by them as equally essential to their theology. Ancient Christians knew that the earth was spherical and that the universe is immensely large compared to the earth. And although they all believed (until about the fourteenth century) that the earth was the centre of the universe, they did not think that there was anything special about being there, since it was hell, rather than the terrestrial surface, that lay at the very centre. From the ancient perspective, it was the periphery of the cosmos, and not the centre, that took pride of place. The outermost sphere was the source of all terrestrial life and motion. The centre was a kind of sump in which all that was gross and base settled.[49]

Nancy Pearcey and Charles Thaxton explain that 'in medieval cosmology . . . humanity's central location was no compliment, nor was its loss a demotion. In fact, in Copernicus's own day a common objection to his theory was that it elevated mankind *above* his true station . . . the idea that Copernican theory threatened the Christian teaching of human significance is an anarchronism.'[50] Galileo argued that the Copernican revolution actually *promoted* humanity: 'we seek to ennoble and perfect [the earth] when we strive to make it like the celestial bodies, and, as it were, place it in heaven, from which your philosophers [i.e. Aristotle] have banished it.'[51]

Furthermore, Sagan flatly contradicts his own 'locationist' argument! Under the pre-Copernican scheme, Sagan observes, 'The Earth . . . had all the corruption of the universe localized here'.[52] Yet *in the very next paragraph* Sagan asserts that in the Copernican scheme 'the Earth was demoted'![53] Sagan contradicts his Copernican argument in another way as well, in the very act of attempting to push the supposedly sharp blade of his argument deeper into the heart of theism: 'there was the hope that, well, at least maybe our galaxy was at the centre of all the other galaxies, all those many billions of other galaxies. But modern views have it that there is no such thing as a centre of the universe . . .'[54] In the first sentence Sagan invokes the (false) principle that centrality equals significance whereas non-centrality equals insignificance. He thereby implies that we are insignificant because *not even our galaxy is in a central location.* In the second sentence Sagan informs us that 'there is no such thing as a centre of the universe'. But *if there is no central location in the universe, then there cannot be any non-central location in the universe!* Sagan says that 'one of the central points of special relativity is that there are no privileged frames of reference, that we are not in an important position or state of motion.'[55] But if there are 'no privileged frames of reference', then not only is the concept of an 'important' or 'privileged' position incoherent, *so is the concept of a non-important or under-privileged position!*

Contemporary science stands Sagan's 'Copernican' objection on its head in another way as well; for we now know that the great age, and hence size, of the universe in comparison with Earth (as well as the non-central solar and galactic location of Earth) are just some of the many finely-tuned physical preconditions for the existence of life that make the here and now of planet Earth very special indeed.[56]

The Galileo Affair

Talking of Galileo (as we were a little while back), Sagan invokes a myth when he comments that 'The Catholic Church threatened Galileo with torture as he persisted in the heresy that it was the Earth that moved and not the Sun and the rest of the celestial bodies.'[57] Galileo's problems with the Inquisition stemmed not so much from a conflict between 'science' and 'faith', as the myth holds, as from a conflict of personalities, on the one hand, and a conflict with the scientific mainstream of his day, on the other.

First, historian of science Ronald Numbers explains that Galileo 'had gone out of his way to insult the Pope [Urban VIII], who had previously supported him. He put the Pope's favourite argument against heliocentricism into the mouth of the character Simplicitus – the simple-minded person'[58] – in his *Dialogue on the*

Great World Systems. As Bronowski comments, 'It may be that the Pope felt Simplicitus to be a caricature of himself; certainly he felt insulted.'[59] As a result, Galileo

> was summoned down to Rome by the Inquisition [and] lived in the Tuscan palace. And then when he was asked to move into the Vatican, to the palace of the Inquisition, one of the officials in the Inquisition vacated his three-room apartment so that the distinguished guest, Galileo, could have a nice apartment. And they allowed him to have his meals catered by the chef at the Tuscan embassy. Ultimately, he was under house arrest in his villa outside of Florence . . . for his theological heresies, not for his Copernicanism.[60]

Second, as Steve Fuller recounts,

> Galileo, that 17th century icon of scientific heroism, overplayed his hand by fabricating experimental results and embellishing observational accounts . . . Even Galileo's most sympathetic critics found his appeal to the telescope as a scientific instrument rather puzzling. He lacked any principled explanation – a theory of optics – for how this Dutch toy, essentially a spyglass, enabled him to see lunar craters and sunspots. Moreover, the lenses that Galileo improvised for his own telescope were so full of distortion that observers not already convinced of his interpretation could make little sense of what they saw through them.[61]

While the Catholic Church of the period certainly doesn't come out of the Galileo incident well, the 'science' verses 'faith' portrayal of the affair beloved by Sagan *et al.* is historical revisionism plain and simple.

Evolutionary Considerations

As John O'Leary-Hawthorn opines, 'Ask atheists on the street why they don't believe in God and many will say "Because of evolution". One source of this reaction might be that the atheist takes evolution to be undeniably true, and also takes Christianity to deny evolution.'[62] This popular argument could be disarmed by

a) Rebutting the claim that 'evolution' is 'undeniably true';
b) Rebutting the claim that Christianity denies 'evolution';
c) Pointing out that whether or not Christianity denies 'evolution' is irrelevant to the question of theism, since one needn't be a Christian to be a theist.

I think *all of these rebuttals can and should be advanced* (in suitably nuanced fashion). Daniel Dennett claims that 'there are no reputable scientists . . . Not one'[63] who think that the theory of evolution is false; but this well-poisoning rhetorical gambit shouldn't prevent an open-minded assessment of the arguments made by those raising objections to the grander explanatory pretensions of evolution as a scientific theory.[64] Stripped of the attempt to define a 'reputable' scientist as 'one who believes in evolution', Dennett's claim is demonstrably false.[65] By any non-partisan measure scientists like Lev Beloussov (Russian Academy of Natural Sciences embryologist), Lyle Jensen (Professor Emeritus with the Department of Biological Structure and Department of Biochemistry at the University of Washington, a fellow of the American Association for the Advancement of Science and an elected member of the American Academy of Arts and Sciences),[66] Phillip Skell (Emeritus Evan Pugh Professor at Pennsylvania State University and a member of the National Academy of Sciences)[67] and Richard E. Smalley (Nobel Prize-winning chemist)[68] are 'reputable scientists'; but they all doubt that grander explanatory claims of evolution! In 2001, in response to a television documentary which claimed that virtually no scientists disagreed with Darwinian evolution, 132 scientists signed a joint statement proclaiming, 'We are sceptical of claims for the ability of random mutation and natural selection to account for the complexity of life. Careful examination of the evidence for Darwinian theory should be encouraged.'[69] By April 2007, over 700 international scholars had signed the statement. In point of fact:

> there is a live and growing scientific controversy surrounding neo-Darwinian theory . . . Scientific discoveries of the last few decades have led to greater skepticism over the ability of the mechanisms of biological or neo-Darwinian evolutionary theory to account for the

> complexity of life we see today. [A] growing numbers of scientists
> . . . are skeptical of neo-Darwinism's claim that the undirected
> mechanisms of natural selection and random genetic variation can
> account for the complexity of life . . . Neo-Darwinian theory
> presently remains the dominant theory of origins in the scientific
> community, but serious debate now exists about its sufficiency.[70]

However, lest we get too side-tracked, Francis Fukuyama makes it crystal clear that there is a distinction between *evolution* as a scientific theory and *Darwinism* as a philosophy: 'Since Darwinism maintains that there is no cosmic teleology guiding the process of evolution, what seems to be the essence of a species is just an accidental by-product of a random evolutionary process.'[71] It is, of course, impossible to know that humans are 'nothing but' an *accidental* by-product of *random* evolutionary processes unless one knows that there is no cosmic teleology. But one cannot possibly know *that* without knowing that God doesn't exist. Therefore, one cannot discount God's existence by positing the theory of evolution without begging the question.

The Decline of Demarcation

Scientific descriptions are *in principle* incapable of ruling out teleological notions of intention and purpose. After all, many sciences (e.g. archaeology, cryptography, forensic science) depend upon teleological explanations! Scientific explanations, even when they are constrained by the methodological rule that they should be compatible with naturalism (so-called 'methodological naturalism'), can't rule out the existence or activity of God, because teleological explanations are compatible with non-teleological explanations (e.g. the kettle is boiling because of the laws of thermodynamics *and* because I want a mug of coffee), and because God can act outside empirical detectability (e.g. due to Heizenberg's Uncertainty Principle and/or chaos theory). Moreover, as Dominic J. Balestra writes:

> the last twenty-five years of scientific discussions about origins,
> and the new, post-Kuhnian philosophy of science, present a

significantly transformed context [which] removes an old barrier (the hard demarcation) between science and theology and, thereby, clears a way for new avenues of exchange between these disciplines . . . [This is] a time when the results of science in cosmology and biochemistry have produced findings salutary to religion, and philosophy of science has removed old walls of separation . . . Because certain types of explanations (for example, moral duty as an explanation for someone's behaviour) are ruled out of science for methodological reasons, it does not follow that such explanations *tout court* do not contribute to our understanding . . .'[72]

Hence, even were it not the case that 'Most philosophers of science have abandoned the quest for demarcation . . .',[73] given that it is possible for an explanation in terms of design to be the best explanation for a given set of data *tout court*, one must admit that science defined so as to exclude explanations in terms of design is neither a search for the best explanation, nor a search for the truth! The only solution to such an admission is to allow scientists to *follow the evidence wherever it leads*, even if it leads to a conclusion of design, a conclusion that might be metaphysically interpreted as *divine* design.[74] Interestingly, Richard Dawkins forthrightly rejects the attempt to draw a line of demarcation between science and God. He states that 'The question of whether there exists a supernatural creator, a God, is one of the most important that we have to answer. I think that it is a scientific question.'[75]

Scientism and the Limits of Science

'the claim advanced by the "scientific" world view to represent the only valid approach does not lead anywhere but into sterility . . .'
– Josef Pieper[76]

A variation of the 'science vs. religion' argument is advanced by Richard Dawkins when he writes that 'God cannot be proved by any scientific hypothesis. Therefore he does not exist.'[77] But of course, neither can the proposition that 'unless something can be proved by a scientific hypothesis it does not exist' be proved by any scientific hypothesis. By Dawkins' own standards, his objection to theism doesn't exist! Such 'scientism' – *a repetition of the misunderstanding of reason that underpins both the 'root of all evil' argument and the 'religion is nothing but . . .' argument* – is self-defeating, exhibiting a philosophically untenable account of the relationship between evidence and rationality. As Francis Collins states, 'Science is not the only way of knowing.'[78] Atheist physicist Lawrence M. Krauss likewise cautions that 'Science's success does not mean it encompasses the entirety of human intellectual experience . . . Science does not make it impossible to believe in God. We should recognize that fact and live with it and stop being so pompous about it.'[79]

Atheist Kai Nielson points out that 'Most claims that people make are not scientific; yet they can, for all that, be true or false.'[80] Robert C. Koons elaborates:

> Much of the philosophy of science in the mid-twentieth century was taken up in a quixotic attempt to find a line of demarcation between science, on the one hand, and metaphysics and common-sense knowledge, on the other. Every such attempt to find necessary and sufficient conditions for counting something as 'scientific enquiry' or as a 'scientific theory' ended in utter failure . . . If science really were a distinctive mode of knowing, demonstrably superior to commonsense and all other methods, we might be under a kind of intellectual duty to base all of our beliefs on science alone. However, since science cannot be demarcated from the rest of knowledge, our ordinary ways of warranting beliefs are under no such cloud of suspicion and remain innocent until proven guilty.[81]

Steven Weinberg attempts to be more subtle than Dawkins by affirming that 'When it comes to issues of fact rather than of value, I take it as a point of honour, as a moral rather than a logical necessity, to judge matters by the methods of science, or by their commonsense analogues in everyday life.'[82] However, by assuming that the category of 'facts' (defined as matters that can be judged by the methods of science or their commonsense analogues) doesn't include the category of values, Weinberg undermines his own appeal to the moral *value* of his vaunted point of honour!

A misplaced belief in the omnicompetence of science under-girds Peter Atkins' affirmation that, 'There is no necessity for God because science can explain everything.'[83] Freeman likewise asserts that, 'To invoke the supernatural is unnecessary, because we can explain all aspects of our life without it.'[84] But of course, *science cannot even explain everything about which we currently know.* As Stephen Weinberg says, 'There are still countless things in nature that we cannot explain . . .'[85] For example, Ned Block admits that, 'We have no conception of our physical or func-tional nature that allows us to understand how it could explain our subjective experience . . . in the case of consciousness we have nothing – zilch – worthy of being called a research programme, nor are there any substantive proposals about how to go about starting one . . . Researchers are stumped.'[86] Responding to The *Edge* Annual Question 2005, 'What Do You Believe Is True Even Though You Cannot Prove It?', Block wrote, 'I believe that the "Hard Problem of Consciousness" will be solved by conceptual advances made in connection with cognitive neuroscience.'[87] He explained further:

> No one has a clue (at the moment) how to answer the question of why the neural basis of the phenomenal feel of my experience of red is the neural basis of that phenomenal feel rather than a dif-ferent one or none at all. There is an 'explanatory gap' here which no one has a clue how to close . . . The mind-body problem is so singular that no appeal to the closing of past explanatory gaps really justifies optimism, but I am optimistic nonetheless.[88]

One could not hope for a clearer admission that we lack a naturalis-tic account of consciousness and that optimism about the possibility of such an account is based upon blind faith in naturalism.

I am *not* pointing out that science doesn't currently explain every-thing in order to lay the ground for a 'god-of-the-gaps' argument from ignorance. Rather, my pointing out that science doesn't cur-rently explain everything is a legitimate rebuttal of the atheological argument based upon the premise that is thereby shown to be false. Moreover, fear of invalid theistic arguments from ignorance should not be permitted to legitimize the question-begging assumption that every mystery must have an explanation consistent with the metaphysics of naturalism. Nor should such fear exclude the possibility that increased scientific knowledge might furnish natural theology with (more) data that is best explained by a theistic worldview.

Atkins' affirmation that, 'There is no necessity for God because science can explain everything'[89] might be more charitably interpreted as proclaiming his faith that science *will one day* explain everything; or at least that science is *in principle* capable of explaining everything. However, it's hard to see how he could evidentially justify these assertions without laying claim to an omniscience that would be hard to explain scientifically. After all, if we have not yet even discovered everything we might want to explain (and surely we have not), how else can Atkins rule out the possibility that we may discover a counter-example to his scientism – something science cannot explain? Indeed, many scholars think that we have already discovered counter-examples to Atkins' unlimited faith in the explanatory capacities of science. As Steve Jones, Professor of Genetics at University College London, points out, 'Science cannot answer the questions that philosophers – or children – ask'.[90] As Stephen Hawking admits, 'Although science may solve the problem of how the universe began, it cannot answer the question: why does the universe bother to exist?'[91]

In their paper 'Several Open Problems in Physics and Cosmology', Mikuláš Blazek (professor of physics at the University of Trnava, member of the Slovak Academy of Sciences) and Miroslav Karaba (lecturer in philosophy at the University of Trnava) argue that:

> the universe began from a hot and dense state of matter. It originated as a whole . . . There is no serious evidence for the existence of an oscillating universe . . . There are only hypotheses on the physical properties of the universe before the start of its expansion. Let us admit that some kind of 'primordial' matter (either in its vacuum or some excited state) existed before the start of that expansion. In such a kind of matter there existed different fluctuations and one of them, energetically very rich, might decay leading to the birth of our universe . . . Of course, *such a possibility does not solve the problem of the origin of matter: this model shifts it only one*

step further into the past. Questions related to the origin (or eternity) of matter are answered within the framework of religion . . . it is interesting to notice that *not all questions formulated in the field of serious science will be met with adequate serious (scientific) answers . . .* in this way the mutual complementarity between religion and science is clearly manifested.[92]

Nor is science equipped to deal with questions of value (truth, goodness, beauty) and meaning upon which the very practice of science depends. As Erwin Schrödinger said, 'the scientific picture of the world around me is very deficient. It gives a lot of factual information, puts all our experience in a magnificently consistent order, but is ghastly silent about all and sundry that is really near to our heart . . .'[93] Some respond to such remarks by rejecting the objective reality of all and sundry that is really near to our heart; but to limit knowledge or existence to that which falls within the competency of science is an unjustified and self-defeating leap of blind faith.

J.P. Moreland notes that, 'Science . . . assumes that the universe is intelligible and not capricious, that the mind and senses can be applied to the world, that knowledge is possible, that there is a uniformity in nature that justifies inductive inferences . . . and so forth.'[94] In other words, there are propositions that science itself depends upon but which are not scientific propositions or propositions that science is equipped to defend. As philosopher of science Del Ratzsch argues:

> if we are rationally justified in accepting science then we must be rationally justified in accepting those foundational presuppositions [that science depends upon]. But not being *results* of science, their rational justification cannot rest upon science, but must lie *beyond* science. Thus, if we take science and its results to be rationally justified, science is not the only source of rational justification. There must then evidently be some *deeper* source of rational justification. Historically religion played a significant role here.[95]

The view that science is the only valid path to knowledge, or that only the scientifically knowable is real (a position known as 'hard scientism'), is itself neither the conclusion of scientific reasoning, nor a proposition within the purview of science. Like Charles Hartshorne, we should therefore acknowledge that 'empirical evidence . . . is not sufficient for all our cognitive needs'.[96] As Fraser Watts, lecturer in theology and natural science at Cambridge University, concludes, 'I do not know of any research that conflicts with religion. The problem comes from the ideological position, held by a minority of scientists, that science is the only valid form of knowledge and has got all the answers.'[97]

The view that science is the only valid form of knowledge, and that this form of knowledge is necessarily in tension with religious claims, is surprising when one considers the fact that the pioneers of modern science were theists whose theism functioned as a deeper source of rational justification than science and which justified their very engagement in science. In fact, 'many recent historians . . . have argued that science grew out of a theistic milieu and that a number of theological beliefs were essential to the rise of science in Western Europe in the sixteenth and seventeenth centuries . . .'[98] J.J. Haldane explores the synergy between theism and science, writing that:

> science involves an absolutely fundamental and extensive commitment to the nature of reality; one that is presupposed rather than derived from it; and one that makes ineliminable reference to the idea that what there is is intelligible. So viewed, it should seem odd to oppose scientific and religious ways of thinking about the nature of reality. On the contrary, it is plausible to regard them as similar; for a central idea of theism is that we and the world we inhabit constitute an objective order that exhibits intrinsic intelligibility . . . the Judaeo-Christian-Islamic doctrine of creation serves to underwrite science by assuring us that its operative assumptions of order and intelligibility are correct and by providing a motivation for pure science, namely understanding the composition and modes of operation of a vastly complex mind-reflecting artifact.[99]

A.C. Grayling asserts that 'As real knowledge and mastery advance, there is diminishing need to invoke supernatural agencies to explain the world. Deities inhabit the dark places over the horizon of knowledge, and retreat as light approaches.'[100] However, by claiming that deities inhabit the dark places beyond the bright horizon of the 'real knowledge and mastery' provided by 'science's careful and thorough hypotheses . . . [that make] use of no materials or speculations beyond what the world itself offers',[101] Grayling banishes philosophy to the outer darkness, and thereby embraces a self-contradictory scientism. Moreover, by making the falsifiable claim that as scientific knowledge advances, so the need to invoke supernatural agencies *decreases*, Grayling lays his position open to falsification by the observation that today it is precisely the *advance* of scientific understanding that has indirectly lent *increased* vigour to natural theology.

Behind the Spirit of the Times

The main gist of the 'science vs. religion' argument is summarised by C.S. Lewis' caricature of 'Mr Enlightenment' in *The Pilgrim's Regress*:

> 'They are a shrewd lot, those Stewards [religious leaders]. They know which side their bread is buttered on, all right. Clever fellows . . .'
> 'But do you mean that the Stewards don't believe it themselves?'
> 'I dare say they do. It is just the sort of cock and bull story they would believe. They are simple old souls most of them – just like children. They have no knowledge of modern science and they would believe anything they were told.' John went silent for a few minutes. Then he began again: 'But how do you know there is no Landlord [God]?'
> 'Christopher Columbus, Galileo, the earth is round, invention of printing, gunpowder!!' exclaimed Mr Enlightenment . . .
> 'I don't quite understand,' said John . . .
> 'Your people in Puritania believe in the Landlord because they have not had the benefits of a scientific training. For example, now, I dare say it would be news to you to hear that the earth was round . . .'[102]

In the final analysis, the 'science vs. religion' objection expresses a prejudice exemplified by Peter Atkins' remarks that religion is 'outmoded and ridiculous' and that it is 'not possible to believe in gods and be a true scientist'.[103] Feuerbach brushed aside the question of God's existence as being out of date, saying, 'The question as to the existence or non-existence of God . . . belongs to the sixteenth and seventeenth centuries, not to the nineteenth. I deny God.'[104] The New Atheists repeat this old mantra; but substituting new dates doesn't patch the hole in its logic. The primary emphasis of Nietzsche's mature writings was that 'belief in the Christian God has become unbelievable',[105] a statement that, as McGrath observes, 'represents a cultural observation rather than a philosophical argument.'[106] Nietzsche admitted that 'What is now decisive against Christianity is our taste, no longer our reasons.'[107] Contemporary atheologians are caught up in the same 'spirit of the times'. As Kai Nielson comments, 'in cultures such as ours, religion is very often an alien form of life to intellectuals. Living as we do in a post-enlightenment era, it is difficult for us to take religion seriously. The very concept seems fantastic to us . . .'[108] This is an interesting sociological report. It isn't an argument.

Conclusion

'I do not see that committing oneself to science necessarily implies that one thinks that all of religion is false . . .'
– Michael Ruse[109]

C.S. Lewis, who exhorted us to 'take a low view of "climates of opinion"',[110] explained the prevalence of this sort of 'been there, done that' myth as the result of 'chronological snobbery', by which he means:

> the uncritical acceptance of the intellectual climate common to our own age and the assumption that whatever has gone out of date is on that account discredited. You must find why it went out of date. Was it ever refuted (and if so by whom, where, and how conclusively) or did it merely die away as fashions do? If the latter, this tells us nothing about its truth or falsehood. From seeing this, one passes to the realization that our own age is also 'a period,' and certainly has, like all periods, its own characteristic illusions.[111]

The 'Science vs. Religion' objection is just such an illusion. As Peter Kreeft says, trying to tell the truth with a clock instead of an argument is 'as silly as trying to tell time with a syllogism'.[112] As Sociologist David Martin advises, 'if I were an atheist anxious to disturb the faith of an intelligent young friend, I would recommend . . . a bracing course in romantic literary Weltschmertz. But not, definitely not, a bracing course in astrophysics. He or she might rather too easily suppose he or she was tracing "the Mind of the Maker".'[113] The 'Science explains everything' objection to theism is a myth we can and should leave behind.

Recommended Resources

Michael J. Behe, *The Edge of Evolution: The Search for the Limits of Darwinism* (London/New York: Free Press, 2007).

Michael J. Behe, *Darwin's Black Box: The Biochemical Challenge to Evolution* (London/New York: Free Press, 2006).

David Berlinski, *The Devil's Delusion: Atheism and Its Scientific Pretensions* (New York: Crown Forum, 2008).

John Angus Campbell and Stephen C. Meyer (eds.), *Darwinism, Design, And Public Education* (East Lansing: Michigan State University Press, 2003).

Paul Copan, *How Do You Know You're Not Wrong*? (Grand Rapids, MI: Baker, 2005).

Paul Copan and Paul K. Moser (eds.), *The Rationality of Theism* (London/New York: Routledge, 2003).

William Lane Craig and J.P. Moreland (eds.), *Naturalism: A Critical Analysis* (London/New York: Routledge, 2001).

William A. Dembski (ed.), *Uncommon Dissent: Intellectuals Who Find Darwinism Unconvincing* (Wilmington, DE: ISI Books, 2004).

William A. Dembski, *The Design Revolution: Answering the Toughest Questions about Intelligent Design* (Downers Grove, IL: IVP, 2004).

William A. Dembski, *No Free Lunch: Why Specified Complexity Cannot be Purchased without Intelligence* (Larkam, MD: Rowman & Littlefield, 2001).

William A. Dembski and Jonathan Wells, *The Design of Life: Discovering Signs of Intelligence In Biological Systems* (Dallas, TX: Foundation for Thought and Ethics, 2007).

William A. Dembski and Sean McDowell, *Understanding Intelligent Design: Everything You Need to Know in Plain Language* (Eugene, OR: Harvest House, 2008).

Phil Dowe, Galileo, *Darwin and Hawking: The Interplay of Science, Reason, and Religion* (Grand Rapids, MI: Eerdmans, 2005).

Stewart Goetz and Charles Taliaferro, *Naturalism* (Grand Rapids, MI: Eerdmans, 2008).

Edward Grant, *A History of Natural Philosophy: From the Ancient World to the Nineteenth Century* (Cambridge: Cambridge University Press, 2007).

William Hasker, *The Emergent Self* (Ithaca, NY: Cornell University Press, 1999).

Philip E. Johnson, *Darwin on Trial* (Downers Grove, IL: IVP, 1993).

Antony Latham, *The Naked Emperor: Darwinism Exposed* (London: Janus, 2005).

John Lennox, *God's Undertaker: Has Science Buried God?* (Oxford: Lion, 2007).

Angus Menuge, *Agents Under Fire: Materialism and the Rationality of Science* (Oxford: Rowman & Littlefield, 2004).

J.P. Moreland, *Consciousness and the Existence of God: A Theistic Argument* (London/New York: Routledge, 2008).

J.P. Moreland and William Lane Craig, *Philosophical Foundations for a Christian Worldview* (Downers Grove, IL: IVP, 2003).

Terence L. Nichols, *The Sacred Cosmos: Christian Faith and the Challenge of Naturalism* (Grand Rapids, MI: Brazos, 2003).

Nancy R. Pearcey and Charles B. Thaxton, *The Soul Of Science: Christian Faith and Natural Philosophy* (Wheaton, IL: Crossway, 1994).

Alvin Plantinga, *Warranted Christian Belief* (Oxford: Oxford University Press, 2003), www.ccel.org/ccel/plantinga/warranted.html.

Del Ratzsch, *Science and Its Limits: The Natural Sciences in Christian Perspective* (Downers Grove, IL: IVP, 2000.

Robert B. Stewart (ed.), *Intelligent Design: William A. Dembski and Michael Ruse in Dialogue* (Minneapolis, MN: Fortress Press, 2007).

David Swift, *Evolution under the Microscope: A Scientific critique of the theory of evolution* (Stirling: Leighton, 2002).

Keith Ward, *The Big Questions in Science and Religion* (West Conshohocken, PA: Templeton Foundation Press, 2008).

H. Wayne House (ed.), *Intelligent Design 101: Leading Experts Explain the Key Issues* (Grand Rapids, MI: Kregel, 2008).

David DeWolf, John West, Casey Luskin, and Jonathan Witt, *Traipsing Into Evolution: Intelligent Design and the Kitzmiller vs. Dover Decision* (Washington, DC: Discovery Institute, 2006).

Thomas Woodward, *Darwin Strikes Back: Defending the Science of Intelligent Design* (Grand Rapids, MI: Baker, 2006).

Thomas Woodward, *Doubts About Darwin: A History of Intelligent Design* (Grand Rapids, MI: Baker, 2003).

On-Line Papers

Steve Fuller, 'The Darwinian Delusion', www.standpoint-mag.co.uk/node/254/full.

Robert C. Koons, 'The Incompatibility of Naturalism and Scientific Realism', www.leaderu.com/offices/koons/docs/natreal.html.

C.S. Lewis, 'The Cardinal Difficulty of Naturalism', www.philosophy.uncc.edu/mleldrid/Intro/csl3.html.

Art Lindsley, 'C.S. Lewis on Chronological Snobbery', www.cslewisinstitute.org/pages/resources/publications/knowingDoing/2003/LewisChronologicalSnobbery.pdf.

Angus Menuge, 'The Role of Agency in Science', www.4truth.net/site/apps/nl/content3.asp?c=hiKXLbPNLrF&b=1171681&ct=1579247.

Bradley Monton, 'Is Intelligent Design Science? Dissecting the Dover Decision', http://philsci-archive.pitt.edu/archive/00002583/01/Methodological_Naturalism_2.pdf.

J.P. Moreland, 'Does the argument from mind provide evidence for God?', www.boundless.org/features/a0000901.html.

Alvin Plantinga, 'Evolution vs. Naturalism', www.christianitytoday.com/bc/2008/004/11.37.html.

Alvin Plantinga, 'Religion and Science', http://plato.stanford.edu/entries/religion-science/.

Alvin Plantinga, 'Methodological Naturalism?', http://id-www.ucsb.edu/fscf/library/plantinga/mn/home.html.

Charles Thaxton, 'Christianity and the Scientific Enterprise', www.leaderu.com/truth/1truth17.html.

Benjamin Wiker, 'The Atheist's Benchwarmer', www.discovery. org/a/4220.

Dallas Willard, 'Knowledge and Naturalism', www.dwillard. org/Philosophy/Pubs/knowledge_and_naturalism.htm.

Dallas Willard, 'Non-Reductive and Non-Eliminative Physicalism?', www.dwillard.org/articles/artview.asp?art ID=48.

Peter S. Williams, 'Reviewing the Reviewers: Pigliucci *et al* on "Darwin's Rottweiler & the public understanding of science"', www.arn.org/docs/williams/pw_pigliucci_reviewingreviewers.htm.

Peter S. Williams, 'Undermining Richard Norman on "Why Science Undermines Religion"', www.arn.org/docs/ williams/ pw_underminingrichardnorman.htm.

Audio

William Lane Craig, 'Has Science Made Faith in God Impossible?', www.reasonablefaith.org/RF_audio_video/ Other _clips/A97TAMU01.mp3.

William Lane Craig vs. Victor Stenger, 'Does God Exist?', www.bringyou.to/CraigStengerDebate.mp3.

William Lane Craig, 'Scientific Intolerance', www.reasonablefaith.org/site/News2?page=NewsArticle&id=5887.

Alister McGrath, 'Has Science Eliminated God?', www.bethinking.org/resource.php?ID=176&Topic=&Category.

Angus Menuge, 'Agents Under Fire, Part One', http//intelligentdesign.podomatic.com/entry/eg/2008-08-18T17_44_24-7_00.

J.P. Moreland, 'The Argument from Consciousness', www.veritas.org/mediafiles/VTS-Moreland-1997-Georgia-97VFGA02.mp3.

Alvin Plantinga, 'Faith and Science', www.calvin.edu/january/2000/ram/20000118.ram.

Alvin Plantinga, 'Science and Religion – Why does the debate continue?', www.redeemingreason.org/Media2006/ROR2006-03%20Alvin%20Plantinga.MP3.

Alvin Plantinga, 'The evolutionary anti-naturalism argument', www.hisdefense.org/audio/ap_001.ram.

Peter S. Williams, 'An Introduction to Intelligent Design Theory', www.cis-centralsouth.org.uk/media/2006-intelligent-design/PeterWilliams.vbr.mp3.

Peter S. Williams, 'Darwinism vs. Design', www.damaris.org/cm/podcasts/category/peterswilliams.

Video

Robert C. Koons, 'Science and Belief in God: Concord not Conflict', http://webcast.ucsd.edu:8080/ramgen/UCSD_TV/7828.rm.

John Lennox, 'Has Science Burried God?', www.cis.org.uk/upload/cis20080428.mov.

Alister E. McGrath, 'Dawkins' God', www.cis.org.uk/central-south/dawkins-god-http.shtml.

John Polkinghorne, 'Interview', http://video.google.com/videoplay?docid=-625904119099996720.

6

A Significant Absence of Evidence?

'The secular humanist outlook . . . is committed to . . . scepticism of
a theistic God . . . for it finds insufficient evidence'
– Paul Kurtz[1]

Asked what he would say if he found himself standing before God after death and God asked him, 'Why didn't you believe in me?', Richard Dawkins answered, 'I'd quote Bertrand Russell: "Not enough evidence, God, not enough evidence."'[2] There's an interesting difference in *attitude* on this point between Russell and Dawkins, on the one hand, and H.L. Mencken, on the other hand, who answered essentially the same question by saying: 'If I do fetch up with the twelve apostles, I shall say, "Gentlemen, I was wrong".'[3] In this context we should not shy away from the fact that atheists may (and note that I say *may* rather than *will*) fail to appreciate genuine evidence for theism due to the sort of non-rational factors we considered in chapter four. As Piers Benn acknowledges, 'since some theistic religions teach that sin can impair our thinking, we risk begging the question against those religions if we assume that *if* we can see no good reason for believing them, then they are almost certainly false.'[4]

According to Dawkins, 'there is no evidence in favour of the God Hypothesis'.[5] This claim is a rather astonishing one for Dawkins to make, since he *defines* biology as 'the study of complicated things that give the appearance of having been designed for a purpose'.[6] There is, then, according to Dawkins himself, *prima facie* evidence for the God hypothesis. The *Humanist Manifesto* II, drafted by Paul Kurtz and Edwin H. Wilson, more cautiously declares: 'We find insufficient evidence for belief in the existence of a supernatural . . . theism . . . is an unproven and outmoded faith.'[7] (The term 'outmoded' here is a fine example of chronological snobbery.) Manifesto signatory Antony Flew reports that he asked several Christian friends to refer him 'to the work or works they saw as presenting the most formidable intellectual challenge to my unbelief',[8] but that 'they all admitted to great difficulty in thinking of anything they could recommend as adequate . . .'[9] It is testimony to the fact that Christian scholarship has come a long way since Flew's atheistic heyday that I would make no such admission today. For atheist Keith Parsons, one of the problems with theism nevertheless remains the perceived absence of a formidable intellectual challenge to unbelief. He asks:

> What is the appropriate attitude of the atheist when confronted with yet another set of unconvincing arguments for theism? I think it must be the same as his attitude about claims made on behalf of the Loch Ness Monster, UFOs, the Lost Continent of Atlantis, the Bermuda Triangle, and Bigfoot. These are interesting claims, but their proponents are perennially incapable of putting forward any good evidence for them.[10]

Kai Nielson states:

> Starting with the early Enlightenment figures, finding acute and more fully developed critiques in Hume and Kant, and carried through by their contemporary rational reconstructers (e.g., Mackie, and Martin), the various arguments for the existence of God have been so thoroughly refuted that few would try to defend them today and even those few who do, do so in increasingly attenuated forms.[11]

Such claims are out of touch with contemporary practice. As Plantinga affirms, 'Christian belief can be justified, rational, and warranted not just for ignorant fundamentalists or benighted medievals but for informed and educated twenty-first century Christians who are entirely aware of all the artillery that has been rolled up against Christian belief since the Enlightenment.'[12] What William Lane Craig calls 'the obsolete, 18th century objections of

Hume and Kant'[13] have received substantial replies from contemporary philosophers.[14] Amazingly, Nielson singles out Hume for special mention regarding services rendered to the cause of atheology: 'Many contemporary naturalists believe that . . . the critical work – the critique of the truth-claims of theism – [has been] essentially done by Hume . . .'[15] Naturalists who believe this are at best uninformed concerning the contemporary 'resurrection of theism' (after all, the contemporary debate includes arguments that didn't even *exist* in the nineteenth century). According to James F. Sennett and Douglas Groothuis, 'Natural theology is alive and well in contemporary philosophy; the supposed Humean refutation of the enterprise is a myth whose exposure is long overdue.'[16]

Hume was not the atheist one might think from Nielson's comments. Hume expert Nicholas Capaldi states that, 'In none of his writings does Hume say or imply that he does not accept the existence of God. On the contrary, Hume says in several places that he accepts the existence of God.'[17] What Hume *did* reject was the traditional formulations of a number of arguments for God, which is hardly surprising given his general scepticism about metaphysics. John Perry and Michael Bratman conclude that

> the mature Hume was a theist, albeit of a vague and weak-kneed sort. He seems to have been convinced by the argument from design of the proposition 'That the cause or causes of order in the universe probably bear some remote analogy to human intelligence.' But he was also convinced that the argument does not permit this undefined intelligence to be given further shape or specificity . . .[18]

Hume's critique of the design argument (although many scholars think it flawed)[19] is a helpful corrective to any natural theology that seeks to build a case for God from any single a *posteriori* argument (such as the design argument), rather than upon an accumulation of arguments. As Hume rightly warned, 'When we infer any particular cause for an effect we must proportion the one to the other, and can never be allowed to ascribe to any cause any qualities, but what are exactly sufficient to produce the effect.'[20] The Intelligent Design movement agrees with Hume upon this point, noting that the identification of the designer(s) detected by the application of design-detection criteria to nature is a philosophical step beyond the scientific evidence.

Mackie's critique of natural theology was countered by Richard Swinburne.[21] Martin's contribution to the debate has not exactly been without critics (notably Paul Copan).[22] Moreover, many contemporary philosophers give their endorsement to the project of natural theology. As Edward Feser reports:

> There are, of course, a number of standard objections to the traditional arguments for God's existence. But there has also been in recent decades a great revival of interest among philosophers in the philosophy of religion in general and in the traditional theistic arguments in particular. Many contemporary philosophers of religion hold that the traditional arguments can be reformulated in a way that makes them immune to the usual objections, and that many of those objections rest in the first place on misunderstandings or even caricatures . . .[23]

Individual arguments for theism may often be defended in more rigorously cautious terms than was the norm in medieval scholasticism, but today's natural theology can hardly be called 'attenuated' when philosophers like Robert C. Koons are prepared to say that 'the evidence for theism has never been so clear and so strong as it is now'.[24]

Lewis Wolpert's Presumption of Atheism and the 'Insufficient Evidence' Objection

Cell biologist Lewis Wolpert has attained a measure of notoriety, primarily through the publication of his book *Six Impossible Things Before Breakfast: The Evolutionary Origins of Belief* (Faber, 2006) and through his participation in a public debate on the existence of God with Christian philosopher William Lane Craig. This debate was held on 27 February 2007 at Westminster Central Hall in London, chaired by well-known journalist John Humphrys, and reported on by him in a major article for the *Daily Telegraph*,[25] as well as in his book *In God We Doubt*. Professor

Wolpert, who is a vice president of the British Humanist Association, admits that he 'stopped believing in God when I was 15 or 16 because he didn't give me what I asked for'.[26] However, Wolpert has subsequently, and repeatedly, justified his atheism by asserting that 'There is absolutely no evidence for the existence of God.'[27]

Tom Price provides a concise, eye-witness summary of the public debate between Craig and Wolpert, a debate in which Wolpert majored on the 'Insufficient Evidence' objection:

Craig: God exists, here is the evidence.
Wolpert: God doesn't exist, there is no evidence.
Craig: God exists, here is the evidence.
Wolpert: God doesn't exist, who made God?
Craig: God does exist, he is an uncaused eternal being. Here is the evidence.
Wolpert: God doesn't exist. He hasn't done anything in the last 2,000 years.
Craig: That's chronological snobbery. You don't tell the time with an argument, you don't tell if an argument is true or false, or if evidence is good or bad with a watch.
Wolpert: God doesn't exist. We believe because we have a notion of cause and effect, this leads to tool-making, and also to belief in God.
Craig: That's the genetic fallacy. To confuse the origin of a belief with its truth or falsity. You need to deal with the arguments and evidence that I have presented.
Wolpert: God doesn't exist. There is no evidence. Who made God?
Craig: Here is the evidence. God is an uncaused being. God does exist.
Wolpert: God doesn't exist. There is no evidence.
Craig: God does exist. Here is the evidence.[28]

As Humphrys reports:

> you might assume that a debate between someone like Craig and someone like Wolpert – a Jew who lost his faith when he was 15 – would produce a riveting intellectual knockabout at least and a

profound discussion of whether God is delusion or reality at best. Sadly it didn't work out like that. They might as well have been talking in different languages. Here's the essence of Craig's case:

- God created the universe. The proof lies in the premise that whatever begins to exist has a cause. The universe began to exist; therefore it has a cause. It was brought into existence by something which is greater than (and beyond) it. And that something was a 'personal being'.
- God 'fine tunes' the universe . . . There is no other logical explanation for the way things operate.
- Without God there can be no set of [objective] moral values.
- The 'historical facts' of the life of Jesus prove the basis for Christianity.
- God can be known and experienced [in a properly basic manner].

And here's the essence of Wolpert's rebuttal: it's all bunkum. Every bit of it.[29]

Wolpert's defence of atheism consisted of a few irrelevant and invalid arguments against the rationality of belief in God's existence, on the one hand (instances of chronological snobbery and the genetic fallacy respectively) and *a total failure to interact with the purported evidence for God*, on the other hand, apparently on the grounds 'that there is no evidence' with which to interact! Craig comments that:

> Poor Professor Wolpert was clearly out of his depth and had little to offer as evidence that belief in God is a delusion apart from asking, 'Who created God?' My notes from the debate have large, blank spaces across from my arguments for God's existence, indicating a lack of response. So it was a pretty one-sided contest. It's sad that it is this sort of superficial secularism that is so influential in Britain today.[30]

Given Craig's use of the cosmological argument from the temporal finitude of the past, it is interesting to note that Wolpert candidly admits he has no adequate non-theistic explanation for the

Big Bang: 'And then, of course, there's the whole problem of where the universe itself came from. And that is a great mystery. Big bang, big schmang! How did that all happen? I haven't got a clue.'[31] How can someone who makes such repeated use of the 'Insufficient Evidence' objection fail so totally to even deal with the evidence presented by Craig? The answer to this question recently became clear in an interview between Wolpert and another Christian philosopher . . .

Wolpert's Question-Begging Obscurantism

In the hands of Lewis Wolpert, the 'Insufficient Evidence' objection is not at all what it seems. Wolpert says that atheism is justified because 'There is absolutely no evidence for the existence of God.'[32] However, Professor Keith Ward of Oxford University had the following revealing exchange with Wolpert concerning this assertion in the course of an interview for the March 2007 edition of *Third Way* magazine:

Ward: What sort of evidence would count for you? Would it have to be scientific evidence of some sort?

Wolpert: Well, no . . . I think I read somewhere: If he turned the pond on Hamstead Heath into good champagne, it would be quite impressive . . .

Ward: A miracle would be sufficient?

Wolpert: But then you have to remember what David Hume said, that you wouldn't believe in a reported miracle unless 'the falsehood of [the] testimony would be more miraculous than the event which [it] relates.'

Ward: It's one of his worst arguments, in my view.

Wolpert: Hume is the only philosopher I take seriously. I'm big against philosophy . . .[33]

Wolpert justifies his atheism by complaining that there is no evidence for the existence of God. So what sort of evidence would he accept? Would he accept scientific evidence? On Humean grounds (grounds that are widely thought by contemporary philosophers to be defunct), he would not. Later in the same interview Ward asked whether (in principle) there could be evidence of providence in history? Wolpert replied that there 'absolutely [could] not'[34] be any such evidence. Wolpert apparently includes the evidence of religious experience among purported scientific evidence for God, because having suggested an explanation of such experience in terms of evolutionary psychology (and despite admitting 'I don't have a good explanation, to be quite honest'[35] for why he himself has escaped the supposed evolutionary pressure to believe), Wolpert feels that he can dismiss all such experiences as delusional (an unsurprising move for someone who is a self-confessed 'reductionist and a materialist').[36] If Wolpert rules out scientific evidence for theism, will he accept philosophical evidence? He will not, because he is 'big against philosophy' (although he will embrace a double standard in order to allow Hume into the fold, to shore it up against scientific evidence for deity).

Having excluded *a priori* the very possibility of there being any evidence for God, it is perhaps unsurprising that Wolpert can find none, or that he would fail to engage with purported evidence for God offered to him by Professor Craig. What *is* surprising is that having excluded *a priori* the possibility of there being any evidence for God, Wolpert should shirk the task of *showing* why Craig's evidence is insufficient (where exactly do Craig's arguments for God go wrong? Do they have false premises? Do they have invalid logic? Wolpert doesn't say) whilst continuing to justify his atheism primarily by repeating that 'the evidence for God is not very good from my point of view'.[37]

Wolpert's complaint is ultimately *not* that there is insufficient evidence for theism. Rather it is that since the possibility of there being sufficient evidence for theism would require reductionistic materialism to be false, and since reductionistic materialism is true (a mere assertion of Wolpert's part), there can't possibly be sufficient evidence for theism! In other words, Wolpert doesn't merely think that there *isn't* any evidence for God, he thinks that there *can't be* any evidence for God. These are significantly different claims, and so it is nontrivial when Wolpert substitutes one for the other. There would be nothing wrong with taking this approach if Wolpert provided *de facto* arguments purporting to show that materialism is true (or at least that theism is false), if he was prepared to enter into philosophical debate concerning the soundness of those arguments, and if he was prepared to extend the same courtesy to the theistic arguments of academics like Professors Craig and Ward.

Unfortunately Wolpert doesn't appear to be interested in ful-filling any of these conditions. He simply repeats his equivocating mantra that there is no evidence for God. Like doubting Thomas, Lewis Wolpert says, 'I will not believe unless I see'; but unlike doubting Thomas, Wolpert keeps his eyes resolutely shut. In other words, *Wolpert's atheism is a matter of blind faith*. As ex-atheist Antony Flew observes:

> We see how easy it is to let preconceived theories shape the way we view evidence instead of letting the evidence shape our theories. A Copernican leap may thus be prevented by a thousand Ptolemaic epicycles . . . And in this, it seems to me, lies the peculiar danger, the endemic evil, of dogmatic atheism. Take such utterances as 'We should not ask for an explanation of how it is that the world exists; it is here and that's all' or 'Since we cannot accept a transcendent source of life, we choose to believe the impossible: that life arose spontaneously by chance from matter' . . . Now it often seems to people who are not atheists as if there is no conceivable piece of evidence that would be admitted by apparently scientific-minded dogmatic atheists to be a sufficient reason for conceding 'There must be a God after all.' I therefore put to my former fellow-athe-ists the simple central question: 'What would have to occur or to have occurred to constitute for you a reason to at least consider the existence of a superior Mind?'[38]

Wolpert and the Origin of Life

For example, during his interview with Keith Ward, Wolpert commented that 'How the cell came about is just . . . Wow! It's absolutely mind-blowing. It's truly miraculous – almost in a reli-gious sense. I think we understand quite a lot about evolution – although even in later evolution there are problems for which we don't have good explanations – but the origin of life itself, the origin of the cell itself, that's not solved at all.'[39] Following this interesting admission, Ward asked Wolpert whether he was happy to be described as a neo-Darwinian, and the following revealing exchange ensued:

Wolpert: I'm afraid I would have to say that, yes.

Ward: So, even though you find it 'miraculous', you think we must account for the emergence of life purely in terms of random mutation and natural selection?

Wolpert: That's the line we must pursue, yes.

Ward: Why 'must'?

Wolpert: Because there really is no other way. Otherwise, you can only invoke God.[40]

In other words, Wolpert believes that the inherent capacities of the natural world (putting aside the cosmological question of why there is a natural world in the first place) *must* account for – and therefore must be *capable* of accounting for – both the origin and diverse nature of life on Earth because this conclusion is philosophically deduced (*not* because it is scientifically inferred) from the assumption that God could not possibly feature in the true account of these matters. This is presumably because, as a materialist, Wolpert believes that there is no God to feature in the true account of these matters. Wolpert closes his eyes to the possibility of evidence pointing towards God's existence by the simple expedient of assuming that God doesn't exist! Once again, Wolpert's use of the 'Insufficient Evidence' objection to belief in God is exposed as a rhetorical façade hiding a circular argument.

Wolpert isn't an isolated example of question-begging 'dogmatic atheism'. Biologist Franklin Harold asserts that 'Life arose here on earth from inanimate matter, by some kind of evolutionary process.'[41] But as Harold admits, this assertion is not grounded in scientific evidence, but in naturalistic metaphysical assumptions: 'This is not a statement of demonstrable fact, but an assumption . . .'[42] As William Lane Craig comments:

> evolutionary theory's status as the best explanation of biological complexity depends crucially on excluding from the pool of live explanatory options [teleological] hypotheses . . . Were we to admit into the pool of live explanatory options [teleological] hypotheses, then it would no longer be evident that evolutionary theory is the best explanation of the data. It is in this sense that the theory presupposes naturalism. The theory itself does not imply naturalism; rather it is the theory's current exulted position as the

best explanation that depends crucially upon excluding from consideration [teleological] alternatives . . . The question we need to
face squarely, then, is, What happens to evolutionary theory if we
do not assume, metaphysically or methodologically, anti-teleolog-
ical naturalism?[43]

Richard Dawkins will not face Craig's question: 'The kind of
explanation we come up with must . . . *make use of the laws of
physics, and nothing more than the laws of physics.*'[44] Richard
Lewontin is explicit about the way in which his naturalistic
assumptions drive his scientific conclusions, writing:

> we have a prior commitment to materialism. It is not that the
> methods . . . of science somehow compel us to accept a material
> explanation of the . . . world, but, on the contrary, that we are
> forced by our . . . adherence to material causes to create . . . a set of
> concepts that produce material explanations, no matter how coun-
> terintuitive, no matter how mystifying . . .[45]

'Moreover', says Lewontin, 'that materialism is absolute, *for we
cannot allow a Divine foot in the door* . . .'[46]

Abiogenesis and Design

In a 2004 letter to *Philosophy Now* magazine Antony Flew discussed
'the limits of the negative theological implications of Darwin's
Theory of Evolution by Natural Selection'. Flew notes that the theory of evolution by natural selection logically cannot account for
the origin of life capable of evolving, and observed that, 'Probably
Darwin himself believed that life was miraculously breathed into
that primordial form of not always consistently reproducing life by
God . . .'[47] Flew noted that 'the evidential situation of natural (as
opposed to revealed) theology has been transformed in the more
than fifty years since Watson and Crick won the Nobel Prize for
their discovery of the double helix structure of DNA. It has become
inordinately difficult even to begin to think about constructing a
naturalistic theory of the evolution of that first reproducing organism.'[48]

The idea that the prerequisites of evolution could simply
'arise', perhaps from some 'warm little pond' of chemicals, is

known as *abiogenesis*, from the Greek *a* (without), *bios* (life) and *ginomai* (to form). The concept is popularly known today under the rubric of the hypothetical 'primal soup'. Dawkins considers the question of *abiogenesis* in *The God Delusion*, writing:

> the spontaneous arising by chance of the first hereditary molecule strikes many as improbable. Maybe it is – very very improbable . . . The origin of life is a flourishing, if speculative, subject for research. The expertise required for it is chemistry and it is not mine. I watch from the sidelines with engaged curiosity, and I shall not be surprised if, within the next few years, chemists report that they have successfully midwifed a new origin of life in the laboratory. Nevertheless it hasn't happened yet, and it is still possible to maintain that the probability of it happening is, and always was, exceedingly low – although it did happen once![49]

The hypothesis that *abiogenesis* happened without the aid of intelligence, as Dawkins' comments make clear, is *a philosophical deduction entailed by the assumption of naturalism*. Many of those with the expertise Dawkins admits to lacking (including Wolpert – see above) are not so confident. For example, Robert Shapiro writes:

> A profound difficulty exists . . . with the idea of RNA, or any other replicator, at the start of life. Existing replicators can serve as templates for the synthesis of additional copies of themselves, but this device cannot be used for the preparation of the very first such molecule, which must arise spontaneously from an unorganized mixture. The formation of an information-bearing [RNA chain or equivalent] through undirected chemical synthesis appears very improbable.[50]

According to biochemist Stuart Pullen:

> The hypothesis [of *abiogenesis*] is found in almost all biology books where it is put forth as the generally accepted theory. Yet in the scientific journals, scientists routinely dismiss many aspects of the hypothesis as highly improbable . . . While several amino acids can be created under plausible conditions, proteins cannot be . . . many biologists mistakenly believe that it is quite easy to synthesize all

of the required biological molecules. Nevertheless, a quick review of the relevant literature reveals that this is not true.[51]

A *New Scientist* cover story on 'The 10 Biggest Mysteries of Life' (*New Scientist*, 4 September 2004) included the question 'How did life begin?' as one of the 'biggest unanswered questions' in biology. Writing in the 50th Anniversary special edition of *New Scientist* in 2006, Paul Davies confirmed that 'One of the great outstanding mysteries is the origin of life', affirming that 'The truth is, nobody has a clue.'[52] In February 2007 *Wired* magazine ran an article entitled 'What We Don't Know About' which included a section on 'Where did life come from?' by Gregg Easterbrook, who wrote,

> What creates life out of the inanimate compounds that make up living things? No one knows. How were the first organisms assembled? Nature hasn't given us the slightest hint. If anything, the mystery has deepened over time. After all, if life began unaided under primordial conditions in a natural system containing zero knowledge, then it should be possible – it should be *easy* – to create life in a laboratory today. But determined attempts have failed . . . no one has come close . . . Did God or some other higher being create life? . . . Until such time as a wholly natural origin of life is found, these questions have power. We're improbable, we're here, and we have no idea why. Or how.[53]

Having restudied the evidence, Nobel laureate Richard Smalley recently affirmed that life must have been created by design.[54] Against this inference, Dawkins argues that:

> The . . . alternative to the design hypothesis is statistical. Scientists invoke the magic of large numbers . . . a billion billion is a conservative estimate of the number of available planets in the universe. Now, suppose the origin of life, the spontaneous arising of something equivalent to DNA, really was a quite staggeringly improbable event . . . If the odds of life originating spontaneously on a planet were a billion to one against, nevertheless that stupefying improbable event would still happen on a billion planets . . . I do not for a moment believe the origin of

life was anywhere near so improbable in practice . . . Even accepting the most pessimistic estimate of the probability that life might spontaneously originate, this statistical argument completely demolishes any suggestion that we should postulate design . . .[55]

Odds of 'a billion to one against' can be expressed as odds of 1 in 10^9. In *Climbing Mount Improbable* Dawkins calculates that 'the probability that any particular sequence of, say 100, amino-acids will spontaneously form is [roughly] 1 in 20^{100}. This is an inconceivably large number, *far greater than the number of fundamental particles in the entire universe.*'[56] And yet Dawkins argues that any suggestion that design might be the best explanation for the origin, not merely of a single chain of amino-acids at odds of 1 in 20^{100}, but of *life capable of undergoing evolution,* is demolished by the 'statistical argument' that it only had to 'spontaneously originate' on one planet out of 'a billion-billion'! Dawkins *vastly* underestimates the odds against the spontaneous generation of life. Stephen C. Meyer calculates that to generate a single functional protein of 150 amino acids exceeds '1 chance in 10^{180}', and comments that 'it is extremely unlikely that a random search through all the possible amino acid sequences could generate even a single relatively short functional protein in the time available since the beginning of the universe . . .'[57]

As Dean L. Overman observes, 'the difficulties in producing a protein from the mythical prebiotic soup are very large, but more difficult still is the probability of random processes producing the simplest living cell which represents an overwhelming increase in complexity'.[58] David Swift comments:

> Biologists have become increasingly aware that the real stumbling block to the origin of life is its complexity – complexity in terms of the interdependence of molecules and biochemical pathways within cell metabolism, and complexity at the molecular level of individual components. The combination of complexities at these different levels presents insurmountable difficulties to getting anything that is remotely life-like . . . the complexity of even the simplest forms of life, a bacterium is much closer to a human being than it is to any

cocktail of organic compounds in some putative primeval soup . . . the core of the problem is the considerable complexity of even the 'simplest' forms of life, or even of some notional system that is stripped down to the theoretical bare necessities of life.[59]

Fazale Rana and Hugh Ross report that, 'Theoretical and experimental studies designed to discover the bare minimum number of gene products necessary for life all show significant agreement. Life seems to require between 250 and 350 different proteins to carry out its most basic operations.'[60] The simplest self-reproducing organism known outside the laboratory is the bacterium *Mycoplasma Genitalium*, which has 482 genes (two thirds of which have been shown to be necessary to its survival in the laboratory). Outside of the laboratory *Mycoplasma Genitalium* is: 'unable to sustain itself without parasitizing on an even more complex organism . . . Therefore a hypothetical first cell that could sustain itself would have to be even *more* complex.'[61] Rana and Ross argue that:

> the minimum complexity for independent life must reside somewhere between about 500 and 1,500 gene products. So far, as scientists have continued their sequencing efforts, all microbial genomes that fall below 1,500 belong to parasites. Organisms capable of permanent independent existence require more gene products. A minimum genome size (for independent life) of 1,500 to 1,900 gene products comports with what geochemical and fossil evidence reveals about the complexity of Earth's first life. Earliest life forms displayed metabolic complexity that included photosynthetic and chemoautotrophic processes, protein synthesis, the capacity to produce amino acids, nucleotides, fatty acids and sugars [as well as] the machinery to reproduce. Some 1,500 different gene products would seem the bare minimum to sustain this level of metabolic activity . . . *neither enough matter nor enough time in the universe exist for even the simplest bacterium to emerge by undirected chemical and physical processes.*[62]

Paul Davies states that the odds against producing *just the proteins* necessary for a minimally complex life form by chance are 'something like $10^{40,000}$ to one'.[63] As Swift writes:

it is no longer tenable to hide behind millions or even billions of years – trying to argue that even the improbable becomes probable given time – nor even behind the argument that life did not have to evolve on earth but could have arisen on any one of an astronomical number of possible planets. The conclusion is plain and simple: the universe is not big enough or old enough, not by a factor of trillions of trillions . . . for the complexities of life to have arisen by random associations of simple organic molecules or of random mutations of proteins or nucleic acids[64]

Appealing to the existence of a billion billion hypothetical life friendly planets (and they have to be *life friendly* planets) doesn't rescue the theory of spontaneous origination when the odds against producing *just the proteins* necessary for a *minimally complex* life form by chance are 'something like $10^{40,000}$ to one'.[65]

Moreover, Dawkins' appeal to the existence of a billion billion life friendly planets is made in the teeth of the evidence. As astronomer Danny R. Faulkner writes, 'it is unlikely that there are many, if any, other earth-like planets in the universe'[66] able to sustain life. Astronomer Hugh Ross reviews 200 parameters required for a life-bearing planet. Comparing the chances of a planet falling within these parameters by chance alone with our best estimate of the total number of planets in the universe (10^{22}) he estimates that there is 'less than 1 chance in 10^{215}' of a habitable planet existing in the universe.[67] Ross argues that 'fewer than a trillionth of a trillionth of a percent of all stars will have a planet capable of sustaining advanced life. Considering that the observable universe contains less than a trillion galaxies, each averaging a hundred billion stars, we can see that not even one planet would be expected, by natural processes alone, to possess the necessary conditions to sustain life.'[68]

Offering an updated 'Drake equation' for calculating the number of intelligent civilizations in our Galaxy, astronomer Guillermo Gonzalez and philosopher Jay W. Richards conclude that 'the probability that the Milky Way Galaxy contains even one advanced civilization is likely to be much less than one. This is an interesting result, of course, since we exist.'[69] Naturalistic astrobiologists Peter D. Ward and Donald Brownlee concede that 'If some god-like being could be given the opportunity to plan a sequence of events with the express goal of duplicating our "Garden of Eden", that power would face a formidable task. With the best intentions, b*ut limited by natural laws and materials*, it is unlikely that Earth could ever be truly replicated.'[70]

The design inference from the 'specified complexity' (note, *not* the mere 'complexity') of evolvable life (and its preconditions) is *not* an argument from ignorance. It is an inference from our knowledge of evolvable biological systems, on the one hand, and the cause and effect structure of reality on the other. Discussing SETI in *The God Delusion* Dawkins comments that, 'It is a non-trivial question . . . what kind of signal would convince us of its intelligent origin . . . Metronomic rhythms can be generated by many non-intelligent phenomena . . . Nothing simply rhythmic . . . would announce our intelligent presence to the waiting universe.'[71] The specified but uncomplicated pattern of a pulsar doesn't require explanation in terms of design. Neither, of course, does the unspecified complexity of static. So what sort of signal would convince us of its intelligent origin? Dawkins has an answer: 'Prime numbers are often mentioned as the recipe of choice, since it is difficult to think of a purely physical process that could generate them.'[72] Dawkins thereby affirms that specified complexity is a type of pattern, discoverable by empirical investigation, which it is difficult to explain in purely physical terms, and the discovery of which rightly triggers a design inference: 'A pile of detached watch parts tossed in a box is . . . as improbable as a fully functioning, genuinely complicated watch. What is specified about a watch is that it is improbable in the specific direction of telling the time . . .'[73] Likewise, a random bunch of amino acid sequences may be just as improbable as a fully functioning, genuinely complicated suite of proteins; but what is specified about the proteins is that they are improbable in the specific direction of biological function. As J.T. Trevors and D.L. Abel argue in their paper 'Three subsets of sequence complexity and their relevance to biopolymeric information', published in the Journal *Theoretical Biology and Medical Modeling*:

> We can hypothesize that metabolism 'just happened' independent of directions, in a prebiotic environment billions of years ago. But we can hypothesize anything. The question is whether such

hypotheses are plausible . . . when multiple biopolymers must all converge at the same place at the same time to collectively interact in a controlled biochemically cooperative manner, faith in 'self organization' becomes 'blind belief'. No empirical data or rational scientific basis exists for such a metaphysical leap . . . Bone fide organization [specified complexity] always arises from choice contingency [intelligent design], not chance contingency or necessity . . . Biopolymeric matrices of high information retention are among the most complex entities known to science. They do not and can not arise from low-informational, self-ordering phenomena. Instead of order from chaos, the genetic code was algorithmically optimized to deliver highly informational, aperiodic, specified complexity.[74]

Fred Hoyle and Chandra Wickramasinghe reach the same conclusion:

the enormous information content [specified complexity] of even the simplest living systems . . . cannot in our view be generated by what are often called 'natural' processes . . . There is no way in which we can expect to avoid the need for information, no way in which we can simply get by with a bigger and better organic soup, as we ourselves hoped might be possible . . . The correct position we think is . . . an intelligence, which designed the biochemicals and gave rise to the origin of carbonaceous life . . .[75]

Dawkins admits that '[Design theorists] correctly pose the problem of specified complexity as something that needs explaining,'[76] but pulls back from accepting the design hypothesis for reasons we shall examine (and find wanting) in chapter seven. Until then, let us simply note that the existence of evolvable life provides multiple pieces of data for which naturalistic assumptions have consistently failed to provide a plausible account, and that, when analyzed using a design detection criterion accepted by Dawkins (and other atheists),[77] clearly signals an intelligent design for which God is an obvious candidate explanation. Readers might wish to withhold judgement on this argument until they have considered Dawkins' objections and the responses offered to them in chapter seven. Nevertheless, it should be clear that there is evidence here that provides *prima facie* support for the God hypothesis over-and-above metaphysical naturalism. Like Dawkins, one may think that this case can be rebutted; but one cannot think this whilst simultaneously adopting Wolpert's refusal to engage with the arguments for theism, or his mantra, 'There is absolutely no evidence for the existence of God.'[78]

Wolpert's Slumber Party

'The basic argument from no evidence relies on the idea that in order to rationally believe something we need evidence for it. But from the perspective of many philosophers, the latter claim represents a gross oversimplification.'
– John O'Leary-Hawthorne[79]

Wolpert's charge that there is no evidence for God implicitly assumes that theism is irrational because it lacks evidential support. However, the charge that theism is irrational because it lacks evidential support commits two mistakes. On the one hand, few theists would concede Wolpert's assumption that their belief in God is predicated upon an absence of evidence. Natural theology has emerged from the doldrums of the positivist era in philosophy in robust health. Wolpert simply refuses to engage with the evidence. On the other hand, it should be remembered that *evidence is not always necessary for rational belief*. Contra the likes of Lewis Wolpert and Sam Harris, belief without evidence is in fact considered a mark of rationality and common sense in many areas of life (i.e. where 'properly basic beliefs' are concerned). Hence 'being rational' and 'having evidential support' are not one and the same thing (indeed, on pain of self-contradiction, they *can't be* one and the same thing). It is all well and good to demand that people hold all their beliefs *rationally* (for example, we shouldn't pick our beliefs at random, and we shouldn't hold them in the face of overwhelming counter-evidence); but there is no sense in demanding that people hold *all* their beliefs *on the basis of evidence*. Sam Harris may affirm that, 'An atheist is simply a person who believes that [theists] should be obliged to present evidence for [God's] existence . . .';[80] but the fact that the demand that every belief be justified with evidence is self-defeating (on the one hand, what is the evidence for *this* claim? On the other hand, how would one ever satisfy this demand?) means that the 'not enough evidence' argument deployed by Harris and Wolpert is demonstrably unsound.

Theists can respond to Wolpert's charge by noting that the existence of God is a 'properly basic belief' for them. Interestingly, as Keith Ward points out, the availability of this rebuttal to Wolpert's 'no evidence' objection is supported by the common sense philosophy of the only philosopher Wolpert has time for, namely David Hume:

> On [Hume's] own common sense principle, we might think that if the religious tendency is a general feature of common human nature, as he says it is, then we might expect to find it as well established as belief in physical objects, causality or other minds – for which he could find no rational justification either . . . Generations of philosophy students have stayed in bed all day, because they have no justification for getting up. How do they know that the world outside their bedroom still exists? Since their beliefs have to be strictly proportioned to the available evidence, they cannot get out of bed until they have more evidence. So they are forced to stay where they are. That's their story, anyway. To all of which Hume replies that we must let common sense take over and assume without evidence that the world still exists. If we can do that, why can't we assume without evidence that God exists too? Belief in God is widespread and natural. Millions of people think they apprehend God . . . the fact that other people do not apprehend God does not show that God does not exist. So on Hume's own principles we would expect him to think that belief in God is a pretty commonsense, if not absolutely universal, belief. As such, it ought to be perfectly acceptable. But on the topic of religion the greatest Scottish philosopher of common sense refuses to accept common sense . . .[81]

Wolpert follows Hume, complaining that there is no evidence for the existence of a world outside the bedroom of his dogmatic slumbers, and lazily refusing to look out the window.

The Presumption of Atheism

*'if there were no evidence at all for belief in God, this would [at best]
legitimize merely agnosticism unless there is evidence against the
existence of God.'*
– Scot A. Shalkowski[82]

As Robert A. Harris writes:

> a common sense look at the world, with all its beauty, apparent
> design, meaning, and vibrancy, would seem to predispose a neutral
> observer to presume that God exists unless good evidence for his
> non-existence could be brought to bear . . . The fact that materialists
> often struggle with this issue, working to explain away the design
> of the creation, for example, would seem to back up this claim.[83]

Nevertheless, Richard Norman asserts that: 'the onus is on those
who believe in a god to provide reasons for that belief. If they
cannot come up with good reasons, then we should reject the
belief.'[84] It was Antony Flew who most famously urged that the
'onus of proof must lie upon the theist'[85] and that unless compelling reasons for God's existence could be given there should
be a 'presumption of atheism'. However, by 'atheism' Flew
meant merely 'non-theism'. Hence Paul Copan points out that
'even if the theist could not muster good arguments for God's
existence, atheism still would not be shown to be true'.[86] Kai
Nielsen acknowledges that, 'To show that an argument is invalid
or unsound is not to show that the conclusion of the argument is
false . . . All the proofs of God's existence may fail, but it still may
be the case that God exists.'[87]

Indeed, given Plantinga's account of theistic belief as properly
basic, all the proofs of God's existence may fail and belief in God
may still be warranted for people with appropriate grounding
experiences. Aside from its questionable insistence upon the necessity of 'proof' or 'evidence' for belief in God to be warranted, the
presumption of atheism is therefore not particularly interesting
unless (as with Richard Norman) it really is the presumption of
atheism rather than the presumption of *agnosticism*. Copan
dispatches the former presumption, as:

the 'presumption of atheism' demonstrates a rigging of the rules of philosophical debate in order to play into the hands of the atheist, who himself makes a truth claim. Alvin Plantinga correctly argues that the atheist does not treat the statements 'God exists' and 'God does not exist' in the same manner. The atheist assumes that if one has no evidence for God's existence, then one is obligated to believe that God does not exist – whether or not one has evidence *against* God's existence. What the atheist fails to see is that atheism is just as much a claim to know something ('God does not exist') as theism ('God exists'). Therefore, the atheist's denial of God's existence needs just as much substantiation as does the theist's claim; the atheist must give plausible reasons for rejecting God's existence . . . in the absence of evidence for God's existence, agnosticism, not atheism, is the logical presumption. Even if arguments for God's existence do not persuade, atheism should not be presumed because atheism is not neutral; pure agnosticism is. Atheism is justified only if there is sufficient evidence against God's existence.[88]

As Steven Lovell points out, one cannot rationally defend atheism merely on the basis that there is insufficient evidence for belief in God. To avoid a double standard, the atheist cannot use the 'insufficient evidence' argument alone, but must combine it with one or more of the other objections to belief. He recounts:

Time and again I've heard people say that they don't believe in God because they think there is insufficient evidence for His existence. If the person saying this is an atheist (one who thinks that God doesn't exist, that 'God exists' is a false statement), then they imply that they *do* have enough evidence for their atheism. Clearly, if we reject belief in God due to (alleged) insufficient evidence, then we would be irrational to accept atheism, if the evidence for God's non-existence were similarly insufficient. It would be a radical inconsistency. If theistic belief requires evidence, so must atheistic belief. If we have no evidence either way, then the logical conclusion would be agnosticism.[89]

Reliance upon the 'insufficient evidence' objection is a risky gambit, as atheist William Rowe observes, because 'To fail to provide any arguments for the non-existence of God is . . . to virtually con-cede the debate to the person who at least gives some arguments, however weak, on behalf of the position that God exists.'[90] Non-theism posited on the basis that there is insufficient evidence for belief stands before the constant possibility that new evidence, or a better formulation and appreciation of old evidence, just might turn up. Such non-theism cannot afford to be dogmatic.

The *De Facto* 'less evidence than we'd expect' Argument

If the 'less evidence than we'd expect' argument is framed in terms of God's purported failure to meet a certain expectation about the amount of evidence God *ought* to provide for his exis-tence here and now, it becomes a version of the problem of evil. Aside from calling upon concepts such as wish-fulfilment, 'defective father syndrome', or the example of Lewis Wolpert to explain why people may fail to perceive God, or to hide from what they do perceive of God, the theist can question the prem-ise that we are in a good epistemic position to rationally warrant the expectation that God's existence should be more obvious to us than is the case. As J.P. Moreland and William Lane Craig explain:

> the absence of evidence is evidence of absence only in cases in which, were the postulated entity to exist, we should expect to have some evidence of its existence. Moreover, the justification conferred in such cases will be proportional to the ratio between the amount of evidence that we do have and the amount of evi-dence that we should expect to have if the entity existed. If the ratio is small then little justification is conferred on the belief that the entity itself does not exist . . . But if this is correct, then our jus-tification for atheism depends on (1) the probability that God would leave more evidence of his existence than what we have and (2) the probability that we have comprehensively surveyed the field for evidence of his existence . . . Suddenly the presumer of atheism, who sought to shirk his share of the burden of proof, finds himself saddled with the very considerable burden of prov-ing (1) and (2) to be the case.[91]

Moreover, on the Christian view of things it is a matter of relative indifference to God whether humans believe in his existence, since God is interested in establishing a loving relationship with us, not merely in getting us to believe that he exists. As Moreland and Craig observe:

> Of course, in order to believe *in* God, we must have belief *that* God exists. But there is no reason at all to think that if God were to make his existence more manifest, more people would come into a saving relationship with him. Mere showmanship will not bring about a change of heart (Luke 16:30–31) . . . If God were to inscribe his name on every atom or place a neon cross in the sky, people might believe that he exists; but what confidence could he have that after time they would not begin to chafe under the brazen advertisement of their Creator and even come to resent such effrontery?[92]

It is pertinent to contemplate the dogmatic attitude displayed by J.J.C. Smart in his comments upon the possibility of God trying to convince him to become a believer by providing more evidence. On his view:

> someone who has naturalistic preconceptions will always in fact find some naturalistic explanation more plausible than a supernatural one . . . Suppose that I woke up in the night and saw the stars arranged in shapes that spelt out the Apostle's Creed. I would know that astronomically it is impossible that stars should have changed their positions. I don't know what I would think. Perhaps I would think that I was dreaming or that I had gone mad. What if everyone else seemed to me to be telling me that the same thing had happened? Then I might not only think that I had gone mad – I would probably *go* mad.[93]

As Robert A. Harries says that 'the crux of the problem is not the lack of evidence, but the worldview of the person who can see none.'[94] Smart's attitude towards such hypothetical evidence illustrates Moreland and Craig's point about the attitude of the heart being at least as important as the availability of evidence. God cannot guarantee the former by providing the latter. As Michael J. Murray argues, 'if God were to make the truths of the faith evident to us in too forceful a way, it would be tantamount to the coercion one experiences when threatened by a mugger.'[95] On the other hand, 'God cannot leave the truths of the faith entirely hidden from us either.'[96] Thus 'the epistemic forceful-ness of the truth of Christianity must fall somewhere short of what constitutes coercion, leaving creatures free to determine their own course in a morally significant way, but somewhere beyond total absence of evidence, in order to ensure that the creatures can make a decision responsibly.'[97]

Conclusion

In sum, the objection that there is a significant lack of evidence for theism is easily overcome, partly because a lack of evidence for the-ism would not be particularly significant, but partly because there isn't a lack of evidence for theism – a much disputed contention that is the centre of attention in our next and final chapter.

Recommended Resources

John Angus Campbell and Stephen C. Meyer (eds.), *Darwinism, Design, and Public Education* (East Lansing: Michigan State University Press, 2003).

William Lane Craig, 'Naturalism and Intelligent Design', in Robert B. Stewart (ed.), *Intelligent Design: William A. Dembski & Michael Ruse in Dialogue* (Minneapolis, PA: Fortress, 2007).

Guillermo Gonzalez and Jay Richards, *The Privileged Planet: How Our Place in the Cosmos Is Designed for Discovery* (Washington, DC: Regnery, 2004).

Daniel Howard-Snyder and Paul K. Moser (eds.), *Divine Hiddenness: New Essays* (Cambridge: Cambridge University Press, 2002).

John Lennox, *God's Undertaker: Has Science Buried God?* (Oxford: Lion, 2007).

Stuart Pullen, *Intelligent Design or Evolution? Why the Origin of Life and the Evolution of Molecular Knowledge Imply Design* (Raleigh, NC: Intelligent Design Books, 2005).

Fazale Rana and Hugh Ross, *Origins of Life* (NavPress, 2004).

James F. Sennett and Douglas Groothuis (eds.), *In Defence of Natural Theology: A Post-Humean Assessment* (Downers Grove, IL: IVP, 2005).

Charles B. Thaxton, Walter L. Bradley, and Roger L. Olson, *The Mystery of Life's Origin: Reassessing Current Theories* (Addison, TX: Lewis and Stanley, 1992), www.themysteryoflifes-origin.org/.

Peter D. Ward and Donald Brownlee, *Rare Earth: Why Complex Life Is Uncommon in the Universe* (New York: Copernicus, 2000).

Papers

Stephen C. Meyer, 'DNA and Other Designs', www.arn.org/docs/meyer/sm_dnaotherdesigns.htm.

Stephen C. Meyer, 'DNA and the Origin of Life', www.discovery.org/a/2184.

J.T. Trevors and D.L. Abel, 'Chance and Necessity Do Not Explain the Origin of Life', *Cell Biology International*; Volume 28, Issue 11, 1 November 2004, www.discovery.org/a/2664.

J.T. Trevors and D.L. Abel, 'Three subsets of sequence complexity and their relevance to biopolymeric information', *Theoretical Biology and Medical Modelling*, (2005, 2: 29), www.pubmedcentral.nih.gov/articlerender.fcgi?artid=1208958.

Peter S. Williams, 'The Design Inference from Specified Complexity Defended by Scholars Outside the Intelligent Design Movement – A Critical Review', *Philosophia Christi*, Volume 9, Number 2, 2007, pp. 407–428, www.discovery.org/a/4499 and http://epsociety.org/ library/articles.asp?pid=54.

Øyvind Albert Voie, 'Biological function and the genetic code are interdependent,' *Chaos, Solutions and Fractals*, Volume 28, Issue 4, May 2006, pp. 1000–1004, http://home.online.no/~albvoie/index.cfm.

Video

Is God a Delusion? A debate between William Lane Craig and Lewis Wolpert chaired by John Humphrys at Central Hall Westminster, 2007 (UCCF, 2007).

Unlocking the Mysteries of Life (Illustra Media), www.theapologiaproject.org/media/unlocking_the_mystery_of_life.ram.

The Emperor has no Clothes: Natural Theology and the God Hypothesis

'Dawkins has written, perhaps, the most powerful set of arguments against the alleged supernatural god ever written . . . Dawkins quickly exposes each of [the theistic arguments] as vacuous . . .'
– Jim Walker[1]

Richard Dawkins is the unofficial Emperor of the New Atheism. With the publication of *The God Delusion* he has embarked on an undoubtedly well-intentioned mission to liberate theists from what he sees as their false beliefs: 'If this book works as I intend, religious readers who open it will be atheists when they put it down.'[2] Dawkins thinks that if he fails, this can only be because 'dyed-in-the-wool faith-heads are immune to argument, their resistance built up over years of childhood indoctrination using methods [such as issuing] a dire warning to avoid even opening a book like this, which is surely a work of Satan.'[3] However, anyone 'open-minded' whose 'indoctrination was not too insidious . . . or whose native intelligence is strong enough to overcome it [will] need only a little encouragement to break free of the vice of religion altogether.'[4] In other words, anyone who disagrees with Dawkins is either brainwashed or thick. I leave it to readers to decide which I am, or whether Dawkins is posing a false dilemma.

Those who repeat the 'lack of evidence for God' objection often simply assume, like Lewis Wolpert, that all of the arguments for God are unsound. One is fortunate to come across more than the few paragraphs dedicated by Daniel Dennett to dealing with some of the better-known classical arguments for theism. Richard Dawkins' critical analysis of natural theology in *The God Delusion* (together with his attempt to argue positively for atheism) is broadly representative of the treatment these subjects receive from contemporary popular atheology in general, and from the New Atheism in particular. However, Dawkins' critique is the most sustained to emerge from the New Atheism. As such, it has received some over-enthusiastic praise. James Swingle reports that Dawkins 'goes through the different arguments in favour of God, showing the fallacies behind each'.[5] P.Z. Myers writes, '*The God Delusion* delivers a thorough overview of the logic of belief and disbelief. Dawkins reviews, dismantles, and dismisses the major arguments for the existence of the supernatural and deities . . . *The God Delusion* is . . . a classic . . .'[6] According to Jim Walker, 'Dawkins has written, perhaps, the most powerful set of arguments against the alleged supernatural god ever written . . . No matter how much the theist tries to run or hide, he will only run into the face of Dawkins' powerful arguments. At best he can only shout *ad hominems* . . . Dawkins quickly exposes each of [the theistic arguments] as vacuous . . .'[7]

In reality, Dawkins' unscholarly procedure takes the following route to what Terry Eagleton dubs a 'victory on the cheap'.[8]

1) Select a far from comprehensive subset of theistic arguments.

Dawkins' overview is *not* 'thorough' (although it is the most thorough review provided by any of the New Atheist books).

2) Caricature the selected arguments – referring to (but not quoting) medieval rather than contemporary versions.

As John Cornwell observes, 'there is hardly a serious work of philosophy of religion cited in his extensive bibliography . . .'[9] *The God Delusion* is liberally sprinkled with imaginary opponents ('Here is the message that an imaginary "intelligent design theorist" might broadcast . . .'; 'the following statement from an imaginary apologist . . .'; 'My imaginary religious apologist . . .'; 'Let's invent an imaginary quotation from a moral philosopher . . .').[10]

3) Give the appearance of blowing away these arguments using assertion rather than argument, or a charge of logical invalidity that depends upon the fact that you are attacking a straw man, or which misses the point of the argument you are attacking.

The God Delusion is the work of a passionate and rhetorically savvy writer capable of making good points against the easy targets provided by religious fundamentalism. As Stephen Law (editor of the Royal Institute of Philosophy's periodical *Think*) observes, 'what Dawkins attacks is typically a highly *Authoritarian* brand of religion'.[11] However, when it comes to the philosophy of religion, Dawkins simply doesn't recognize that he is way out of his depth. As Antony Latham laments, 'Dawkins clearly has an inflated idea of his competence in metaphysics.'[12] Philosopher Barney Zwartz writes that Dawkins 'is not nearly as good a philosopher as he supposes . . . On nearly every page I found myself wanting to argue, not just with his arguments (or mere assertions), but with the often slipshod or superficial way he puts them . . . He is spectacularly inept when it comes to the traditional philosophical arguments for God . . .'[13]

Moreover, *The God Delusion* is 'marred by its excessive reliance on bold assertion and rhetorical flourish, where the issues so clearly demand careful reflection and painstaking analysis . . .'[14] As Alister McGrath comments, 'Dawkins' engagement with theology is superficial and inaccurate . . . His tendency to misrepresent the views of his opponents is the least attractive aspect of his writings.'[15] Terry Eagleton concurs. 'Imagine', he says:

> someone holding forth on biology whose only knowledge of the subject is the *Book of British Birds*, and you have a rough idea of what it feels like to read Richard Dawkins on theology. Card-carrying rationalists like Dawkins . . . are in one sense the least well-equipped to understand what they castigate, since they don't believe there is anything there to be understood, or at least anything worth understanding. This is why they invariably come up with vulgar caricatures of religious faith that would make a first-year theology student wince . . . critics of the richest, most enduring form of popular culture in human history have a moral obligation to confront that case at its most persuasive, rather than

grabbing themselves a victory on the cheap by savaging it as so much garbage and gobbledygook.[16]

Jim Holt's assessment of *The God Delusion* is, in my opinion, understated; he writes, 'There is lots of good, hard-hitting stuff about the imbecilities of religious fanatics and frauds of all stripes, but the tone is smug and the logic occasionally sloppy.'[17] Let us turn to the arguments themselves.

Religious Experience

Richard Swinburne defends the need of placing the burden of proof upon those skeptical of perceptual claims, including religious perceptual claims. He writes that 'we ought to believe that things are as they seem to be, until we have evidence that we are mistaken . . . If you say the contrary – never trust appearances until it is proved that they were reliable – you will never have any beliefs at all. For what would show that appearances were reliable, except more appearances?'[18] This 'principle of credulity' encourages us to take religious experience at face value, unless there is sufficient reason to doubt it. If you lack religious experience yourself, it is nevertheless reasonable to trust the reports of those with such experience, for 'it is another basic principle of knowledge that those who do not have an experience of a certain type ought to believe many others when they say that they do – again, in the absence of evidence of mass delusion.'[19] As H.H. Price argued, one should 'Accept what you are told, unless you see reason to doubt it.'[20]

Dawkins' response to this kind of argument (which he doesn't bother spelling out) is merely to point out that experiences *can be* delusional, that 'the brain's simulation software . . . is well capable of constructing "visions" and "visitations" of the utmost verdical power. To simulate a ghost or an angel or a Virgin Mary would be child's play to software of this sophistication.'[21] This single observation concludes Dawkins' attempted rebuttal: 'This is really all that needs to be said about personal 'experiences' of gods or other religious phenomena. If you've had such an experience, you may well find yourself believing firmly that it was real. But don't expect the rest of us to take your word for it, espe-cially if we have the slightest familiarity with the brain and its powerful workings.'[22] However, this is *not* 'all that needs to be said', since Dawkins' failure to advance more than one premise means that his supposed rebuttal *doesn't even rise to the level of an argument*. Against the argument from religious experience, all Dawkins gives us is the following:

> Premise 1) Experiences can be delusional
> Premise 2)
> Conclusion) Therefore, all religious experiences are delusion

Merely observing that the brain *can* create illusions provides no support for the conclusion that all religious experiences *are* illusions. Indeed, without a second premise that both links *and* restricts the illusion-giving power of the brain to religious expe-riences, Dawkins' rebuttal would count equally against *all* expe-riences, including those leading him to believe that humans have brains 'capable of constructing "visions" and "visitations" of the utmost verdical power'!

Cosmological Argument

In a typically quotation-free discussion, Dawkins claims that the famous 'five ways'[23] of Aquinas 'are easily – though I hesitate to say so, given his eminence – exposed as vacuous'.[24] Dawkins should have hesitated more. For example, noting Aquinas' use of the principle that a causal regress must terminate somewhere (lest it become infinite), Dawkins complains that Aquinas' cos-mological argument makes 'the entirely unwarranted assump-tion that God himself is immune to the regress'.[25] In other words, Dawkins asks the notorious question, 'Who made God?' Dawkins thereby fails to recognize that the cosmological argu-ment *just is* an argument for the necessity of postulating the exis-tence of something that is immune to the regress of causality.

> Dawkins writes that Aquinas 'makes the entirely unwarranted *assumption* that God is immune to the regress.' It is a commonly

made criticism. Lumbering dutifully in Dawkins' wake, Victor Stenger makes it as well. But Aquinas makes no such assumption, and thus none that could be unwarranted. It is the *conclusion* of his argument that causes in nature cannot form an infinite series. If they are prepared to reject this conclusion, Dawkins and Stenger must show that the argument on which it depends is either invalid or unsound. This they have not done.[26]

But why identify this 'something that's immune to the regress of causality' with God? Dawkins complains that even if the cosmological argument were sound, 'there is absolutely no reason to endow that terminator [of the causal regress] with any of the properties normally ascribed to God.'[27] But this is incorrect. Two of the properties normally ascribed to God are a) being uncreated, and b) being creator of the universe. The cosmological argument (assuming it is sound) proves that there is a being with precisely these divine properties!

Moreover, in conjunction with other sound examples of natural theology, Occam's Razor guides us into building up a composite picture of this uncreated creator. Dawkins' 'divide and conquer' approach to natural theology is unreasonable, as sev-eral arguments that individually fail to prove the existence of God may do exactly that when taken together, just as several clues that are individually insufficient to warrant conviction in a court of law may nevertheless be jointly sufficient to that end. As atheist J.L. Mackie advised, 'It will not be sufficient to criticize each argument on its own by saying that it does not prove the intended conclusion . . . For a set of arguments of each of which, on its own, this adverse comment is true may together make the conclusion *more* likely than not.'[28]

Unfortunately, Dawkins' use of the 'Who made God?' question is typical of the shoddy treatment received by the cosmological argument in the work of contemporary atheists. Sam Harris writes:

> The argument runs more or less like this: everything that exists has a cause; space and time exist; space and time must, therefore, have been caused by something that stands outside of space and time; and the only thing that transcends space and time, and yet retains the power to create, is God . . . As many critics of religion have pointed

out, the notion of a creator poses an immediate problem of an infinite regress. If God created the universe, what created God? To say that God, by definition, is uncreated simply begs the question.[29]

Like Dawkins, Harris fails to notice that the cosmological argument actually *argues* for the conclusion that there must exist an uncaused cause. The argument does *not* beg the question.

Dennett critiques

> The Cosmological Argument, which in its simplest form states that since everything must have a cause the universe must have a cause – namely, God . . . Some deny the premise [that everything must have a cause] . . . Others prefer to accept the premise and then ask: What caused God? The reply that God is self-caused (somehow) then raises the rebuttal: If something can be self-caused, why can't the universe as a whole be the thing that is self-caused?[30]

Indeed, *theists* deny both the premise that everything must have a cause *and* the incoherent suggestion that anything, including God, can be 'self-caused'![31] The first premise of the cosmological argument proper doesn't contain the stipulation that 'everything must have a cause'. Rather, it contains the stipulation that all caused things must (by definition) have a cause. The conclusion of the argument is not that there exists a 'self-caused' cause, but that there exists an *un-caused* cause.

In short, according to many atheists,[32] the cosmological argument goes as follows:

> Premise 1) *Everything* has a cause
> Premise 2) The universe is a thing
> Conclusion) Therefore, the universe has a cause ('God')

This straw-man naturally invites the 'Who caused God?' objection.[33] But consider the following argument:

> Premise 1) Something is caused
> Premise 2) It is impossible for everything to be caused (there can't be an infinite regress of causes)
> Conclusion) Therefore, there must exist an uncaused cause ('God')

This argument is logically valid, and the first premise seems to be beyond dispute, so the only question is whether or not it is possible for everything that exists to be caused. As soon as one asks 'caused by what?', one can see the problem with saying that everything is caused. Outside of *everything* is nothing, and 'from nothing, nothing comes'. The important point to note is that the cosmological argument actually depends upon the *denial* of the very premise, namely 'everything has a cause', falsely attributed to it by many atheists!

Grayling suggests that religious people

> need to believe in [supernatural] agencies because they cannot otherwise understand how there can be a natural world – as if invoking 'Chaos and old night' (in one Middle Eastern mythology the proginators of all things) explained anything, let alone the universe's existence. Doing so might satisfy a pathological metaphysical need for what Paul Davies calls 'the self-levitating superturtle,' but is obviously enough not worth discussing.[34]

I admit that I cannot, besides a belief in some sort of a god, understand how there can be a natural world. I do not admit that this is due to some peculiar failure of imagination on my part. Grayling's comments evince a frankly astonishing refusal to engage with the complex philosophical issues surrounding various versions of the cosmological argument defended by leading contemporary philosophers of religion; an evasion which substitutes armchair psychoanalysis and straw-man references to mythology for rational dialogue. Grayling intimates that theists suffer from some sort of mental block that prevents them sharing in the naturalist's superior insight into the whys and wherefores of reality. But what understanding of how there can be a natural world or set of caused, contingent things does Grayling offer? None.[35]

Ontological Argument

Dawkins summarises Anselm's ontological argument (OA) as follows:

It is possible to conceive, Anselm said, of a being than which nothing greater can be conceived. Even an atheist can conceive of such a superlative being, though he would deny its existence in the real world. But, goes the argument, a being that doesn't exist in the real world is, by that very fact, less than perfect. Therefore we have a contradiction and, hey presto.[36]

He calls this argument 'infantile',[37] complaining, 'The very idea that grand conclusions could follow from such logomachist trickery offends me aesthetically . . . isn't it too good to be true that a grand truth about the cosmos should follow from a mere word game?'[38] Dawkins' response is clearly more of a psychological report than an argument (he simply *asserts* that the OA is 'trickery' and a 'mere word game'). Indeed, Dawkins admits he has

> an automatic, deep suspicion of any line of reasoning that reached such a significant conclusion without feeding in a single piece of data from the real world. Perhaps that indicates no more than that I am a scientist rather than a philosopher. Philosophers down through centuries have indeed taken the ontological argument seriously, both for and against.[39]

But perhaps Dawkins' suspicion is grounded in the mistaken belief that the OA reaches its conclusion 'without feeding in a single piece of data from the real world', where 'data' and 'the real world' are taken to mean, not merely *empirical* data from the *natural* world, but any propositional content at all beyond that contained within the definition of God as 'a being than which nothing greater can be conceived'. However, as Stephen T. Davis observes, while many critics see the OA as trying to prove the existence of God by simply analyzing the concept of God:

> This oft-repeated claim is . . . quite mistaken. It is true that Anselm's definition of God – 'that being than which no greater can be conceived' – is crucial to his argument . . . but merely analysing that concept will get one nowhere in proving the existence in reality of anything. One must also bring into consideration what Anselm surely took to be certain necessary truths (e.g. *a thing is greater if it exists both in the mind and in reality than if it exists merely*

in the mind and the existence of the [greatest conceivable being] is possible). These claims are essential aspects of the OA, and do not follow merely from an examination of any concept of God.[40]

One *suspects* that Dawkins mistakenly believes that 'non-empirical data' is a contradiction in terms. One would of course respond to such a view by pointing out that since the proposition 'non-empirical data is a contradiction in terms' isn't something that could be known through empirical data, it is itself a self-contradictory proposition!

According to Dawkins, 'The most definitive refutations of the ontological argument are usually attributed to the philosophers David Hume (1711–76) and Immanuel Kant (1724–1804).'[41] Christopher Hitchens likewise attempts to dismiss the OA by quoting Bertrand Russell noting how 'Kant objects that existence is *not* a predicate.'[42] According to Kant,

> 'Being' is obviously not a real predicate, that is, it is not a concept of something which could be added to the concept of a thing . . . The proposition 'God is omnipotent' contains two concepts, each of which has its object – God and omnipotence. The small word 'is' adds no new predicate, but only serves to posit the predicate in its relation to the subject. If, now, we take the subject (God) with all its predicates . . . and say 'God is,' or 'There is a God,' we attach no new predicate to the concept of God, but only posit it as an object that stands in relation to my concept. The content of both must be one and the same; nothing can have been added to the concept, which expresses merely what is possible . . .[43]

However, this vaunted 'definitive refutations' of the OA (Hume makes essentially the same point) is rejected by many contemporary philosophers. As Charles Hartshorne notes, 'Logicians, including some who would rather be seen in beggars' rags than in the company of the Ontological Argument, have held that existence is, after all, a sort of predicate, even of ordinary things.'[44] For example, Stephen T. Davis argues:

> If a property or a real predicate is something that appears in the predicate position of a sentence and that increases our knowledge

of the subject, then 'exists' sometimes does fail to be a property or real predicate. But it seems to me that this will only be true in cases where the existence of the thing is already presupposed . . . But sometimes we . . . talk about things that are, or possibly are, non-existent . . . And in those cases it might well add to our knowledge of a thing to say that it does (or does not) exist. In such cases, 'exists' appears to be a property or real predicate.[45]

Moreover, even if saying that something 'exists' could never add to the list of its properties, to say that something 'exists necessarily' certainly *does* add to its list of properties. As Keith E. Yandell writes, 'One may hold . . . that *necessary existence* and *contingent existence* are properties and agree with Hume that we have no general notion of existence – i.e. of *existence, neither necessary nor contingent*.'[46] Hence the 'existence is not a predicate' objection to the OA is a red herring. As Jim Holt observes, Dawkins

> dismisses [Anselm's] ontological argument as 'infantile' and 'dialectical prestidigitation' without quite identifying the defect in its logic. He seems unaware that this argument, though medieval in origin, comes in sophisticated modern versions that are not at all easy to refute. Shirking the intellectual hard work, Dawkins prefers to move on . . . Dawkins' failure to appreciate just how hard philosophical questions about religion can be makes reading [*The God Delusion*] an intellectually frustrating experience.[47]

Alvin Plantinga defines God as a 'maximally great being' and argues that a maximally great being *must exist if its existence is possible*, because 'necessary existence is a great making property'.[48] A great-making property is one that (like goodness, power, knowledge or existence) is objectively good and admits of a logical maximum. Given that 'the existence of a maximally great being is *possible*',[49] it follows that a maximally great being 'exists, and exists necessarily'.[50] Contra Dawkins, the ontological argument *can* be expressed as a logically valid syllogism as follows:

> Premise 1) By definition, if it is possible that God exists, then God exists

Premise 2) It is possible that God exists
Conclusion) Therefore, God exists

As Michael L. Peterson *et al.* argue:

> Although existence per se is not a property, *necessary existence is.* Consequently, for any two objects, if one exists necessarily and the other not (that is, exists contingently, such that it could either exist or not exist), the first is greater than the second. It follows, then, that if God's existence were contingent . . . he would not be the best conceivable being. But God, as the greatest possible being, possesses necessary existence. Therefore, God's existence is either logically necessary or logically impossible. God's existence is not logically impossible. Hence, it is *logically necessary.*[51]

The OA shows that 'the person who wishes to deny that God exists must claim that God's existence is impossible.'[52] Denying the existence of God is not on a par with denying the existence of the Loch Ness monster. To deny the existence of the Loch Ness monster one needn't claim that its existence is logically impossible, because one can coherently claim that Nessie simply fails to exist despite its existence being logically possible. However, to deny the existence of God one does have to make the claim that God's existence is logically impossible (one must reject premise 2 of the above argument), because the OA shows that one cannot coherently claim that God fails to exist *despite being logically possible.* God isn't the sort of thing that could just happen not to exist. By definition, God's existence is either necessary (and actual) or impossible (and non-actual). Hence *if* God's existence isn't impossible, *then* God's existence is necessary (and hence actual). But claiming that a thing's existence is impossible seems to be a stronger claim than the claim that its existence is possible but non-actual, at least when the thing in question is not obviously an incoherent concept like a round square. And no-one thinks that the statement 'God exists' is like the statement 'Round squares exist'! Nevertheless, many non-theists are willing to pay the 'price' of making the stronger claim in order to avoid the conclusion of the OA; and this despite the fact that no independent argument has shown the concept of God to be incoherent.[53]

Since the OA is valid, and since the first premise is true by definition, the question is whether or not its second premise is true. If the second premise is true, then this argument is sound. Naturally, anyone who already believes that God exists will believe that it is possible for God to exist, and hence that this OA is indeed sound. The person in this position might believe in God in a properly basic manner. They might think that a combination of theistic arguments (e.g. the moral, cosmological and design arguments) indicate the existence of a being who is plausibly to be identified as a 'maximally great being' (perhaps on grounds of simplicity). As Charles Hartshorne observes, 'the [Ontological] Argument as it stands does not suffice, except for one who grants that . . . the . . . idea of God is self-consistent. But here the other theistic arguments may help.'[54] Either way (and these 'ways' are not mutually exclusive), anyone with independent grounds for belief in God has independent grounds for thinking that it is possible for God to exist. And if one has independent grounds for thinking that, then one has independent grounds for thinking that the OA is sound.

Of course, if one's acceptance of the OA is wholly dependent upon such independent grounds, then the OA adds nothing to one's grounds for belief in God, although it might add much to one's *understanding of* God. As Charles Taliaferro writes, 'the ontological argument may be seen as a natural, formal attempt to refine a full-scale concept of excellence or greatness.'[55] But are there any grounds for accepting the crucial second premise of the OA that don't depend upon a prior belief in God, or upon other theistic arguments? Plantinga answers this question by noting that if we carefully consider the second premise, and the alleged objections to it, in the context of our overall system of beliefs, and we find insufficient reason to think that the denial of this premise is more plausible than its acceptance, then 'we are within our rational rights in accepting it'.[56] Hence Plantinga argues that the OA shows that theism is *at least rational*, because while

> it must be conceded that not everyone who understands and reflects on its central premise – that the existence of a maximally great being is *possible* – will accept it. Still, it is evident, I think, that there is nothing contrary *to reason* or *irrational* in accepting this

premise. What I claim for this argument, therefore, is that it establishes, not the *truth* of theism, but its rational acceptability.[57]

For example (granted objectivism concerning values) it seems plausible to say that knowledge and power are both great-making properties. And we know that they are compatible properties because humans have both of them to a finite degree. It therefore seems plausible to think that a being could have both great-making properties to a maximal degree. And the same goes for other great-making properties such as goodness or beauty. Moreover, consider Josef Seifert's argument that great-making properties

> must be all compatible with each other, for it contradicts the nature of that, which it is absolutely speaking, better to possess than not to possess to exclude any other such perfection. Otherwise a logical contradiction would arise in that it would be simultaneously better to possess perfection A . . . and not to possess it (because it would exclude another perfection B).[58]

If Seifert is right (and assuming that the objective theory of value is true), then the concept of God as a maximally great being is a provably coherent concept; which is to say that the crucial premise 'God's existence is possible' is demonstrably true.

Let's think a little more about the position of the non-theist faced with the OA. The argument proves that if 'God exists' is a coherent proposition then it must also be a true proposition. And as Charles Taliaferro writes, 'it is at least not obvious that the belief that God exists is incoherent. Indeed, a number of atheists think God might exist, but conclude God does not.'[59] But anyone who believes that God might exist but nevertheless happens not to exist on the one hand, and who understands the OA, on the other hand, will see that they form a self-contradictory set of beliefs. One way to resolve this contradiction, and perhaps the most plausible way, is by accepting the existence of God. Consider the conclusion to Trent Dougherty's discussion of the OA:

> Since all efforts to show that the concept of God is contradictory have failed heretofore I conclude, somewhat reluctantly, that God exists

. . . I realize that to the average person, this seems like a trick, but the average person is not particularly accustomed to following logical arguments at all, much less highly specialized forms of logical calculi developed by professional philosophers. Most professors at the University level don't even know modal logic and many have never studied it and some have never heard of it. What do those who know it, but don't believe in God say? They say that the concept of God is incoherent. I have not yet seen an even slightly plausible argument to that effect. Until I do, the OA will be cogent to me.[60]

The Argument from Degrees of Perfection

In his fourth 'way', Aquinas argued that

Among beings there are some more and some less good, true, noble and the like. But 'more' and 'less' are predicated of different things, according as they resemble in their different ways something which is the maximum, as a thing is said to be hotter according as it more nearly resembles that which is hottest; so that there is something which is truest, something best, something noblest and, consequently, something which is uttermost being [i.e. maximally ontologically secure]; for those things that are greatest in truth are greatest in being, as it is written in [Aristotle's] Metaph. ii. Now the maximum in any genus is the cause of all in that genus; as fire, which is the maximum heat, is the cause of all hot things. Therefore there must also be something which is to all beings the cause of their being, goodness, and every other perfection; and this we call God.[61]

After merely summarizing Aquinas' argument Dawkins attempts a 'reduction to absurdity', writing:

That's an argument? You might as well say, people vary in smelliness but we can make the comparison only by reference to a perfect maximum of conceivable smelliness. Therefore there must exist a pre-eminently peerless stinker, and we call him God.[62]

That's a rebuttal? Dawkins fails to notice that Aquinas' argument utilizes 'great-making properties', a class of properties into which 'smelliness' – the subject of Dawkins' rebuttal – doesn't fall. As Christopher F.J. Martin observes, 'Aquinas is only concerned with the existence of more and a less in terms of properties that by definition admit of an intrinsic and logical maximum'.[63] E.L. Mascall explains that 'Goodness, so the argument claims, demands as its cause a God who is good; while heat, though it necessarily demands a God whose knowledge of possible being includes an idea of heat, does not demand a God who is hot as its cause, but only a God who can create.'[64] Aquinas is arguing along the following lines.

1) Things exist that exhibit finite degrees of great-making properties (e.g. being, goodness, truth, beauty).
2) The existence of something exhibiting a great-making property to a finite degree implies the existence of something that possesses the property in question to a maximal degree.
3) Therefore, all great-making properties possessed in finite degree by beings in the world around us, including being, are possessed to a maximal degree by something.
4) An effect cannot exceed the greatness of its cause.
5) Therefore, there exists a maximally ontologically secure being that possess every great-making property possessed by its effects to a maximal degree; and this we call God.

Contrary to what Dawkins thinks, this argument cannot be dismissed with a jeering reference to smelly people.

The Moral Argument

As Paul Copan writes, the moral argument urges that although '*Belief* in God isn't a requirement for being moral . . . the *existence* of a personal God is crucial for a coherent understanding of objective morality.'[65] Here, then, are the two core claims made by the moral argument:

1) Moral value is objective.
2) The existence of a personal deity is entailed by the existence of objective moral value.

Given these two premises it follows that:

> 3) Therefore, a personal deity exists.

Dawkins rightly observes that belief in God isn't a requirement for *knowing* about morality, or for *being* moral; but he fails to engage with the question of whether or not the very *existence* of objective moral value entails theism. In other words:

> non-theists can and do endorse objective moral values . . . These non-theistic moral realists will tell us, 'you don't need God to be good.' Yet the deeper question is, how did we come to *be* morally responsible, rights-bearing beings? . . . The basic issue . . . is this: why think humans have rights and dignity if they're products of valueless, physical processes in a cause-and-effect series from the big bang until now? The more plausible context or scenario is that human value and moral responsibility come from a good God who created us intrinsically valuable, morally responsible creatures . . . from nothing, nothing comes (*ex nihilo nihil fit*); similarly, *from valuelessness, valuenessness comes* . . . If we're just material beings produced by a material universe, then objective value or goodness . . . can't be accounted for. One will search in vain for any physics textbook describing moral value as one of matter's properties![66]

If the premises of the moral argument are true, then atheism entails the denial of moral objectivism (one cannot be morally obligated to, or commanded by, anything other than a person; but by definition no finite person can ground the existence of an objective moral law). Indeed, Dawkins' naturalism leads him to reject moral objectivism: 'The universe that we observe has precisely the properties we should expect if there is, at bottom, no design, no purpose, *no evil, no good*, nothing but pitiless indifference.'[67] No God (no design, no purpose) means no objective values (no evil, no good). As Dawkins concedes, 'It is pretty hard to defend absolutist morals on grounds other than religious ones.'[68] Denying the objectivity of moral value lets Dawkins off the hook of the moral argument (and, given their dependency on objective value, of the OA and the Fourth Way as well), *but at a terribly high price.* For example, it renders his moral critique of religion either self-contradictory or toothless. It also removes any objective basis for Dawkins' evident expectation that we *should* attend carefully to his arguments and that we *ought* to change our views if we find them convincing. But how can anyone be convinced to adopt a worldview which denies that anyone *should* ever be convinced of anything?

The Anthropic Design Argument

'Although I was once sharply critical of the argument to design, I have since come to see that, when correctly formulated, this argument constitutes a persuasive case for the existence of God.'
– Antony Flew[69]

Dawkins recognizes that the most general, 'anthropic' version of the design argument is particularly popular today, and I shall therefore pay particular attention to his treatment of this argument. Dawkins notes that 'Physicists have calculated that, if the laws and constants of physics had been even slightly different, the universe would have developed in such a way that life would have been impossible.'[70] There are, according to Dawkins, two main explanations given for the fact that our universe permits the existence of life. 'The design theory says that God . . . deliberately set up all the details for our benefit.'[71] Bizarrely, according to Dawkins, the alternative non-design explanation *is the anthropic principle itself*:

> It is a strange fact . . . that religious apologists love the anthropic principle. For some reason that makes no sense at all, they think it supports their case. Precisely the opposite is true. The anthropic principle . . . is an *alternative* to the design hypothesis. It provides a rational, design-free explanation for the fact that we find ourselves in a situation propitious to our existence. I think the confusion arises in the religious mind because the anthropic principle is only ever mentioned in the context of the problem it solves, namely the fact that we live in a life-friendly place. What the religious mind then fails to grasp is that two candidate

solutions are offered to the problem. God is one. The anthropic principle is the other. They are *alternatives*.[72]

However, the 'problem' that needs to be solved is *not* 'the fact that we live in a life-friendly place',[73] as Dawkins says (we obviously couldn't exist in a life-unfriendly place), but rather *the fact that a life-friendly place exists*. The anthropic principle 'provides a rational, design-free explanation for the fact that we find ourselves in a situation propitious to our existence',[74] but it doesn't answer the question of why a situation propitious to our existence should exist in the first place.

As Thomas Woodward explains, sometimes 'the name anthropic principle is brought in as a quasi-synonym for fine-tuning.'[75] When this substitution happens, as in *The God Delusion*, one obviously cannot appeal to the 'anthropic principle' to *explain* 'fine tuning'. That would be like using the concept of 'bachelors' to explain the existence of unmarried men! This, in effect, is precisely what Dawkins attempts to do, deploying the anthropic principle as an *explanation* for the observation of fine tuning, when it is in fact a restatement of the observation: 'It follows from the fact of our existence that the laws of physics must be friendly enough to allow life to arise.'[76] Of course it follows from the observation that we exist that the laws of physics are compatible with our existence; but it does *not* follow that the laws of physics are *necessarily* compatible with our existence, unless one assumes that the existence of humans is a necessary truth about reality! Dawkins' anthropic 'explanation' flounders by equivocating over the meaning of the term 'must'; and by treating the data to be explained as an explanation of the data to be explained. As Jimmy H. Davies and Harry L. Poe explain, 'The Weak Anthropic Principle is a tautology; it states the obvious. If the universe was not fit for life, then we would not be here.'[77] This tautology does nothing to explain the surprising existence of a life friendly universe.

Dawkins actually repudiates his false claim that the anthropic principle is an 'explanation' of fine tuning, referencing John Leslie's analogy of a man sentenced to death by firing squad who survives being shot at to muse 'Well, obviously they all missed, or I wouldn't be here thinking about it.'[78] Dawkins admits that 'he could still, forgivably, wonder why they'd all missed, and toy with the hypothesis that they were bribed . . . [i.e. missed by design]'.[79] The prisoner's *observation* that his continued existence depends upon an unlikely set of preconditions (the squad missing) does nothing to *explain* his continued existence, exclude the hypothesis of intelligent design, or guarantee the truth of a non-design explanation. Noting that the sentenced man wouldn't exist if the firing squad hadn't missed doesn't explain *why* they missed. Likewise, noting that humans wouldn't exist if the laws of nature weren't fine tuned doesn't explain why the laws of nature are fine tuned. As Guillermo Gonzalez observes:

> The [anthropic principle] has been acknowledged for about a quarter of a century, but it was not until John Barrow and Frank Tipler published their massive technical work *The Anthropic Cosmological Principle* in 1986 that it was widely discussed. *The Weak Anthropic Principle* (WAP) is the most basic version – the simple recognition that the parameters we observe in our environment must not be incompatible with our existence . . . We should not be surprised to observe, for example, that we are living on a planet with an oxygen-rich atmosphere, for the simple reason that we require oxygen to live. The WAP 'explains' why we should not observe ourselves to be living on, say, Titan, but it fails to account for the origin of the oxygen in our atmosphere . . . Barrow and Tipler . . . have burdened the basic physical interpretation of the WAP with unwarranted philosophical extrapolations. In considering the WAP with regard to the observable universe, they claim that we ought not be surprised at measuring a universe so finely tuned for life, for if it were different, we would not observe it. But as Richard Swinburne first explained and as William Lane Craig and John Leslie later argued, we should indeed be surprised at observing features of the universe that are highly improbable and are necessary for our existence . . .[80]

Richard Swinburne famously used the example of a card-shuffling machine to advance the design argument from cosmic fine-tuning:

> Suppose that a madman kidnaps a victim and shuts him in a room with a card-shuffling machine. The machine shuffles ten decks of

cards simultaneously and then draws a card from each deck and exhibits simultaneously the ten cards. The kidnapper tells the victim that he will shortly set the machine to work and it will exhibit its first draw, but that unless the draw consists of an ace of hearts from each deck, the machine will simultaneously set off an explosion which will kill the victim, in consequence of which he will not see which cards the machine drew. The machine is then set to work, and to the amazement and relief of the victim the machine exhibits an ace of hearts drawn from each deck. The victim thinks that this extraordinary fact needs an explanation in terms of the machine having been rigged in some way. But the kidnapper, who now reappears, casts doubt on this suggestion. 'It is hardly surprising', he says, 'that the machine draws only aces of hearts. You could not possibly see anything else. For you would not be here to see anything at all, if any other cards had been drawn.' But of course the victim is right and the kidnapper is wrong . . . The fact that this peculiar order is a necessary condition of the draw being perceived at all makes what is perceived no less extraordinary and in need of explanation. The teleologist's starting-point is not that we perceive order rather than disorder, but that order rather than disorder is there. Maybe only if order is there can we know what is there, but that makes what is there no less extraordinary and in need of explanation.[81]

The fact that an event is a pre-condition of its being observed does not explain the occurrence of the event, or negate the obvious fact that 'the victim is right and the kidnapper is wrong' about design being the best explanation for the specified complexity of the event described (which Swinburne offers as a parallel to the fine-tuning of the cosmos).

Dawkins admits that the anthropic principle does *not* negate surprise at our existence:

> The evolution of complex life, indeed its very existence in a universe obeying physical laws, is wonderfully surprising – or would be but for the fact that surprise is an emotion that can exist only in a brain which is the product of that very surprising process. There is an anthropic sense, then, in which our existence should not be surprising. I'd like to think that I speak for my fellow humans in insisting, nevertheless, that it is desperately surprising.[82]

According to Dawkins, 'This objection [to the no-design hypothesis] can be answered by the suggestion . . . that there are many universes. . . .'[83] It is important to note that Dawkins clearly accepts that the anthropic principle is *not* 'an alternative to the design hypothesis',[84] as he previously states, but is rather a description of the problem to which the design hypothesis is one answer and the many world's hypothesis is another. As Gonzalez comments, '[Many worlds] advocates are obviously driven by the desire to avoid the "God-hypothesis," and, in adopting such extravagant and unnecessary assumptions, they are effectively conceding that the WAP has been impotent in discrediting the teleological interpretation.'[85] It is the 'many worlds' hypothesis that competes with the design inference (but not the design hypothesis)[86] to explain the observation of a 'life friendly' universe, *not* the anthropic principle. The reason 'religious apologists love the anthropic principle' is *not* 'some reason that makes no sense at all', as Dawkins opines, but the belief that design is a better explanation of the anthropic principle than the many world's hypothesis.

Cosmic fine tuning is appears to be an example of specified complexity, and (as we saw in chapter six) Dawkins admits that specified complexity is a reliable signal of design. To avoid drawing a design inference from cosmic fine tuning, Dawkins observes that the specified lifefriendly tuning of the observed universe wouldn't be complex (unlikely) enough to warrant a design inference *if* there were 'many worlds'. *If* there were many differently tuned universes, *then* it wouldn't be unlikely that one of them would just happen to be lifefriendly. But even granting this premise, in order to validly reach the conclusion that the lifefriendly tuning of the observed universe *isn't* complex enough to warrant a design inference, Dawkins must additionally assume that there actually *are* 'many universes'. But why think that this crucial second premise is true? Given enough time, typewriters, and monkeys one might well obtain the works of William Shakespeare by chance; but in that case, why does no one actually explain Shakespeare's works using the 'many monkeys' hypothesis? In the absence of independent evidence for the existence of enough time, typewriters and monkeys, the 'written by design' explanation is clearly preferable.[87] Likewise, even granting that given 'multiple worlds' one could obtain the fine-tuning of our universe by chance, in the absence of independent evidence for the existence of 'multiple worlds', the design explanation is clearly preferable.

Indeed, according to cosmologist Paul Davies, the *scientific* 'multiple worlds' hypothesis

> merely shift the problem [of 'fine tuning'] up a level from universe to multiverse. To appreciate this, one only has to list the many assumptions that underpin the multiverse theory. First, there has to be a universe-generating mechanism . . . This mechanism is supposed to involve natural, law-like processes – in the case of eternal inflation, a quantum 'nucleation' of pocket universes, to be precise. But that raises the obvious question of the source of the quantum laws (not to mention the laws of gravitation, including the causal structure of space-time on which those laws depend) that permit inflation. In the standard multiverse theory, the universe-generating laws are just accepted as given: they don't come out of the multiverse theory . . . Furthermore, if we accept that the multiverse is predicted by string/M theory, then that theory, with its specific mathematical form, also has to be accepted as given . . . the multiverse theory [cannot] provide a complete and final explanation of why the universe is fit for life . . .[88]

As philosopher Robin Collins argues:

> even if [a] many-universe generator exists, it along with the background laws and principles could be said to be an *irreducibly complex* system . . . with just the right combination of laws and fields for the production of life-permitting universes: if one of the components were missing or different . . . it is unlikely that any life-permitting universes could be produced. In the absence of alternative explanations, the existence of such a system suggests design.[89]

Not only does the 'many worlds' hypothesis commit the 'inflationary fallacy' of multiplying explanatory probabilistic resources without independent evidence, but as Antony Flew complains, 'If we are trying to understand why the universe is bio-friendly, we are not helped by being told that all possible universes exist . . . The idea of a multiverse replaces the rationally ordered real world with an infinitely complex charade and makes the whole idea of "explanation" meaningless.'[89]

Dawkins' 'Unrebuttable Refutation' of the God Hypothesis, Rebutted

> 'the postulate of a designer or creator only raises the unanswerable question of who designed the designer or created the creator.'
> – Christopher Hitchens[91]

Dawkins argues that, while he can't disprove the God hypothesis, he can show that is at an *improbable* hypothesis. He champions 'a very serious argument against the existence of God, and one to which I have yet to hear a theologian give a convincing answer despite numerous opportunities and invitations to do so. Dan Dennett rightly describes it as "an unrebuttable refutation . . ."'[92] (This objection is common atheistic coinage.)[93] Dawkins writes that this 'unrebuttable refutation' is 'the central argument of my book', the heart of which runs as follows:

> One of the greatest challenges to the human intellect . . . has been to explain how the complex, improbable appearance of design in the universe arises. The natural temptation is to attribute the appearance of design to actual design itself. In the case of a man-made artefact such as a watch, the designer really was an intelligent engineer. It is tempting to apply the same logic to an eye or a wing, a spider or a person. This temptation is a false one, because the designer hypothesis immediately raises the larger problem of who designed the designer. The whole problem we started out with was the problem of explaining statistical improbability. It is obviously no solution to postulate something even more improbable. We need a 'crane', not a 'skyhook', for only a crane can do the business of working gradually and plausibly from simplicity to otherwise improbable complexity. The most ingenious and powerful crane so far discovered is Darwinian evolution by natural selection.[94]

I welcome Dawkins' affirmation that there exists an 'improbable appearance of design in the universe' and that the 'natural' thing to do (via the principle of credulity) is to attribute this 'appearance' to actual design. As philosopher Jakob Wolf argues:

> Biological entities *appear* to be designed. It is very important to note that everybody agrees on *the phenomenological description* of the living organism. Disagreement sets in when it comes to explaining the nature of what everybody observes. Is it possible to account for the evolution of the complex organism by appeal to unintelligent causes alone, or does an intelligent cause need to be invoked? The most obvious conclusion to draw is that . . . an intelligent cause is needed . . . If you think otherwise, the burden of proof rests squarely with you.[95]

Darwinian evolution may be the 'most ingenious and powerful crane so far discovered', but being *the best available explanation compatible with naturalism* doesn't necessarily mean being *a plausible explanation*, let alone being *the best available explanation*. Of course, Dawkins has what he considers an unrebuttable response to this line of thought ready and waiting: 'the designer hypothesis immediately raises the larger problem of who designed the designer. The whole problem we started out with was the problem of explaining statistical improbability. It is obviously no solution to postulate something even more improbable.'[96] There are actually two overlapping objections here: 1) the 'Who designed the designer?' objection; and 2) the 'You can't explain something with something more complex' objection.

The 'Who designed the designer?' question can be asked of *all* design inferences; but as Jay Richards observes, no one would pose this objection to the design inference in any other field of inquiry: 'If someone explains some buried earthenware as the result of artisans from the second century BC, no one complains, "Yeah, but who made the artisans?"'[97] Even if we have no answer to the 'Who designed the designer?' question, this wouldn't invalidate our design inference. Dawkins misunderstands the nature of explanation. As William Lane Craig explains, 'in order for an explanation to be the best explanation, one needn't have an explanation of the explanation (indeed, such a requirement would generate an infinite regress, so that everything becomes inexplicable) . . .'[98]

As for explaining A in terms of B when B is more complex than A, would it be legitimate to explain a painting with reference to an artist? The question answers itself. Plantinga' illustration nails this point:

> we land on an alien planet orbiting a distant star and discover machine-like objects that look and work just like tractors; our leader says 'there must be intelligent beings on this planet who built those tractors.' A first-year philosophy student on our expedition objects: 'Hey, hold on a minute! You have explained nothing at all! Any intelligent life that designed those tractors would have to be at least as complex as they are.' No doubt we'd tell him that a little learning is a dangerous thing . . .'[99]

However, Dawkins argues that 'A designer God cannot be used to explain organized complexity because any God capable of designing anything would have to be complex enough to demand the same kind of explanation in his own right. God presents an infinite regress from which he cannot help us to escape.'[100] That is:

1) Once you posit a designer to explain organized (i.e. specified) complexity you must posit an infinite regress of designers, because all designers would necessarily demand the same kind of explanation in their own right, etc.
2) There can't be an infinite regress of explanations
3) Therefore one shouldn't posit a designer to explain organized complexity

The correct response to this (logically valid) argument is to deny the first premise. Dawkins' second premise rejects explanations framed in terms of an infinite regress, but, strangely, Dawkins objects to the design inference on the basis of a first premise lamenting the supposed necessity of just such a regress in all cases of the design inference, and this *despite the fact that he himself accepts the design inference in some cases*! He can't have it both ways. Consistency requires applying Dawkins' objection to the design inference *in every case, including cases he admits are legitimate* (e.g. the design inference from a sequence of prime numbers in a radio signal). The obvious legitimacy of design inferences in *some* cases constitutes an *ad absurdum* rebuttal of the above argument. Unless Dawkins is prepared to eliminate *all* design inferences (and he isn't), he must reject his 'Who designed the designer?' objection.

Since Dawkins' 'Who designed the designer?' objection is logically valid, he must reject it either by ditching the second premise (an option rightly frowned upon by Dawkins), and/or by rejecting the first premise. Dawkins rejects the first premise, accepting design inferences when the posited designer is an agent he thinks is a physical being that *must* (so he deduces from the question-begging *assumption* that naturalism is true) have a Darwinian explanation: 'The crucial difference between gods and god-like extraterrestrials lies not in their properties but in their provenance. Entities that are complex enough to be intelligent are products of an evolutionary process. No matter how god-like they may seem when we encounter them, they didn't start that way.'[101]

As far as Dawkins is concerned, then, Intelligent Design Theory could be true, *as long as the designer is an alien* (however 'god-like' its properties) *whose provenance tracks back* (avoiding infinite regresses) *to an evolutionary explanation*. But as Mike King points out,[102] Dawkins is confused about properties and provenance, for aliens have a provenance (a source, causal explanation or origin), but God, having the essential property of necessary (un-caused) existence, *does not have a provenance*. Dawkins bends the first premise of his 'Who designed the designer?' objection so that it only applies to a designer who is thought to explain organized physical complexity *in general*. Dawkins thereby simply resorts to *asserting* his naturalistic worldview, begging the question against the possibility of an un-designed designer – designer who is neither the product of design, nor of an evolutionary process – a designer with no 'provenance'. As Woodward comments: 'Dawkins . . . veers here into blatant circular argumentation. He simply asserts – without any evidence-based argument or philosophical proof – that no intelligence can ever exist who is a necessary (uncaused) being . . .'[103]

Thus Dawkins' 'Who designed the designer' objection depends upon his dismissal of the cosmological argument. Yet

Dawkins not only fails to dismiss the cosmological argument (because he only critiques a straw man); he accepts both the premise that *some* things have explanations outside of themselves (e.g. zoologists, aliens, cars), and the premise that explanations framed in terms of infinite regress are illegitimate; from which it follows that there must exist an explanation *that has no explanation outside of itself* (that is, an explanation lacking a provenance). A designer without a provenance doesn't demand any explanation, and so doesn't fall foul of Dawkins' objection.

According to Dawkins, the ultimate explanation for organized physical complexity can't be *God*, because 'God, or any intelligent, decision-making, calculating agent, would have to be highly improbable in the very same statistical sense as the entities he is supposed to explain.'[104] This false assertion rightly fails to convince Antony Flew, who writes:

> Dawkins has rejected [the God hypothesis] on the grounds that God is too complex a solution for explaining the universe and its laws. This strikes me as a bizarre thing to say about the concept of an omnipotent and omniscient spiritual Being . . . Alvin Plantinga recently pointed out that, by Dawkins's own definition, God is simple – not complex – because God is a spirit, not a material object, and hence does not have parts.[105]

As mathematician and philosopher David Berlinski complains, when it comes to matters of 'complexity and information . . . Dawkins is casual about these concepts to the point of slackness . . .'[106] Dawkins confuses 'having a large number of metaphysically distinguishable properties' (e.g. God's omniscience entailing that God has a great many true beliefs) with being 'complex' in the statistical sense of the term – a sense that is co-extensive with the notion of contingency. However, part of the 'crucial difference between [God] and god-like extraterrestrials' is that some of the former's properties are radically different from those of the latter. For example, if God exists he exists necessarily. If an alien exists it exists contingently. Hence, while God's existence may be more or less *evidentially* probable relative to the evidence available to us, God's existence is nevertheless, ontologically speaking, either impossible or necessary (as the *ontological* argument demonstrates).

To borrow a rebuttal made by philosopher James E. Taylor in a related context, Dawkin's claim about the improbability of God 'is a claim about *evidential* rather than *objective* probability, and what is needed for the objection to succeed is the latter'.[107] Hence Dawkins' objection commits a category error.[108] As Plantinga argues:

> if God is a necessary being, if he exists in all possible worlds, then the probability that he exists, of course, is 1, and the probability that he does not exist is 0. Far from its being improbable that he exists, his existence is maximally probable. So if Dawkins proposes that God's existence is improbable, he owes us an argument for the conclusion that there is no necessary being with the attributes of God – an argument that doesn't just start from the premise that materialism is true. Neither he nor anyone else has provided even a decent argument along these lines; Dawkins doesn't even seem to be aware that he *needs* an argument of that sort.[109]

Swinburne explains:

> whether a hypothesis is simple or not is an intrinsic feature of that hypothesis, not a matter of its relation to observable data. Whether the hypothesis is such as to lead us to expect the data is a second and different criterion for assessing a hypothesis . . . whether Newton's theory that all bodies attract each other with forces proportional to $mm1/r2$ is simple is something we can see by studying it. But, to be probably true, the hypothesis must also satisfy the criterion of leading us to expect the data. The postulation of one entity (God) with the stated properties (scientists prefer hypotheses postulating infinite qualities to hypotheses postulating very large finite quantities – other things, that is satisfaction of other criteria, being equal) is intrinsically simple. I also argue that it leads us to expect the enormously complex data.[110]

As 'the greatest possible being', God is *metaphysically simple* in a way that no finite entity can be.[111] With a finite entity one can always ask why it has this or that property to this or that degree. Such questions don't arise with God, since (by definition) God must exhibit, to the greatest possible degree, the greatest co-possible set of great-making properties (e.g. beauty, goodness, power, knowledge, etc.), including the great-making property of 'maximal ontological security' – a quality which entails being uncaused, independent, necessarily existent, and immaterial. Moreover, as Moreland and Craig argue: 'A mind's ideas may be complex, but a mind itself is a remarkably simple thing, being an immaterial entity not composed of pieces or separable parts.'[112]

God isn't a contingent physical object composed of separable parts combined in a contingent order which can be assigned a probability of one possible arrangement out of a certain number of possible arrangements. Not only is God not physical, he is not contingent, and *a pre-requisite of the design inference is that it begins with a contingent object*. As atheist Thomas Nagel comments in response to Dawkins' central argument, 'God, whatever he may be, is not a complex physical inhabitant of the natural world.'[113]

Conclusion

> *'The* God Delusion *is full of bluster and bombast, but it really doesn't give even the slightest reason for thinking belief in God mistaken, let alone a "delusion."'*
> – Alvin Plantinga[114]

Several laudatory reviews of *The God Delusion* share the view, expressed by Tim Gebhart, that theists are inherently unreasonable: 'If *The God Delusion* suffers a flaw, it is an inherent and perhaps ultimately fatal one. It is almost impossible to use logic and reasoning to educate and persuade others on a subject that requires ignoring and rejecting logic and reasoning.'[115] Such comments exhibit wishful thinking rather than a sober assessment of the facts. Dawkins accuses 'dyed-in-the-wool faith-heads' of being 'immune to argument . . .'[116] It is hard to test this assumption using *The God Delusion*, since the arguments against theism therein are conspicuously unsound. Dawkins thinks that 'open-minded' religious believers 'need only a little encouragement to break free of the vice of religion altogether.'[117] Unfortunately for Dawkins' self-admitted 'presumptuous optimism',[118] *The God Delusion* fails to provide even a 'little' rational encouragement to this end. Indeed, Dawkins' critique of theism is one long bluff that deserves to be called. As Thomas Nagel laments: 'Dawkins dismisses, with contemptuous flippancy, the traditional . . . arguments for the existence of God offered by Aquinas and Anselm. I found these attempts at philosophy, along with those in a later chapter on religion and ethics, particularly weak . . .'[119] Jeremy Pierce likewise comments that 'Dawkins is not a philosopher, never mind a well-trained one, and what he says demonstrates that he is hardly familiar with the literature in philosophy of religion. He regularly commits easy-to-spot fallacies . . .'[120]

Dawkins only reviews some of the arguments for God. Having dismissed them as 'vacuous',[121] he leaps to the conclusion that there is therefore 'no evidence to favour the God Hypothesis'.[122] Even if his critique of the arguments he examines were sound, this conclusion wouldn't follow. In point of fact, however, Dawkins' critique is unsound in every case. Dawkins repeatedly attacks straw men and offers rebuttals that are themselves easily revealed as 'vacuous'. As Jay Tolson comments, 'Philosophical arguments for or against God are more sophisticated than one might learn from Dawkins, who sometimes comes close to confirming Francis Bacon's adage that a little philosophy inclineth man's mind to atheism, but depth in philosophy bringeth men's minds about to religion.'[123]

On a 2007 cruise to the Galapogos Islands, Dawkins held a Q&A session with a group of atheists. He was asked this question, 'What would be the best criticism of your book, *The God Delusion*?' He replied, 'I think the best criticism would be any kind of suggestion that there really is good evidence that some kind of supernatural being exists . . . that would be a good criticism if anybody could come up with one. I think it is revealing that nobody has, and I don't believe anybody could.'[124] Readers will have to make of this what they will in light of the above defence of natural theology; but I think that of primary significance is the fact that Dawkins' supposedly 'unrebuttable' refutation of theism is nothing like. As Gregory Clark concludes, 'There are . . . convincing rebuttals to all of Dawkins's claims against theism. He tends to make emotionally bloated, philosophically under-developed and theologically naïve appeals on atheism's behalf, all the while refusing to respond to some of the best arguments *for* theism.'[125] Blowing away worldview houses made from philosophical straw is a praiseworthy endeavour; but Dawkins' substitution of straw houses for the real thing means that his critique is long on hot air and short on bite. The Emperor of New Atheism has no clothes.

Recommended Resources

Francis J. Beckwith, William Lane Craig, and J.P. Moreland (eds.), *To Everyone an Answer: A Case for the Christian Worldview* (Downers Grove, IL: IVP, 2004).

Paul Copan and Paul K. Moser (eds.), *The Rationality of Theism* (New York/London: Routledge, 2003).

William Lane Craig, *Reasonable Faith: Christian Truth and Apologetics*, third edition (Wheaton, IL: Crossway, 2008).

William Lane Craig (ed.), *Philosophy of Religion: A Reader and Guide* (Edinburgh: Edinburgh University Press, 2002).

William Lane Craig, 'Naturalism and Intelligent Design', in Robert B. Stewart (ed.), *Intelligent Design: William A. Dembski & Michael Ruse in Dialogue* (Minneapolis, MN: Fortress Press, 2007).

Brian Davies, *An Introduction To The Philosophy Of Religion* (Oxford: Oxford University Press, 2004).

Paul Davies, *The Goldilocks Enigma: Why Is The Universe Just Right For Life?* (London: Penguin, 2007).

Stephen T. Davis, *God, Reason and Theistic Proofs* (Edinburgh: Edinburgh University Press, 1997).

C. Stephen Evans, *Philosophy of Religion: Thinking About Faith* (Downers Grove, IL: IVP, 2001).

Antony Flew, *There Is a God: How the World's Most Notorious Atheist Changed His Mind* (New York: HarperOne, 2007).

R. Douglas Geivett and Brenden Sweetman (eds.), *Contemporary Perspectives on Religious Epistemology* (Oxford: Oxford University Press, 1992).

C. Stephen Layman, *Letters to Doubting Thomas: A Case for the Existence of God* (Oxford: Oxford University Press, 2006).

John Lennox, *God's Undertaker: Has Science Buried God?* (Oxford: Lion, 2007).

J.P. Moreland, *Scaling the Secular City* (Grand Rapids: Baker, 1987).

J.P. Moreland and William Lane Craig, *Foundations for a Christian Worldview* (Downers Grove, IL: IVP, 2003).

Victor Reppert, *C.S. Lewis' Dangerous Idea: In Defence of the Argument from Reason* (Downers Grove, IL: IVP, 2003).

James F. Sennett and Douglas Groothuis, *In Defence of Natural Theology: A Post-Humean Assessment* (Downers Grove, IL: IVP, 2005).

Richard Swinburne, *The Existence of God* (Oxford: Clarendon, 2004).

Keith Ward, *Why There Almost Certainly Is A God* (Oxford: Lion, 2008).

Benjamin Wiker and Jonathan Witt, *A Meaningful World: How the Arts and Sciences Reveal the Genius of Nature* (Downers Grove, IL: IVP, 2006).

Peter S. Williams, *I Wish I Could Believe in Meaning: A Response to Nihilism* (Southampton: Damaris, 2004).

Websites

William Lane Craig: Reasonable Faith, www.reasonablefaith.org site/PageServer.

Additional Papers

Robin Collins, 'Design and the Many Worlds Hypothesis', http://home.messiah.edu/~rcollins/finetune/ Craig7.htm.

Paul Copan, 'The Moral Argument for God's Existence', www.4truth.net/site/apps/nl/content3.asp?c=hiKXLbPNLrF &b=778665&ct=1264233.

William Lane Craig, 'Richard Dawkins' Argument Against God in *The God Delusion*', www.reasonablefaith.org/site/ News2? page=NewsArticle&id=5493.

Peter May, 'This House Believes That God is a Delusion', www.bethinking.org/resource.php?ID=411.

Alvin Plantinga, 'The Dawkins Confusion', www.christianitytoday.com/bc/2007/002/1.21.html.

Richard Swinburne, 'Response to Richard Dawkins' Criticisms in *The God Delusion*', http://users.ox.ac.uk/~orie0087/frameset-pdfs.shtml.

Audio

William Lane Craig, 'Reasonable Faith: Five Arguments for God – Part I', www.rfmedia.org/RF_audio_video/RF_podcast/ Reasonable_Faith_book_03.mp3.

William Lane Craig, 'Reasonable Faith: Five Arguments for God – Part II', www.rfmedia.org/RF_audio_video/RF_podcast/Reasonable_Faith_book_04.mp3.

William Lane Craig, 'The Big Bang & Fine Tuning', www.rfmedia.org/RF_audio_video/RF_podcast/The-Big-Bang.mp3.

William Lane Craig, 'Reasonable Faith: The New Atheism', www.rfmedia.org/RF_audio_video/RF_podcast/Reasonable_Faith_book_09.mp3.

William Lane Craig, 'Craig's Response to The God Delusion,' www.rfmedia.org/RF_audio_video/Other_clips/UF-Responding-to-Dawkins-The-God-Delusion/UF_Bill_Craig_s_Response_to_The_God_Delusion.mp3.

William Lane Craig, 'Blackwell Companion to Natural Theology,' www.rfmedia.org/RF_audio_video/RF_podcast/Blackwell_Companion_Book.mp3.

William Lane Craig, 'Can we be Good Without God?,' www.rfmedia.org/RF_audio_video/Other_clips/National_Faculty_Leadership_Conf_2008/Can_Be_Good_Without_God.mp3.

Richard Dawkins on Point of Enquiry, 'The God Delusion', http://cdn.libsyn.com/pointofinquiry/10-16-06.mp3.

Douglas Groothuis, 'Cosmological Arguments, Lectures 1, 2, and 3', www.relyonchrist.com/Lecture/Audio/12.mp3; www.relyonchrist.com/Lecture/Audio/13.mp3; www.relyonchrist.com/Lecture/Audio/14.mp3.

Douglas Groothuis, 'The Argument from Religious Experience', www.relyonchrist.com/Lecture/Audio/22.mp3.

John Haldane, 'Why I Believe in God', www.stpt.usf.edu/hhl/radio/whyiamatheist.htm.

Keith Ward, 'WhyThere Almost Certainly Is A God,'www.premierradio.org.uk/listen/ondemand.aspx?mediaid={F4CABBF-859A-45EA-984A-1892586B32EA}.

Peter S. Williams, 'Cosmic Fine Tuning', www.damaris.org/cm/podcasts/category/peterswilliams.

Peter S. Williams Discusses *The God Delusion*, www.damaris.org/content/content.php?type=5&id=512.

Peter S. Williams, 'Dawkins & the Fine-Tuning Argument', www.damaris.org/cw/audio/williams_on_dawkins_fine_tuning.mp3.

Peter S. Williams, 'Dawkins and the Moral Argument', www.damaris.org/cw/audio/williams_on_dawkins_moral_a rgument.mp3.
Peter S. Williams, '*The God Delusion* Deconstructed - South-amp-ton University', www.ecs.soton.ac.uk/~pjb304/ SUCU_talks/ eternity/2007-02-15-PeteWilliams-TheGodDelusion-Deconstructed.mp3.

Video

Unlocking the Mysteries of Life, www.theapologiaproject.org/ media/unlocking_the_mystery_of_life.ram.
The Privileged Planet, www.theapologiaproject.org/media/ the_privileged_planet.ram.
William Lane Craig, 'Response to Dawkins' Central Argument', www.apologetics.com/index.php?option=comcontent-&view=article&id=202:dr-craig-responds-to-dawkins-book-video&catid=57:philosophy-of-science&Itemid=62.
William Lane Craig, 'The Moral Argument', www.leestrobel. com/videos/Creator/strobelT1199.htm.
William Lane Craig vs. Garrett Hardin, 'Christianity vs. Scientific Naturalism', www.uctv.tv/library-test.asp?showID=7334.
William Lane Craig vs. Bill Cooke, www.rfmedia.org/ RF_audio _video/Other_clips/New-Zealand-08/Is-God-a-Delusion-Craig-v-Cooke.php.
William Lane Craig, 'Why Does Anything At All Exist?,' www.rfmedia.org/RF_audio_video/Other_clips/Wake-Forest-Why-Does-Anything-at-All-Exist/index.php.
William A. Dembski, 'Order and Design: Philosophical Issues', www.meta-library.net/perspevo/wdemb-frame.html.
Stephen C. Meyer, 'The New Cosmology: Theistic Implications', www.counterbalance.net/cosmcrea/meyer-frame.html.
J.P. Moreland, 'Right and Wrong as a Key to the Meaning of the Universe', http://webcast.ucsd.edu:8080/ramgen/UCSD_ TV/8008.rm.

Conclusion:

'None Shall Pass'?

'The first to plead his case seems just, until another comes and examines him.'
– Proverbs 18:17

I have reviewed contemporary popular atheology, paying particular attention to so-called 'New Atheists'. I am seriously unimpressed. Philosopher Paul Copan's summation is, in my considered opinion, unerring: 'the new atheists are remarkably out of touch with [contemporary] sophisticated theistic arguments for God's existence. Their arguments against God tend to be very superficial (bordering on village atheist argumentation that is often *ad hominem* or hasty generalization) and often naively tout science as the arbiter of truth, following in the barren footsteps of their positivistic forebears.'[1] As Becky Garrison comments in her book *The New Atheist Crusaders And Their Unholy Grail*, 'when it comes to the actual weapons that the New Atheists lob against their opponents, they seem to be shooting blanks.'[2]

According to Richard Norman,

> the 'New Atheism' is not really new. Its distinctive themes – religion as the enemy of science, of progress and of an enlightened morality – are in a direct line of descent from the 18th-century enlightenment and 19th-century rationalism. The 'new' movement is better seen as a revival, a reassertion of the values of rational thought and vigorous argument.[3]

If by 'vigorous' one means acerbic and rhetorically canny, then the New Atheism is certainly 'vigorous'. However, as a revival of the value of rational thought (something I'm all for) the New Atheism is sadly lacking. This is partly because its narrow, self-defeating misunderstanding of rationality is mired in an eighteenth-/nineteenth-century epistemological foundationalism; and partly because the movement's boosters frequently allow their 'vigour' to bypass their critical faculties. The New Atheists confidently proclaim intellectual, ethical and even (eventual) political victory; but from my perspective they look about as dangerous as the Black Knight in the Monty Python film *Monty Pythan and the Holy Grail*. The Black Knight exhibits blind faith in his ability to beat any opponent ('I'm invincible . . . the Black Knight always triumphs!')[4] and thereby to uphold his assertion that 'None shall pass'[5] by force of arms. Despite having various limbs lopped off in combat with King Arthur, the Black Knight nonetheless vigorously taunts, 'It's just a flesh wound!'[6] He isn't fooling anyone but himself. Likewise, I endorse Peter Berkowitz's conclusion concerning the New Atheists: 'The disproportion between the bluster and bravado of their rhetoric and the limitations of their major arguments is astonishing.'[7]

On the rhetorical side of the ledger, the New Atheists repeatedly flatten straw men (erected by shoddy research and/or data-picking), often using blunt *ad hominem* bayonets, and frequently by substituting an equally blunt, unsubstantiated assertion for the required incisive argument. To believe that such rhetoric constitutes 'a reassertion of the values of rational thought and vigorous argument' is to embrace a delusion on a par with that suffered by the Black Knight.

As for the 'limitations of their major arguments', the New Atheists' apparently have as much trouble spotting a logically valid argument as do the witch-weighing villagers in *Monty Python and the Holy Grail*.[8] Indeed, they have difficulty in recognizing validity both when it is present in the arguments of their opponents, and (as is more often the case than not) when it is absent from their own. As John F. Haught comments, 'I do not expect that philosophers will recommend these writings to their own students . . . although the books might usefully serve as case studies for classes in critical thinking.'[9] Indeed, New Atheist writings offer up such a rich vein of logically fallacious arguments that I have used them as precisely such case studies.

Dawkins calls theism a delusion, but 'a delusion is when some-one persists in a belief after receiving conclusive evidence to the contrary.'[10] While the New Atheists *define* theism as a belief held in the teeth of overwhelming evidence to the contrary, they fail to substantiate the claim that an overwhelming evidential case against theism exists. As Colin Tudge writes, 'on matters of the-ology their arguments are a disgrace: assertive without sub-stance; demanding evidence while offering none; staggeringly unscholarly.'[11] Indeed, contemporary popular atheology spends most of its time launching question-begging attacks upon the warrant of theistic *belief*, rather than substantive attacks upon the truth status of theism. That many New Atheist arguments (of both varieties) are question-begging is ironic for a group so con-cerned to stamp out blind faith; and it highlights their suffocat-ingly narrow understanding of rationality.

The primary intellectual objection to theism promulgated by the New Atheists – an objection that underpins the 'root of all evil' objection, the 'science explains everything' objection and the 'lack of evidence' objection – is that *theists fail to fulfil their intel-lectual obligations*. But how do the New Atheists see our intellec-tual obligations? They see them in terms of (a rather narrow version of) classical foundationalism. In particular, they believe that: a) nothing should be believed in the teeth of evidence, and that b) nothing should be believed without evidence. Well, of course nothing should be believed in the teeth of (overwhelming) contrary evidence – but then faith does *not* require such belief by definition as the New Atheists assert (in the teeth of overwhelm-ing evidence to the contrary); nor, I suggest, does it require it in practice (the fact that contemporary atheology is largely a matter of anti-*belief* objections underlines this fact). The latter claim, that nothing should be believed without evidence (that the only good reason is a scientific reason, that truth-claims should only be taken seriously if they have empirical support, that science is *the* way to know truth, etc.) is self-contradictory. Michael Novak's comment about Daniel Dennett, that his 'concept of reason and science is so narrow that he seems trapped in something like early-period A.J. Ayer',[12] goes for the New Atheist movement as a whole. Like logical positivism, classical foundationalism is self-defeating. Once we open up our epistemological horizons beyond the narrow confines of self-contradiction, we find a host of non-tautological, non-indubitable beliefs that are both clearly rational and analogous to belief in God, but which nevertheless stand without evidential support. Hence belief in God, like my properly basic memory-based belief that I had coffee with friends yesterday, can be perfectly rational without an appeal to evidence.

This said, just as the properly basic nature of a trusted memory doesn't preclude the existence of sound supporting arguments for the same belief, so the properly basic nature of belief in God does not preclude the existence of sound theistic arguments. Are there any? As Alvin Plantinga says: 'At least a couple of dozen or so.'[13] The attempt by the New Atheists to rebut natural theology is philosophically ham-fisted, suffering from many methodological defects, most egregious among which are the consistent preference for attacking a) straw man versions of b) medieval rather than contemporary defences of c) a very narrow range of theistic arguments. For example, when attempting to rebut the cosmological argument, does Dawkins research representative formulations of each sub-species of the argument (e.g. Kalam, Leibnizian sufficient reason and Thomistic contingency variants) by respected contemporary philosophers such as Robert C. Koons, Stephen T. Davis or William Lane Craig?[14] No. Instead, he manfully grapples with his own quotation-free misunderstanding of one of Aquinas' medieval summaries of the argument. The resulting spectacle would have all the drama of watching Tarzan wrestling a rubber crocodile, if it weren't for the fact that on this occasion the crocodile proves to be more resilient than Tarzan's rubber dagger!

As we have seen, of all the New Atheists, it is Richard Dawkins who pays most attention to the philosophical debate concerning God's existence. Yet Alvin Plantinga's professional verdict on Dawkins-the-philosopher is unfortunately apposite: 'You might say that some of his forays into philosophy are at best sophomoric, but that would be unfair to sophomores; the fact is . . . many of his arguments would receive a failing grade in a sophomore philosophy class.'[15] Nor can this assessment be dismissed as the product of religious bias. As Michael Ruse writes in his review of *The God Delusion*:

It is not that the atheists are having a field day because of the brilliance and novelty of their thinking. Frankly – and I speak here as a non-believer myself, pretty atheistic about Christianity and skeptical about all theological claims – the material being churned out is second rate. And that is a euphemism for 'downright awful.' . . . Dawkins is brazen in his ignorance of philosophy and theology (not to mention the history of science) . . . Dawkins . . . is a man truly out of his depth.[16]

The blatant misrepresentation of the cosmological argument as depending upon the premise that 'everything' has a cause (rather than the premise that some specifically defined type of thing – a thing with a beginning, a contingent thing, a dependent thing, etc. – requires a cause) is a persistent myth of popular atheology.[17] So is the widespread failure to understand that the point of the moral argument is *not* that it is impossible for humans to *know* what the right thing to do is, still less that it is impossible for humans to *do* the right thing, without *belief in* God/religion/the Bible; but rather that it is impossible for there to *be* such a thing as an objectively good or evil thing to be known or done without *the existence of God*. Ironically, this is a fact that atheists themselves frequently affirm. 'The universe that we observe has precisely the properties we should expect if there is, at bottom, no design, no purpose, *no evil, no good* . . .'[18] writes Dawkins. Likewise, Julian Baggini argues,

If there is no single moral authority [i.e. if there is no God, then] we have to in some sense 'create' values for ourselves . . . that means that moral claims are not true or false in the same way as factual claims are . . . moral claims are judgments [that] it is always possible for someone to disagree with . . . without saying something that is factually false . . . you may disagree with me but you cannot say I have made a factual error.[19]

Not only do I disagree with Dawkins and Baggini about the nature of moral value, I think they have made a crucially significant factual error. What becomes of the moral critique of the terrible things religious people do if moral debate involves nothing but self-created, non-factual disagreements about claims that 'are not true or false'? I think that the 9/11 terrorists did an object-ively evil thing, and I think that anyone who disagrees with this judgement thereby makes a factual error. The New Atheists superficially *seem* to agree with me, but they expound a world-view that explicitly erases the very concept of an objective dis-tinction between good and evil. Only the theistic worldview on the receiving end of the New Atheists' ethical objections can metaphysically sustain the charges of wrongdoing they wish to press home! Religious people as a notional class may or may not do proportionally more evil in the name of religion than atheists do in the name of atheism; but while things might look different if we factored in atheistic ideologies like communism or eugen-ics: 'The real problem is not that tyrants reject the "dogma" of religion, but that they splash around in the bloodshed permitted by the ultimate relativism of all things.'[20]

And if the death of God entails the death of objective values (and I agree with Dawkins and Baggini that it does), then what becomes of Norman's cherished '*values* of rational thought and vigorous argument'?[21] The New Atheists actively undermine not only their moral critique of religion, but their laudable desire to encourage people to fulfil their intellectual *obligations*. This is truly an example of sawing off the branch upon which one is seated.

Michael Novak observes how 'Jürgen Habermas, possibly the best-known atheist in Europe . . . writes of believers with respect and as equal partners in an important dialogue. A respectful regard for mutual dignity is, Habermas holds, essential to the practice of rationality among human beings.'[22] But as Novak laments:

> it is extremely difficult to engage on the same level with Harris, Dennett, and Dawkins. All of them think that religion is so great a menace that they do not have much disposition for dialogue . . . Surely, one of the noblest works of reason is to enter into respect-ful argument with others, whose vision of reality is dramatically different from one's own, in order that both parties may learn from this exchange, and come to a deeper mutual respect. Our authors engage in dialectic, not science, but they can scarcely be said to do so with respect for those they address.[23]

In a spirit of charity, one can only assume that it is a deficit of the respect for mutual dignity called for by Habermas that leads the New Atheists to eviscerate so many straw men, rather than a deliberate intention to misrepresent their partners in rational dialogue. As Douglas Groothuis wryly comments, 'Dawkins is not the most sympathetic interlocutor.'[24]

I have been at pains to highlight some areas of agreement with the New Atheists. For example,

- The God hypothesis *is* a meaningful hypothesis worthy of serious debate (positivism is false).
- Atheists *shouldn't* be made to feel like an oppressed minority. It's *not* alright to be intolerant of atheists.
- Faith *shouldn't* be 'blind'.
- All religious believers *are* sinners.
- The Christian doctrine of hell *shouldn't* be taught *in an insensitive and theologically un-nuanced way, especially to children.*
- Science and metaphysics *don't* form air-tight compartments.
- The reality of intelligent design in the universe *is* a scientific question; but one to which a positive answer provides indirect support for natural theology.

The New Atheists rarely display an interest in mutual understanding, let alone mutual agreement. And while it is only upon the foundation of mutual understanding and agreement that true debate can make any progress, I for one do not consider the New Atheists a lost cause (that epithet I reserve for the New Atheism). Unlike the fight between Arthur and the Black Knight, there is a sense in which the proper goal of the debate about God should be victory for all. As A.C. Grayling writes:

> The idea of good defeats – those in which you learn, or give, or allow the better to flourish – is an important one. Spinoza wrote that weapons never conquer minds, only magnanimity and love; to be conquered by these things is a great victory in itself, because it is a response to what is best. To recognize an argument as sound, and to defer to it, or to grasp the justice of another's cause and to make way for it, are likewise victorious defeats.[25]

Hence this book should not be misconstrued as an attempt to defeat the New Atheists, but rather as an attempt to encourage them to defer to their own 'victorious defeat'; for as Fr Andrew said, 'There is only one true way of conquering [ideological] enemies in this warring world, and that is to make your enemies your friends.'[26]

In John Humphry's assessment as an agnostic:

> The atheists . . . must do two things. They must prove, rather than merely assert, that mainstream religion is a malign force in the world [but how can they do this whilst denying any objective reality to moral malignancy?]. They cannot rely on a small minority of religious extremists to do that for them or hark back to the brutality of earlier centuries. And they must offer an alternative to the millions who rely on their beliefs to make sense of their lives [but how can they do this whilst denying any objective reality to our intellectual obligations?]. Unlike the militant atheists I do not think people are stupid if they believe in God. For vast numbers of ordinary, thoughtful people it is impossible not to. Of course, this may be the result of indoctrination at a very early age – but it may also be a considered reluctance to accept that the material world is all there is.[27]

It is of course the latter point, concerning God's existence, which lies at the very heart of the matter. For all its 'None shall pass' confidence, I find nothing in contemporary popular atheology to undermine my own considered reluctance to abandon a trusting belief in God. Indeed, I remain a theist (of a specifically Christian variety) because I have yet to see a better account of reality to satisfy my mind, a more powerful source of personal transformation for my heart, or a more meaningful purpose for my life.[28] As Peter said to Jesus, 'Lord, there is no one else that we can go to! Your words give eternal life' (John 6:68, Contemporary English Version).

Appendix:

The Evidence for Jesus

'nowhere do the gods emerge from invisibility and sit down to eat . . .
or drink the wine.'
– Daniel Dennett[1]

Having arrived at a belief in God, Antony Flew observes that 'the question of whether the Divine has revealed itself in human history remains a valid topic of discussion.'[2] He comments:

> In both my antitheological books and various debates I have taken issue with many of the claims of divine relevlation or intervention. My current position, however, is more open to at least certain of these claims. In point of fact, I think that the Christian religion is the one religion that most clearly deserves to be honoured and respected whether or not its claim to be a divine revelation is true. There is nothing like the combination of a charismatic figure like Jesus and a first-class intellectual like St. Paul . . . who had a brilliant philosophical mind . . . If you're wanting omnipotence to set up a religion, this is the one to beat.[3]

You certainly wouldn't come away from reading a new atheist book such as *The God Delusion* with the impression that the Christian revelation claim is 'the one to beat'! Consider a typical selection of the sort of thing Richard Dawkins says about the evidence for Jesus:

> Ever since the nineteenth century, scholarly theologians have made an overwhelming case that the gospels are not reliable accounts of

what happened . . . All were written long after the death of Jesus
. . . then copied and recopied, through many different 'Chinese
Whispers generations' . . . Nobody knows who the four evangelists
were, but they almost certainly never met Jesus . . . Much of what
they wrote was in no sense an honest attempt at history . . .
Although Jesus probably existed, reputable bible scholars do not in
general regard the New Testament . . . as a reliable record of what
actually happened in history . . .[4]

Dawkins' views contrast sharply with those of fellow scientist
Francis Collins, who writes:

the gospels . . . were put down just a few decades after Christ's
death. Their style and content suggests strongly that they are
intended to be the record of eyewitnesses (Matthew and John
were among the twelve apostles). Concerns about errors creep-
ing in by successive copying or bad translations have been
mostly laid to rest by discovery of very ancient manuscripts.
Thus, the evidence for authenticity of the four gospels turns out
to be quite strong.[5]

How can we judge between these contradictory assessments of
the evidence for Jesus? First, we must see through Dawkins'
rhetorical ploy of implying that, by definition, anyone who
thinks that the gospels represent reliable 'accounts of what
happened' are *unscholarly* folk whose *disreputable* opinions are
out of date. Second, we must contend with New Testament
scholar Craig L. Blomberg's affirmation that, 'The gospels may
be accepted as trustworthy accounts of what Jesus did and said
. . . other conclusions, widespread though they are, seem not to
stem from even-handed historical analysis but from religious
or philosophical prejudice.'[6] Let us begin, with a brief 'even-
handed historical analysis' of the evidence (i.e. one that neither
assumes it must be unreliable nor that it must constitute the
infallible word of God), before returning to philosophical
issues.

The Chain of Testimony

When assessing written testimony, a historian wants to know the strength of various 'links' in the 'chain of testimony'. There are four links in the chain:

Link 1) Between the author and the reported events (e.g. Does the author intend to covey truth, and are they in a good position to do so? Were they an eye-witness? Did they get information from an eye-witness?)

Link 2) Between the reported events and the writing down of the report.

Link 3) Between the original report (the autograph) and the surviving copies; and

Link 4) Between the autograph and the text we can reconstruct today from surviving copies.

In every case, the *stronger* the link, the more confidence we can place in the source. Let's test the gospels by these criteria in reverse order.

Link 4

Consider first the *number* of New Testament manuscripts compared to other ancient works:

- The writings of Plato survive in 7 manuscripts.
- The work of the Roman historian Livy comes to us through 10 manuscripts.
- Homer's *Illiad* is the closest comparison, with c. 650 surviving manuscripts.
- The New Testament comes to us through over 24,000 manuscripts (including c. 5,700 Greek manuscripts).

As Norman L. Geisler and Frank Turek note, 'there is nothing from the ancient world that even comes close in terms of manuscript support [to the New Testament] . . . Most other ancient works survive on fewer than a dozen manuscripts, yet few historians question the historicity of the events those works describe.'[7]

Due to this wealth of available manuscripts, the text of today's New Testament is 99.99% percent accurate (with the remaining textual uncertainty not affecting any crucial theological issue).[8] As B.B. Warfield observes, 'The great mass of the New Testament . . . has been transmitted to us with no, or next to no variations.'[9]

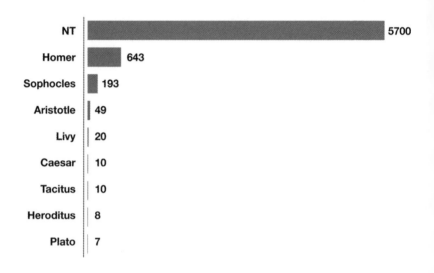

NT — 5700
Homer — 643
Sophocles — 193
Aristotle — 49
Livy — 20
Caesar — 10
Tacitus — 10
Heroditus — 8
Plato — 7

Manuscript Evidence

This chart compares just the *Greek* manuscript evidence for the New Testament text with the *total* manuscript evidence for other ancient texts (including the next closest, which is the *Illiad* by Homer).

Link 3

According to Winfried Corduan, 'No other ancient document equals the New Testament when it comes to the preservation of manuscripts, both in terms of number and closeness in time to the original autographs.'[10] N.T. Wright confirms that 'There is better evidence for the New Testament than for any other ancient book . . . The New Testament we have printed in our Bibles does indeed go back to what the very early Christians wrote.'[11]

Consider the link between the writing of the 'autographs' and the earliest surviving manuscripts in each of the following cases.

- Between Aristotle and our earliest copy lie 1,450 years.
- Between both Plato and Herodotus and our copies lie 1,300 years.
- Between Pliny the Younger and our copies lie 750 years.
- Between Homer and our earliest copy lies 500 years.
- Between the gospel autographs and our complete copies lies c. 250–300 years *at most*.

Indeed, 'The average time span between the original and earliest copy of the other ancient texts is over 1,000 years. However, the New Testament has a fragment within one generation of its original composition. Whole books appear within 100 years of the original, most of the New Testament within 200 years, and the entire New Testament within 250 years from the date of its completion.'[12]

Gap Between Originals and Copies

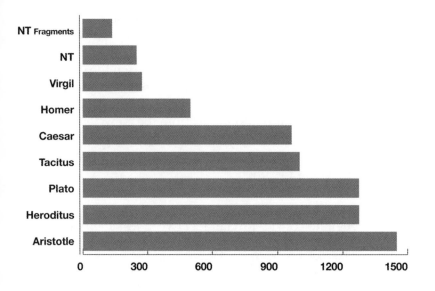

- We have *complete copies of all the gospels* from AD 325–350 (e.g. Codex Vatinicus, Codex Sinaiticus,[13] and Codex Ephraemi Rescriptus).[14]
- *We have major portions of all four gospels* (and Acts) from c. AD 250 (Chester Beatty Papyri).[15]
- We have *several pages of Luke and John* from c. AD 200 (Bodmer Papyri).[16]
- We also have *fragments of gospel* – including the Rylands Papyrus[17] containing John 18:31–33, 37–38 – dating from c. AD 117–138; and perhaps even earlier (e.g. there is a disputed papyri fragment dating from AD 50–70 which some scholars think bears a snatch of Mark's gospel).[18]

Even as an atheist, Antony Flew acknowledged that 'the textual authority, the earliness and the number of manuscripts for most of the Christian documents, is unusually great . . . that's . . . very good authority for the accuracy of the text that is provided in translation in the New Testament.'[19]

Many verses from all four gospels are quoted in extra-biblical texts (usually letters) by the likes of Ignatius (AD 30–107) and Clement (in his letter to the Corinthians of AD 95). On these grounds alone we can note that the gospels must all have been written *before the end of the first century AD*. Indeed, all but eleven verses of the New Testament can be reconstructed from quotations used by the early church fathers in their own works of the first to fourth centuries AD. Between them, the early church fathers quoted over twenty thousand times from the Gospels and Acts, over fourteen thousand times from the New Testament letters, and over six hundred times from Revelation. That's a total of over thirty-six thousand quotations from the New Testament as a whole![20] Hence it has been said that 'if all the copies of the New Testament were destroyed, it could be reconstructed solely from external references by others.'[21]

Link 2

Here we begin to consider the link between Jesus' life (Jesus died c. AD 30) and the gospel autographs. One influential argument for dating the 'synoptic' gospel autographs *before c. AD 62* begins with the observation that the book of Acts, a sequel to Luke, ends with

Paul in prison c. AD 62. That nothing is said about Paul's trial indicates that Acts was written before it took place (especially since Luke worked with Paul, a major character in Acts). Luke's gospel shouldn't be dated later than its sequel; and given that Luke was written after Matthew, and Matthew after Mark, it would therefore seem that the 'synoptic' gospels were written *within thirty years of Jesus' death.*

Other evidence supports the conclusion that the gospels were written prior to AD 70; for example, 'various passages in Matthew refer to details of temple worship, which would be unnecessary anachronisms after AD 70 [when Jerusalem and the temple were destroyed by the Romans], and one passage (17:24–27) would be positively misleading since it approves the payment of the temple tax, which after AD 70 was diverted to the upkeep of the temple of Jupiter in Rome!'[22]

Scholars advocating composition dates for the gospels after AD 70 often rely upon the question-begging assumption that miracles (such as prophecy) are impossible: 'all the Gospels record Jesus prophesying the destruction of Jerusalem. Now, liberal scholars who don't believe anything supernatural can occur, argue that this shows that the Gospels must be written after the fall of Jerusalem [in AD 70] (a main reason they date the Gospels late).'[23]

This table lists the range of 'conservative' and 'liberal' dates proposed for the writing of the gospel autographs.

GOSPEL	'CONSERVATIVE' DATING AD	'LIBERAL' DATING AD
Mark	40s-mid 50s	Late 60s-70s
Matthew	40s-early 60s	80s-95
Luke	50s-early 60s	80s-95
John	Mid 60s-95	90-95

Scholars thus agree that *all four gospels were written within c. 60 years of Jesus' death, by the end of the first century.* Liberals place Mark *within c. 40 years of Jesus' death.* More conservative scholars date all the synoptic gospels *within c. 30 years of Jesus' death,* placing Mark within *c. 10-20 years of Jesus' death.* According to F.F. Bruce, 'even with the later dates, the situation is encouraging from the historian's point of view, for the first three Gospels were written at a time when many were alive who could remember the things that Jesus said and did, and some at least would still be alive when the fourth Gospel was written.'[24] However, 'in recent years, there has been a trend in New Testament studies towards dating the Gospels earlier.'[25] For example, Dr James G. Crossley, of the Department of Biblical Studies at the University of Sheffield and co-chair of the Jesus Seminar for the British New Testament Conference, recently published a book arguing that the gospel of Mark was written *between the mid-30s and mid-40s AD*! As Carsten Peter Thiede reports, 'those who argue for early dates of authentic Gospels as sources of information about an historical Jesus . . . are no longer the conservative or fundamentalist outsiders.'[26]

Link 1

J.P. Moreland states that 'a strong case could be made for the fact that much of the New Testament, including the Gospels and the sources behind them, was written by eyewitnesses.'[27] Most of these eye-witnesses were martyred for refusing to renounce their claims, a fact which speaks to their *sincerity* if not their accuracy.[28] R.T. France writes:

> Luke, the doctor who was a companion of Paul (Colossians 4:14; 2 Timothy 4:11; Philemon 24) is the most widely accepted, as the author of both the third gospel and its sequel, the Acts of the Apostles. Mark, similarly a colleague of Paul (Acts 12:25; 15:37–41; Colossians 4:10; 2 Timothy 4:11; Philemon 24), but also, if the same Mark is intended, a companion of Peter (1 Peter 5:13), is accepted by many as at least a possible author of the second gospel . . . There are in fact weighty defenders today of the traditional authorship of all four gospels . . . I find all four traditional ascriptions at least plausible.[29]

Walter A. Elwell and Robert W. Yarbrough note that 'according to the best evidence available from the early years of the church, three of the four gospels are directly linked to the apostles; the fourth, Luke, by his own testimony (Luke 1:1–4), was dependent on eye-witnesses and those who had known Jesus from the beginning.'[30] According to Blomberg, 'a good case can still be made for

Matthew, Mark, Luke, and John as the authors of the Gospels that have traditionally been attributed to them'.[31] Christians probably wouldn't attribute gospels to such peripheral characters as Mark, Luke, and even Matthew, if they didn't write them: 'Mark and Luke, after all, were not among Jesus' twelve apostles . . . Though an apostle, Matthew is best known for . . . his unscrupulous past as a [tax-collector].'[32]

The synoptic gospels were probably all written (by – or at least with the input of – the people whose name they now bare) *within 30 years of the crucifixion*; in the order of: Mark (40s to mid 50s), Matthew (mid 50s to early 60s) and Luke (late 50s to early 60s). France testifies, 'It is . . . probable that some . . . of the gospels were written in substantially their present form within thirty years of the events, and that much of the material was already collected and written a decade or two before that.'[33] Mark is widely accepted as the first gospel to have been written, and hence 'the gospel with the highest claims to be accepted as a reliable historical source'.[34] Moreover, 'Many gospel critics will accept the earlier existence of a written collection of Jesus' sayings (usually called 'Q') on which both Matthew and Luke drew . . .'[35] This 'source' material, absent from Mark but common to Matthew and Luke, would date from the mid 50s *or earlier*.

Of course, the gospels are not our only extant historical source of information about Jesus.

Paul's Letters
According to Moreland, 'an objective historian would agree that we possess from seven to thirteen letters from the hand of Paul. Most of these letters are dated from 49 to 65.'[36] Alister McGrath confirms that 'The New Testament letters . . . date mainly from the period AD 49-69, and provide confirmation of the importance and interpretations of Jesus in this formative period.'[37] That is, 'a concept of a divine Jesus was already present, at the latest, within sixteen to twenty years after the crucifixion.'[38] Moreover:

Paul's letters contain a number of creeds and hymns (Rom 1:3–4; 1 Cor. 11:23 ff.; 15:3–8; Phil. 2:6–11; Col. 1:15–18; 1 Tim. 2:8 . . .) . . . they use language which is not characteristically Pauline, they often translate easily back into Aramaic, and they show features of Hebrew poetry and thought-forms. This means that they came into existence while the church was heavily Jewish and that they became standard, recognized creeds and hymns well before their incorporation into Paul's letters.[39]

These creeds and hymns testify to 'the death, resurrection, and deity of Christ. They consistently present a portrait of a miraculous and divine Jesus who rose from the dead . . . In sum, the idea of a fully divine, miracle-working Jesus who rose from the dead was present during the first decade of Christianity. Such a view was not a legend which arose several decades after the crucifixion.'[40]

1 Corinthians was written c. AD 55 to a Gentile congregation. Paul closes his letter using the Aramaic phrase *maranatha* (from the Aramaic *mar*, meaning 'God' or 'Deity'), imploring Jesus *as God* to 'come quickly':

> Why would Paul use an Aramaic word of closing to a Greek-speaking congregation which did not understand Aramaic? The answer would seem to be that this had become a standard form of address by the time Paul had visited Corinth in [AD] 50 . . . Where did this form of address arise? It would surely be in the early Jewish church. Thus, once again we have historical evidence that belief in a divine Jesus . . . originated in [an early] Jewish context.[41]

Moreover, 1 Corinthians 15 contains what 'virtually all scholars agree'[42] is an ancient creed recording the death, burial and resurrection appearances of Jesus: 'scholars generally agree that this report has an extremely early origin.'[43] Joachim Jeremias calls it 'the earliest tradition of all'.[44]

> typically, scholars date Paul's reception of this formula to two to eight years after the crucifixion itself, or from about AD 32–38. Most of those who comment on the issue hold that Paul most likely received this material shortly after his conversion during his visit to Jerusalem with Peter and James, who are included in the list of appearances (1 Cor 15:5; 7; Gal 1:18–19).[45]

Blomberg argues that 'it is plausible to date this information to the year of Paul's conversion, perhaps as early as AD 32.'[46] And if Paul received this creed from Peter and James, they had to have it before they gave it to him! Thus 'this ancient formula is an invaluable report of the original eye-witnesses' experience.'[47]

Non-Christian Confirmation
Michel Onfray asserts that there are only 'two or three vague references' to Jesus 'in ancient texts'.[48] However, Gary R. Habermas explains that:

> a number of ancient secular sources mention various aspects of Jesus' life, corroborating the picture presented by the Gospels. The writers of these sources include ancient historians such as Tacitus, Suetonius, and Thallus. Jewish sources such as Josephus and the Talmud add to our knowledge. Government officials such as Pliny the Younger and even Roman Caesars Trajan and Hadrian describe early Christian beliefs and practices. Greek historian and satirist Lucian and Syrian Mara Bar-Serapion provide other details . . . at least seventeen non-Christian writings record more than fifty details concerning the life, teachings, death, and resurrection of Jesus, plus details concerning the earliest church. Most frequently reported is Jesus' death, mentioned by twelve sources. Dated approximately 20 to 150 years after Jesus' death, these secular sources are quite early by the standards of ancient historiography.[49]

These sources tell us that

- Jesus lived during time of Tiberius Caesar.
- He was virtuous.
- He worked wonders.
- He had a brother named James.
- He was acclaimed as the Messiah.
- He was crucified under Pontius Pilate.
- He was crucified on the eve of the Jewish Passover.
- Darkness and an earthquake occurred when he died.
- His disciples believed he rose from the dead.
- His disciples were willing to die for their belief.

- Christianity spread rapidly as far as Rome.
- His disciples denied the Roman gods and worshiped Jesus as God.[50]

Blomberg points out that, by combining the evidence from first- to third-century Greco-Roman writers, including Thallus, Pliny the Younger, Tacitus, Lucian of Samosata, and Mara bar Serapion: 'one can clearly accumulate enough evidence to refute the fanciful notion that Jesus never existed, without even appealing to the testimony of Jewish or Christian sources. [This evidence includes] references to his crucifixion, being worshipped as a god, working miracles, having an unusual birth, and being viewed as a sage, king and an instigator of a controversy . . .'[51]

Archaeological Confirmation
Archaeology can be used to check the reliability of the gospel writers in various matters, and when a reporter proves accurate in matters we can check for ourselves, our confidence concerning their accuracy in matters we cannot check for ourselves is increased: 'Besides the general outline of New Testament history confirmed by secular sources close to Christ, there is specific confirmation of specific facts of New Testament history from archaeology . . . There are literally hundreds of archaeological finds that support specific persons, events, and facts presented in Luke-Acts . . .'[52] For example:

> During the excavation of a Roman theatre in Caesarea, a stone was found in the landing of a flight of steps. It bears the inscription 'To the people of Caesarea Tiberium Pontius Pilate Prefect of Judea.' Another line seems to indicate the word meaning 'dedication.' It is likely the stone was originally placed on an outside wall to commemorate the theatre's construction.[53]

Then again, two stone ossuries (boxes for the re-burial of bones) discovered outside Jerusalem in 1945 by Eleasar L. Sukenik were marked with four crosses and the words *Iesous iou* ('Jesus, help') and *Iesous aloth* ('Jesus, let him rise'). These ossuries have been dated to c. AD 50, just twenty years after Jesus' crucifixion.

Good to Go

A.N. Sherwin-White studied the rate at which legend accumulated in the ancient world. He concluded that a span of two generations is not sufficient for legend to wipe out a sold core of historical facts. But as Moreland writes, 'The picture of Jesus in the New Testament was established well within that length of time.'[55] Paul Copan argues:

> Given (1) the importance of memorization and oral tradition in first-century Palestine, (2) the practice of (occasionally) writing down and preserving the teachings of rabbis by their disciples, (3) the fact that the vast majority of Jesus' teaching was in poetic (and easily memorable) form, (4) the importance and revered status of religious traditions in Palestine, and (5) the presence of apostolic authority in Jerusalem to ensure the accurate transmission of tradition (and to check potential heresy), we have good reason to believe that the material in the Gospels was carefully and correctly set down.[56]

I agree with Blomberg that: 'on sheer historical grounds alone there is substantial reason to believe in the *general* trustworthiness of the Gospel tradition.'[57]

Who Was Jesus?

Historian Jaroslav Pelikan points out that the oldest Christian sermon, the oldest account of a Christian martyr, the oldest pagan report of the church, and the oldest liturgical prayer (1 Corinthians 16:22) *all* refer to Jesus as Lord and God. Turning to the gospels, we find that while Jesus didn't go around saying 'I'm God', he *did* lay claim to divinity in a host of ways. As Paul Copan notes:

> *Jesus claimed certain functions and abilities that were reserved for God alone.* He said that he had authority to forgive sins – a claim understood to be a usurpation of divine prerogatives (Mark 2:1–12). He claimed that he was the *ultimate judge* of all, the one to determine

every human's destiny (Matt. 7:21–23; 25:31ff.). He identified himself as *David's "Lord"* (Matt. 22:41–46). He used the language of
kingship and expressed his intent to set up a new rule that included his disciple's ruling with him (Matt. 19:28). *He challenged
others to follow him and required that their devotion to him surpass even
familial commitments* (Matt. 10:34–33) . . . He maintained that his
words will never pass away (Mark 13:31) – a claim made about
God's words in Isaiah 40:8.[58]

William Lane Craig reports that 'New Testament critics have
reached something of a consensus that the historical Jesus came
on the scene with an unprecedented sense of divine authority, the
authority to stand and speak in God's place. That's why the
Jewish leadership instigated his crucifixion for the charge of blas-
phemy . . .'[59] As N.T. Wright concludes, Jesus 'believed himself
called to do and be what, in the scriptures, only Israel's God did
and was'.[60]

After investigating Jesus' claims, John Rist, Professor of
Classics and Philosophy at the University of Toronto, concluded
that:

> the full range of Christian claims must go back to the very earli-
> est followers of Jesus, and in all probability to Jesus himself. The
> solution that either Jesus was a lunatic or his earliest followers
> were all blatant liars again seemed the only alternative possibil-
> ity if their claims were false. I could no longer delude myself that
> 'real' scholarship told us that we have no evidence that Jesus him-
> self, as well as the earliest generation of his followers, made
> claims for his divinity. The attempt of the biblical critics to show
> that such claims grew up (or were fabricated) within the Church
> seemed to be a tissue of bad argument, unhistorical treatment of
> the sources and wishful thinking: the wish being to make
> Christianity acceptable to the conventional 'liberal' orthodoxy . . .
> of the nineteenth and twentieth centuries. The resulting 'scholar-
> ship' was defective to a degree that would not be acceptable in
> other philological disciplines. When I saw this clearly . . . I had to
> decide only whether the totality of Jesus' recorded behaviour
> looked like that of a madman; it was not difficult to see that it did
> not.[61]

Jesus' claims raise the questions, 'Was he lying? Was he mad?' If he wasn't lying, then he must have been sincere. And if he was sincere, then his claim was either true or false. If it was false, then Jesus was sincerely deluded about his selfhood in such a fundamental way that it can only be described as madness. Therefore, given his claims, *if Jesus was neither lying nor mad, then he was both sincere and correct.* Dawkins attempts to dispense with this argument by suggesting that Jesus was simply 'honestly mistaken'. But as Mike King writes, 'anyone "honestly mistaken" in such a way would inevitably by considered insane. But why should Dawkins *et al.* not be content to simply dismiss Jesus as mad or bad? Quite clearly, it is because even a rudimentary flick through Jesus' life demonstrates both of these possibilities to be untenable.'[62]

Conclusion

Concerning doubts about the historical reliability of the New Testament witness to Jesus, it is important to distinguish between: a) doubts based upon naturalistic philosophical assumptions (e.g. that miracles can't happen), and b) doubts about the chain of evidence from the historical events to the gospels we have today. Dawkins is no expert on the New Testament, and a perusal of his sources shows that he depends upon scholars like Bart Ehrman, who follows David Hume's notorious arguments against the supportability of miracles. However, as William Lane Craig writes, 'those who are familiar with contemporary philosophy . . . know that Hume's arguments are today widely rejected as fallacious.'[63] For example, agnostic philosopher John Earman concludes, 'I find it astonishing how well posterity has treated "Of Miracles," given how completely the confection collapses under a little probing.'[64] And as Antony Flew affirms, if one is even agnostic about the existence of God, then one must be open to the possibility of revelation, for 'You cannot limit the possibilities of omnipotence except to produce the logically impossible. Everything else is open to omnipotence.'[65] Craig thus comments that 'If we are at least open to [God], then miraculous events cannot be ruled out in advance.

We have to be open to looking honestly at the evidence . . .'[66] Dawkins' critique of the New Testament in general (and his failure to even consider the evidence for Jesus' resurrection in particular) is grounded in an unsustainable philosophical commitment to naturalistic explanations, rather than in objective historical analysis.

This *a priori* dynamic is common currency among the New Atheists. For example, Michel Onfray asserts that when it comes to 'so-called holy books . . . We should approach the whole corpus from a . . . historical, philosophical . . . standpoint hostile to the belief that these texts were inspired . . . by God. None of them is a work of revelation. Who would have done the revealing?'[67] Hence, with New Testament scholar R.T. France, we should recognize that:

> At the level of their literary and historical character we have good reason to treat the gospels seriously . . . Indeed, many ancient historians would count themselves fortunate to have four such responsible accounts written within a generation or two of the events and preserved in such a wealth of manuscript evidence . . . Beyond that point, the decision as to how far a scholar is willing to accept the record they offer is likely to be influenced more by his openness to a 'supernaturalist' world-view than by strictly historical considerations.[68]

Recommended Resources

Francis J. Beckwith (ed.), *To Everyone an Answer: A Case for the Christian Worldview* (Downers Grove, IL: IVP, 2004).

F.F. Bruce, *The New Testament Documents: Are They Reliable?, with a new foreword by N.T. Wright* (Grand Rapids, MI: Eerdmans, 2000).

John F. Ankerberg (ed.), Gary R. Habermas and Antony G.N. Flew, *Resurrected? An Atheist and Theist Dialogue* (Larkam, MD: Rowman & Littlefield, 2005).

Richard Bauckham, *Jesus and the Eyewitnesses: The Gospels as Eyewitness Testimony* (Grand Rapids, MI: Eerdmans, 2006).

Paul Barnett, *Is The New Testament Reliable?* (Downers Grove, IL: IVP, 2005).

Paul Barnett, *The Truth About Jesus: The Challenge of Evidence* (Sydney: Aquila Press, 2004).[3]

Craig L. Blomberg, *The Historical Reliability of the Gospels* (Downers Grove: IL: Apollos, 2007).

Paul Copan (ed.), *Will The Real Jesus Please Stand Up? A Debate between William Lane Craig and John Dominic Crossan* (Grand Rapids, MI: Baker, 1998).

Paul Copan and William Lane Craig (eds.), *Passionate Conviction: Contemporary Discourses on Christian Apologetics* (Nashville, TN: B&H Academic, 2007).

Paul Copan and Ronald K. Tacelli (eds.), *Jesus' Resurrection: Fact or Figment? A debate between William Lane Craig & Gerd Ludemann* (Downers Grove, IL: IVP, 2000).

William Lane Craig, *Reasonable Faith: Christian Truth and Apologetics* (Wheaton, IL: Crossway, 2008).[3]

William Lane Craig, *The Son Rises* (Eugene, OR: Wipf & Stock, 2000).

Stephen T. Davies, *Risen Indeed: Making Sense of the Resurrection* (London: SPCK, 1993).

John Earman, *Hume's Abject Failure: The Argument Against Miracles* (Oxford: Oxford University Press, 2006).

Craig A. Evans, *Fabricating Jesus: How Modern Scholars Distort the Gospels* (IVP, 2006).

R.T. France, *The Evidence for Jesus* (London: Hodder & Stoughton, 1986).

R. Douglas Geivett and Gary R. Habermas (eds.), *In Defence of Miracles: A Comprehensive Case for God's Action in History* (Leicester: Apollos, 1997).

Gary R. Habermas and Michael R. Licona, *The Case for the Resurrection of Jesus* (Grand Rapids, MI: Kregel, 2004).

Gary R. Habermas, *The Historical Jesus: Ancient Evidence for the Life of Christ* (Joplin, MO: College Press, 2001).

Gary R. Habermas, *Ancient Evidence for the Life of Jesus: Historical Records of His Death and Resurrection* (Nashville, TN: Thomas Nelson, 1984).

Timothy Paul Jones, *Misquoting Truth: A Guide to the Fallacies of Bart Ehrman's "Misquoting Jesus"* (Downers Grove, IL: IVP, 2008).

C.S. Lewis, *Miracles* (London: Fount, 1998).

Terry L. Miethe (ed.), Gary R. Habermas and Anthony Flew, *Did Jesus Rise from the Dead? The Resurrection Debate* (San Francisco, CA: Harper & Rowe, 1987).

Michael R. Molnar, *The Star of Bethlehem: The Legacy of the Magi* (New Brunswick, NJ: Rutgers University Press, 2000).

Amy Orr-Ewing, *Why Trust The Bible? Answers to 10 tough questions* (Leicester: IVP, 2005).

Randall Price, *The Stones Cry Out: What Archaeology Reveals About the Truth of the Bible* (Eugene, OR: Harvest House, 1997).

Charles L. Quarles (ed.), *Buried Hope or Risen Savior? The Search For The Jesus Tomb* (Nashville, TX: Holman, 2008).

Jeffery L. Sheler, *Is The Bible True?* (San Francisco, CA: Harper Collins, 2000).

Graham N. Stanton, *The Gospels and Jesus* (Oxford: Oxford University Press, 2002²).

Lee Strobel, *The Case For The Real Jesus: A Journalist Investigates Current Attacks on the Identity of Christ* (Grand Rapids, MI: Zondervan, 2007).

Lee Strobel, *The Case for Christ: A Journalists' Personal Investigation of the Evidence for Jesus* (San Francisco: Harper Collins, 1998).

Richard Swinburne, *The Resurrection of God Incarnate* (Oxford: Clarendon Press, 2003).

Richard Swinburne, *Was Jesus God?* (Oxford: Oxford University Press, 2008).

Peter Walker, *The Weekend that Changed the World: The Mystery of Jerusalem's Empty Tomb* (London: Marshall Pickering, 1999).

John Wenham, *Easter Enigma: Are the resurrection accounts in conflict?* (Carlisle: Paternoster, 1992).

Michael J. Wilkins and J.P. Moreland (eds.), *Jesus Under Fire – Modern Scholarship Reinvents the Historical Jesus* (Carlisle: Paternoster, 1996).

N.T. Wright, *What Saint Paul Really Said: Was Paul of Tarsus the Real Founder of Christianity?* (Grand Rapids: Eerdmans, 1997).

N.T. Wright, *The Resurrection of the Son of God* (London: SPCK, 2003).

Websites

Apollos, 'Historical Reliability of the New Testament', www.apollos.ws/nt-historical-reliability/.

Bethinking.org, 'Jesus & History', www.bethinking.org/categories.php?CategoryID=2.

Bethinking.org, 'Resurrection & Miracles', www.bethinking.org/ categories.php?CategoryID=5.

William Lane Craig: Reasonable Faith, www.reasonablefaith. org/site/PageServer.

Gary R. Habermas, www.garyhabermas.com.

Lee Strobel, www.leestrobel.com/index.html.

Additional Sources

Craig L. Blomberg, 'The Historical Reliability of the Gospels', www.4truth.net/site/apps/nl/content3.asp?c=hiKXLbPNLrF &b=784441&ct=981289&printmode=1.

Craig L. Blomberg, 'The Historical Reliability of John', www.4truth.net/site/apps/nl/content3.asp?c=hiKXLbPNLrF &b=784441&ct=981291&printmode=1.

Craig L. Blomberg, 'In Search of the Historical Jesus', www.veritas.org/mediafiles/VT-Blomberg%20UCSB-XC.mov.

F.F. Bruce, 'The New Testament Documents: Are They Reliable?', http://ananswer.org/school/certification/ntdocumentsand-reliability/new%20testament%20documents%20are%20they% 20reliable_%20ff%20bruce.pdf.

Paul Copan, 'You Can't Trust the Gospels. They're Unreliable', www.countercult.com/r14ac.html.

William Lane Craig, 'The Problem of Miracles: A Historical and Philosophical Perspective', www.reasonablefaith.org/site/ News2?page=NewsArticle&id=5212.

William Lane Craig and Bart Ehrman, 'Is There Historical Evidence for the Resurrection of Jesus?', www.holycross.edu/ departments/crec/website/resurrdebate.htm.

William Lane Craig, 'Defending the True Historical Jesus', www.isucru.com/debate/audio/Defending%20the%20True% 20historical%20Jesus%20by%.

William Lane Craig vs. John Dominic Crossan, 'Will the real Jesus please stand up?', www.bringyou.to/CraigCrossanDebate. mp3.

William Lane Craig vs. Gerd Ludemann, 'Jesus' Resurrection: Fact or Figment?', www.bringyou.to/CraigLudemannResur-rectionDebate.mp3.

William Lane Craig vs. Hector Avalos, 'The Resurrection: Fact or Fiction?', www.bringyou.to/CraigAvalosResurrectionDebate. mp3.

William Lane Craig, 'Who Does Jesus Think He Was?,' www.rfmedia.org/RF_audio_video/Otherclips/National-FacultyLeadershipConf-2008/Who-Jesus-Think-He-Was.mp3.

Stephen T. Davis, 'Was Jesus Mad, Bad or God?', www.apollos.ws/trilemma/microsoft%20word%20-%20davis-stephentt1.pdf.

R.T. France, 'The Gospels as Historical Sources for Jesus', www.leaderu.com/truth/1truth21.html.

Gary R. Habermas, 'The Da Vinci Code', www.bringyou.to/apologetics/HabermasDaVinciCode.mp3.

Peter Kreeft and Ronald Tacelli, 'Evidence for the Resurrection of Christ', http://hometown.aol.com/philvaz/articles/num9.htm.

Peter Kreeft, 'The Divinity of Christ', http://catholiceducation.org/articles/religion/re0020.html.

J.P. Moreland, 'The Historicity of the New Testament', www.apologetics.org/books/historicity.html.

J.P. Moreland, 'A Legendary Jesus and New Testament Dating', www.trueu.org/Academics/LectureHall/A000000262.cfm.

J.P. Moreland, 'The Modern Search for the Historic Jesus', www.veritas.org/mediafiles/VTS-Moreland-1997-UNCA-97VFNC04.mp3.

J.P. Moreland, 'The Search for the Historical Jesus', Parts 1–7, www.youtube.com/watch?v=HA2d5jOpsH0&feature=PlayList&p=5C3ED050A38A301B&index=0.

Doug Smith, 'Dispelling Muslim Myths about the Gospels', www.ses.edu/journal/articles/3.1Smith.pdf.

Richard Swinburne, 'Historical Evidence for the Resurrection', www.blackhawkmedia.org/MP3/Swinburne3.mp3.

Peter S. Williams, 'The Impossible Planet & The Satin Pit', www.damaris.org/content/content.php?type=5&id=492.

Peter S. Williams, 'The Shroud of Turin: A Cumulative Case for Authenticity', www.case.edu.au/uploads/media/The_20Shroud_20of_20Turin.pdf.

Ravi Zacharias and William Lane Craig, 'The Top 5 Questions: Part IV – The Resurrection of Jesus', www.rzim.org/radio/archives.php?p=LMPT&v=detail&id=219.

Videos

Gary R. Habermas Video Clips, www.youtube.com/profile_videos?user=toolsfortalks&p=r.

Lee Strobel and Garry Poole, *Discussing the Da Vinci Code* (Zondervan, 2006).

N.T. Wright, *Resurrection* (IVP Connect, 2003).

Selected Resources

General Responses to 'The New Atheism'

Aikman, David, *The Delusion of Disbelief: Why the New Atheism Is a Threat to Your Life, Liberty, and Pursuit of Happiness* (Carol Stream: Salt River, 2008).

Beattie, Tina, *The New Atheists: The Twilight of Reason and The War On Religion* (London: DLT, 2007).

Berlinski, David, *The Devil's Delusion: Atheism and Its Scientific Pretensions* (New York, NY: Crown Forum, 2008).

Day, Vox, *The Irrational Atheist: Dissecting the Unholy Trinity of Dawkins, Harris, and Hitchens* (Dallas, TX: BenBella, 2008).

D'Souza, Dinesh, *What's So Great About Christianity?* (Washington, DC: Regnery, 2007).

Garrison, Becky, *The New Atheist Crusaders And Their Unholy Grail* (Nashville, TN: Thomas Nelson, 2007).

Johnson, George, 'A Free-for-All on Science and Religion', *New York Times*, 23 Nov 2006, www.nytimes.com/2006/11/21/science/21belief.html?_r=2&oref=slogin&pagewanted=print.

Marshall, David, *The Truth Behind The New Atheism* (Eugene, OR: Harvest House, 2007).

Robertson, David, 'The New Atheism – A Publishing Phenomenon', www.freechurch.org/issues/2007/sept07.htm.

Spencer, Robert, *Religion of Peace? Why Christianity Is And Islam Isn't* (Washington, DC: Regnery, 2007).

Steinfels, Peter, 'Books on Atheism Are Raising Hackles in Unlikely Places', *New York Times*, 3 March 2007, www.nytimes.com/2007/03/03/books/03beliefs.html?_r=1&ref=us&oref=slogin.

Stewart, Robert B., (ed.), *The Future of Atheism: Alister McGrath and Daniel Dennett in Dialogue* (Minneapolis, PA: Fortress, 2008).

Ward, Keith, *Is Religion Dangerous?* (Oxford: Lion, 2006).

Williams, Thomas D., *Greater Than You Think: A Theologian Answers the Atheists About God* (New York, Faith Words, 2008).

Wolf, Gary, 'The Church of the Non-Believers', *Wired* Magazine, Nov 2006, www.wired.com/wired/archive/14.11/atheism_pr.html.

Zacharias, Ravi, *The End of Reason: A Response to the New Atheists* (Grand Rapids, MI: Zondervan, 2008).

Audio

David Berlinski (interviewed by Casey Luskin), 'The Devil's Delusion', http://intelligentdesign.podomatic.com/entry/2008-04-16T16_23_01-07_00#.

The Kindlings Muse, 'The New Atheists: Part 1', www.thekindlings.com/wp-content/uploads/tkm021207newatheist1.mp3.

The Kindlings Muse, 'The New Atheists: Part 2', www.thekindlings.com/wp-content/uploads/tkm021207newatheist2.mp3.

'Unbelievable: David Marshall and Barry Duke discuss The New Atheism', http://media.premier.org.uk/unbelievable/a92b0e86-c5af-4740-ac40-a7d584ed8843.mp3.

Unbelievable, www.premierradio.org.uk/shows/saturday/unbelievable.aspx?mod_page=0.

Wired Interview with Gary Wolf, http://sonibyte.com/audio/raw/1569.mp3.

Vdeo

David Berlinski, 'The Devil's Delusion: Atheism and Its Scientific Pretensions', www.booktv.org/program.aspx?ProgramId=9256&SectionName=&PlayMedia=No.

Nicky Gumbel, 'Is God a Delusion Series', www.htb.org.uk/audio/is-god-a-delusion.

Albert R. Mohler, 'W. H. Griffith Thomas Memorial Lectureship 2008: The New Atheism– Parts I—IV', www.dts.edu/media/series/?SeriesID=77.

Responses to Richard Dawkins' *The God Delusion*

Beckwith, Francis J., 'The Irrationality of Richard Dawkins', www.firstthings.com/onthesquare/?p=776.

Brown, Andrew, 'Dawkins the Dogmatist', www.prospect-magazine.co.uk/article_details.php?id=7803.

Cornwell, John, *Darwin's Angel: An Angelic Reposte to The God Delusion* (London: Profile, 2007).

Craig, William Lane, 'Dawkins' argument against God', www.reasonablefaith.org/site/News2?page=NewsArticle&id=5493.

Crean, Thomas, *A Catholic Replies to Professor Dawkins* (Family Publications, 2007).

Eagleton, Terry, 'Lunging, Flailing, Mispunching', *London Review of Books*, 28 (20), 19 October 2006, www.lrb.co.uk/v28/n20/eagl01_.html.

Edwards, Chuck, 'Dawkins' Delusional Arguments Against God', www.summit.org/resource/tc/archive/0407/.

Hahn, Scott and Benjamin Wiker, *Answering the New Atheism: Dismantling Dawkins' Case Against God* (Steubenville, OH: Emmaus Road Publishing, 2008).

Holt, Jim, 'Beyond Belief', www.nytimes.com/2006/10/22/books/review/Holt.t.html?_r=2&ei=5070&en=4269d64c4939d0f6&ex=1189828800&pagewanted=a&oref=slogin&oref=slogin.

King, Mike, *The God Delusion Revisited* (Lulu, 2007).

Kirk, Richard, 'An Exercise in Contempt', www.spectator.org/dsp_article.asp?art_id=10729.

McGrath, Alister, *The Dawkins Delusion* (London: SPCK, 2007).

Nagel, Thomas, 'The Fear of Religion', The New Republic Online, www.tnr.com/doc.mhtml?i=20061023&s=nagel102306.

Orr, H. Allen, 'A Mission to Convert', www.nybooks.com/articles/1977[5.]

Penfold, Michael J., 'Atheist Delusion', www.atheistdelusion.net/.

Plantinga, Alvin, 'The Dawkins Confusion', www.christianitytoday.com/bc/2007/002/1.21.html.

Robertson, David, *The Dawkins Letters: Challenging Atheist Myths* (Tain: Christian Focus, 2007).

Swinburne, Richard, 'Response to Richard Dawkins's Criticisms in *The God Delusion*', http://users.ox.ac.uk/~orie0087/ framesetpdfs.shtml.

Ward, Keith, *Why There Almost Certainly Is a God: Doubting Dawkins* (Oxford: Lion, 2008).

Wilson, Andrew, *Deluded by Dawkins? A Christian Response to The God Delusion* (Eastbourne: Kingsway, 2007).

Williams, Peter S., 'The Big Bad Wolf, Theism and the Foundations of Intelligent Design Theory', www.arn.org/docs/williams/pw_goddelusionreview.htm.

Williams, Peter S., 'Whose Afraid of the Big Bad Wolf? Richard Dawkins' Failed Rebuttal of Natural Theology', www.arn.org/docs/williams/pw_goddelusionreview2.htm.

Williams, Peter S., 'Who's Afraid of the Big Bad Wolf?', www.damaris.org/content/content.php?type=5&id=501.

Williams, Peter S., 'Calling Dawkins' Bluff', www.damaris.org/content/content.php?type=5&id=503.

Zwartz, Barney, 'The God Delusion', www.theage.com.au/news/book-reviews/the-god-delusion/2006/11/24/1164341383277.html?page=fullpage.

Audio

William Lane Craig, 'Craig's Response to *The God Delusion*', www.rfmedia.org/RF_audio_video/Other_clips/UF-Responding-to-Dawkins-The-God-Delusion/UF_Bill_Craig's_Response_to_The_God_Delusion.mp3.

McGrath, Alister, 'Is God a Delusion?', www.atheistdelusion.net/www.citychurchsf.org/openforum/Audio/OF_Alister_McGrath.mp3.

Williams, Peter S., 'Richard Dawkins' *The God Delusion*', www.damaris.org/content/content.php?type=5&id=512.

Williams, Peter S., '*The God Delusion* Deconstructed – Southampton University', www.ecs.soton.ac.uk/~pjb304/SUCU_talks/eternity/2007-02-15-PeteWilliams-TheGodDelusionDeconstructed.mp3.

Video

William Lane Craig, 'Response to Dawkins' Central Argument,' www.apologetics.com/index.php?option=com_content&view

=article&id=202:dr-craig-responds-to-dawkins-book-video&catid=57;philosophy-of-science&Itemid=62.

Responses to Daniel Dennett's *Breaking the Spell*

Cornwell, John, 'Religion as a Natural Phenomenon', www.timesonline.co.uk/tol/news/uk/science/article730931.ece.

Hart, David B., 'Daniel Dennett Hunts the Snark', www.firstthings.com/article.php3?id_article=5394.

Kirsch, Adam, 'If Men Are From Mars, What's God', www.nysun.com/article/27182.

Orr, H. Allan, 'The God Project', www.newyorker.com/archive/2006/04/03/060403crbo_books?currentPage=1.

Wieseltier, Leon, 'The God Genome', www.nytimes.com/2006/02/19/books/review/19wieseltier.html.

Winchester, Chris, 'Breaking the Spell: Religion as a Natural Phenomenon', www.reasons.org/resources/apologetics/other_papers/breaking_the_spell.shtml.

Audio

Dennett, Daniel vs. David Cook, 'Discussing Religion', http://archive.wgnradio.com:8080/ramgen/wgnam/shows/ex720/Audio/religion060215mr.rm.

Video

Dennett, Daniel vs. Dinesh D'Souza, 'Is God a Human Invention?', http://media.richarddawkins.net/video/2007/ DennettDinesh_all.mov.

Responses to Sam Harris' Letter to a Christian Nation

Leahy, Michael Patrick, *Letter to an Atheist* (Thompsons Station, TN: Harpeth River, 2007).

Metcalf, R.C., *Letter to a Christian Nation: Counter Point* (Lincoln, NI: iUniverse, 2007).

Audio

Craig, William Lane, 'Thoughts on Sam Harris' Claims', www.rfmedia.org/RF_audio_video/Other_clips/Thoughts-on-Sam-Harris-claims.mp3.

Responses to A.C. Grayling's *Against All God's*

Williams, Peter S., 'A Christian Response to *Against All Gods*. Part One: Intellectual Respectability', www.bethinking.org/resource.php? ID=385.
Williams, Peter S., 'A Christian Response to *Against All Gods*. Part Two: Ethical Respectability', www.bethinking.org/resource.php?ID=392.

Responses to Christopher Hitchen's *God Is not Great*

Hitchens, Peter, 'Hitchens v. Hitchens', www.dailymail.co.uk/pages/live/articles/news/newscomment.html?in_article_id=459427&in_page_id=1787&in_a_source.
Roberts, Mark, 'God is not Great by Christopher Hitchens: A Response', www.markdroberts.com/htmfiles/resources/godisnotgreat.htm.
Skapinker, Michael, 'Here's the Hitch', www.ft.com/cms/s/0/6afa3a28-1ecd-11dc-bc22-000b5df10621.html.

Audio

Hitchens, Christopher vs. Mark Roberts, www.bringyou.to/HitchensRobertsDebate.mp3.

Video

Hitchens, Christopher vs. Dinesh D'Souza, 'Is Christianity the Problem?', http://216.75.61.152/xstream/neproductions/tkc/debate.wmv.
Hitchens, Christopher vs. Alister McGrath, 'Poison or Cure? Religious Belief in the Modern World', www.eppc.org/publications/pageID.390/default.asp.

Hitchens, Christopher vs. Peter Hitchens, 'God Does Not Exist: And He Is Not Great: Part 1 & ff.', www.youtube.com/watch?v=M5cxwq6QK7o&feature=PlayList&p=D235CA219715C124&index=4.

Responses to Victor Stenger's *God: The Failed Hypothesis*

George Ellis, 'Case Not Proved', http://physicsworld.com/cws/article/print/27736.
Benjamin Wiker, 'The Atheist's Benchwarmer', www.discovery.org/a/4220.
Audio

William Lane Craig vs. Victor Stenger, 'Does God Exist?', www.bringyou.to/CraigStengerDebate.mp3.

Responses to Michel Onfray's *In Defence of Atheism*

Amarnath Amarasingam, 'A Review of Michel Onfray's *In Defense of Atheism: The Case Against Christianity, Judaism, and Islam*', www.theotherjournal.com/article.php?id=320.
Benjamin A. Plotinsky, 'The Fanatical Philosopher: Michel Onfray's weak case against monotheism', www.city-journal.org/html/rev2007-02-01bp.html.

General Resources

Websites

Access Research Network: www.arn.org.
Apollos: www.apollos.ws/.
Bethinking: www.bethinking.org/.
Discovery Institute Centre for Science and Culture: www.discovery.org/csc/.
William Lane Craig – Reasonable Faith: www.reasonablefaith.org/site/PageServer.

Paul Copan: www.paulcopan.com/.

William A. Dembski: www.designinference.com/.

Gary R. Habermas: www.garyhabermas.com.

Peter Kreeft: www.peterkreeft.com/home.htm.

Alvin Plantinga: www.homestead.com/philofreligion/Plant-ingapage.html.

Richard Purtill, *Reason to Believe* (Grand Rapids, MI: Eerdmans, 1974), http://members.core.com/~tony233/Reason_to_Believe.htm.

Richard Swinburne: http://users.ox.ac.uk/~orie0087/frameset-pdfs.shtml.

Video

Apologia Project Video Library (mainly on science related issues), www.theapologiaproject.org/video_library.htm.

Lee Strobel – Investigating Faith, www.leestrobel.com/index.html.

Audio

Bethinking Audio Files, www.bethinking.org/audio.php.

William Lane Craig Audio-Visual, www.reasonablefaith.org/site/PageServer?pagename=audio_visuals.

William Lane Craig Pod-Casts, www.reasonablefaith.org/site/PageServer?pagename=podcasting_main.

ID The Future Podcast (Podcast about Evolution and Intelligent Design Theory), http://intelligentdesign.podomatic.com/.

Douglas Groothuis Apologetics Audio Lectures, www.relyonchrist.com/lecture.htm.

Lennox, John, 'Richard Dawkins', www.bethinking.org/resource.php?ID=290.

Lennox, John, 'Has Science Buried God?', http://media.premier.org.uk/unbelievable/8547ae5c-d48e-4221-b3a5-68d0df27df2a.mp3.

Peter S. Williams

ID.Plus Blog: http://idpluspeterswilliams.blogspot.com/.

ARN Featured Author: www.arn.org/authors/williams.html.

Evangelical Philosophical Society Web Author Profile, http://epsociety.org/library/authors.asp?mode=profile&pid=37.

Peter S. Williams' Podcasts, www.damaris.org/cm/podcasts/category/peterswilliams.

Peter has authored, co-authored or contributed to the following books:

The Case for God (Crowborough: Monarch, 1999).

The Case for Angels (Carlisle: Paternoster, 2002).

I Wish I Could Believe in Meaning: A Response to Nihilism (Southampton: Damaris, 2004).

Steve Couch, Tony Watkins and Peter S. Williams, *Back in Time: A Thinking Fan's Guide to Doctor Who* (Southampton: Damaris, 2005).

Steve Couch (ed.), *Matrix Revelations: A Thinking Fan's Guide to the Matrix Trilogy* (Southampton: Damaris, 2004).

Tony Watkins (ed.), *Truth Wars: Talking About Tolerance* (Southampton: Damaris, 2005).

Tony Watkins (ed.), *Sex and the Cynics: Talking About the Search for Love* (Southampton: Damaris, 2005).

Tony Watkins (ed.), *Playing God: Talking About Ethics in Medicine and Technology* (Southampton: Damaris, 2006).

Tony Watkins (ed.), *Spooked: Talking About the Supernatural* (Southampton: Damaris, 2006).

Endnotes

Preface

1. W.B. Yeats, 'To a Poet, who would have me Praise certain Bad Poets, Imitators of his and Mine', http://books.google.com/books?id= LhFLwsrI31MC&pg=PA76&lpg=PA76&dq=%E2%80%9CTo+a+Poet, +Who+Would+Have+Me+Praise+Certain+Bad+Poets,+Imitators+of +His+and+Mine.%E2%80%9D&source+=web&ots=Mn6gBd_n1P&s ig=pA5sOWqTsangh0ic9eSPCrp-ha4&hl=en.
2. See http://richarddawkins.net/article,2482,Flea-of-the-week,Rich-ardDawkinsnet.
3. Plato's *Apology*, translated by Benjamin Jowett, http://classics.mit. edu/Plato/apology.html.
4. Mario Beauregarde and Denyse O'Leary, *The Spiritual Brain: A Neuroscientist's Case for the Existence of the Soul* (New York: HarperOne, 2007), p. 167. On the Subject of Scepticism, I highly recommend J. Budziszewski's delightful essay, 'A Sceptical View Of Christianity', www.boundless.org/1999/regulars/office_hours/ a0000011.html.
5. Dinesh D'Souza, *What's So Great About Christianity?* (Washington, DC: Regnery, 2007), p. xvi.
6. Carl Sagan, *Pale Blue Dot: A Vision of the Human Future in Space* (Ballentine Books, 1994), p. 55.
7. C.S. Lewis, 'Myth Become Fact', in *God in the Dock* (London: Fount, 1998).

1. Atheism is Dead

1. Roy Abraham Varghese, *Great Thinkers On Great Questions* (Oxford: Oneworld, 1998), p. 2.

[2] Richard Dawkins, *The God Delusion* (London: Bantam, 2006), p. 13.

[3] Within the Judeo-Christian tradition God is of course no more male than female; rather, God's essential nature unites the *spiritually* (not physiologically!) *masculine and feminine* in a perfect unity; a spiritual unity the tradition considers to be reflected in the 'one-flesh' union of one male and one female in the institution of marriage. Biblical language about God is predominantly (but *not* exclusively) masculine, but one must remember that this is *analogical* language drawn from the culture of the writers. Since God is a personal being, rather than an impersonal thing, the English language forces us to use either 'he' or 'she' (a linguistic choice not faced in German, for example), or else the unwieldy 'he/she'. I will use 'he' with reference to God throughout this book, but the above comments should be borne in mind.

[4] David Robertson, 'The New Atheism – A Publishing Phenomenon', *The Scotsman*, 10 August 2007, www.freechurch.org/issues/2007/sept07.htm.

[5] Madeleine Bunting, 'The New Atheists loathe religion far too much to plausibly challenge it', www.guardian.co.uk/Columnists/Column/0,,2074075,00.html.

[6] David Aikman, 'The Atheist Onslaught', *Implications: A Journal from The Trinity Forum*, www.ttf.org/index/journal/detail/the-atheist-onslaught/.

[7] Christopher Hitchens, *Letters to a Young Contrarian* (Basic Books, 2001), quoted by http:en.wikipedia.org/wiki/Antitheism.

[8] Gary Wolf, 'The Church of the Non-Believers', *Wired Magazine*, November 2006, p. 184, www.wired.com/news/wiredmag/0,71985-0.html?tw=wn_index_1

[9] John Humphrys, *In God We Doubt: Confessions of a Failed Atheist* (London: Hodder & Stoughton, 2007), pp. 15–16.

[10] John Gray, 'The Atheist Delusion', *The Guardian*, 15 March 2008, http://books.guardian.co.uk/departments/politicsphilosophyandsociety/story/0,,2265446,00.html.

[11] Jeremy Stangroom, 'An Intelligent Person's Guide to Atheism', *New Humanist*, Winter 2001, p. 36.

[12] F.C. Copleston, in Bertrand Russell, *Why I Am Not A Christian* (London: Routledge, 1996), p. 133.

[13] Julian Baggini, *Atheism: A Very Short Introduction* (Oxford: Oxford University Press, 2003), p. 4.

[14] Ibid.

15 Ibid., p. 2.
16 Ibid., pp. 3–4.
17 Corliss Lamont, *The Philosophy of Humanism* (New York: Frederick Ungar, 1977), pp. 12–13.
18 An exemplary collection of papers critical of naturalism is William Lane Craig and J.P. Moreland (eds.), *Naturalism: A Critical Analysis* (London: Routledge, 2000). Papers include: Stewart Goetz, 'Naturalism and Libertarian Agency', www.independent.org/newsroom/article.asp?id=1756; Robert C. Koons, 'The Incompatibility of Naturalism and Scientific Realism', www.leaderu.com/offices/koons/docs/natreal.html; and Dallas Willard, 'Knowledge and Naturalism', www.dwillard.org/Philosophy/Pubs/knowledge_and_naturalism.htm. See also William Hasker, *The Emergent Self* (Cornell University Press, 1999); Angus Menuge, *Agents Under Fire: Materialism and the Rationality of Science* (Oxford: Rowman & Littlefield, 2004); Victor Reppert, *C.S. Lewis' Dangerous Idea: In Defence of the Argument from Reason* (Downers Grove: IVP, 2003); Alvin Plantinga, 'Against Materialism', http://maclaurin.org/mp3s/the_maclaurin_institute__copyright_2002.mp3.
19 John G. West, *Darwin Day in America* (Wilmington, DE: ISI, 2007), p. 370.
20 Steve William Fuller, 'Rebuttal of Dover Expert Reports', www2.ncseweb.org/kvd/all_legal/2005-03_expert_witnesses/2005-05-13_Fuller_Ds_expert_rebuttal_OCR.pdf.
21 Paul M. Zulehner, quoted by Uwe Siemon-Netto, 'God not so dead: Atheism worldwide in decline', www.worldtribune.com/worldtribune/WTARC/2005/cs_atheism_03_03.html.
22 See John Blanchard, *Does God Believe in Atheists?* (Darlington: Evangelical Press, 2000), p. 18.
23 B.A. Robinson, 'Religions of the World', www.religioustolerance.org/worldrel.htm.
24 Phil Zuckerman, 'Atheism: Contemporary Rates and Patterns', www.pitzer.edu/academics/faculty/zuckerman/atheism.html.
25 *Catholic Encyclopedia*, www.newadvent.org/cathen/01215c.htm.
26 C. Stephen Evans, *Pocket Dictionary of Apologetics and Philosophy of Religion* (Leicester: Apollos, 2002), p. 8.
27 Ibid, p. 9.
28 Norman L. Geisler, *Christian Apologetics* (Grand Rapids, MI: Baker, 1996), p. 20.

29 Ibid., p. 27.

30 Ibid., p. 26.

31 Francis Collins, *The Language of God* (New York: Free Press, 2006), p. 168.

32 George H. Smith, *Atheism: The Case Against God* (Amherst, NY: Promethius Books, 1989), pp. 8, 13.

33 Somerset Maugham, quoted by Colin Chapman, *Christianity on Trial* (Oxford: Lion, 1981), p. 198.

34 Stephen D. Schwarz, 'Introduction – Philosophy', in Roy Abraham Varghese (ed.), *The Intellectuals Speak Out about God* (Chicago, IL: Regnery Gateway, 1984), p. 116.

35 John Allen Paulos, 'The Self Is a Conceptual Chimera', in John Brockman (ed.), *What Is Your Dangerous Idea?* (London: Pocket Books, 2006), p. 154.

36 See 'May you live in interesting times', http://en.wikipedia.org /wiki/May_you_live_in_interesting_times.

37 Gavin Hyman, 'Atheism in Modern History', in Michael Martin (ed.), *The Cambridge Companion to Atheism* (Cambridge: Cambridge University Press, 2007), p. 32.

38 E.O. Wilson, 'Can biology do better than faith?', *New Scientist*, 5 November 2005, p. 49.

39 Keith Ward, *Is Religion Dangerous?* (Oxford: Lion, 2006), p. 91.

40 Zuckerman, 'Atheism: Contemporary Rates and Patterns', www.pitzer.edu/academics/faculty/zuckerman/atheism.html.

41 Vexen Crabtree, 'Religion in the United Kingdom: Diversity, Trends and Decline', 5 July 2007, www.vexen.co.uk/UK/religion.html.

42 Ibid.

43 Jonathan Petre, 'Migrants fill empty pews as Britons lose faith', *Daily Telegraph*, 18 September 2006, www.telegraph.co.uk/news/main.jhtml;jsessionid=T2GZX4THAYLE1QFIQMFCFWAV-CBQYIV0?xml=/news/2006/09/18/nchurch18.xml.

44 Jonathan Petre, http://blogs.telegraph.co.uk/ukcorrespondents/jonathanpetre/sept06/stateofthenation.htm.

45 Peter Brierley, 'The U.K. Church in 2020: If Trends Continue', www.lausanneworldpulse.com/trendsandstatistics/10-2005.

46 'Church "will be dead in 40 years time"', *The Independent*, 30 November 2006, http://news.independent.co.uk/uk/this_britain/article281604.ece.

47 'Church Attendance on the Rise', www.voice-online.co.uk/content.php?show=10278.

48 Tom Baldwin, 'Where God meets big business – and it's soon coming to a church near you', *The Times*, 27 December 2006.

49 Kelly James Clark, *Philosophers Who Believe*, Introduction, www.calvin.edu/academic/philosophy/writings/pwbintro.htm.

50 Ibid.

51 A.J. Ayer, *Language, Truth and Logic* (London: Victor Gollancz, 1946), p. 115.

52 Ibid., p. 175.

53 Victor Reppert, *C.S. Lewis's Dangerous Idea* (Downers Grove, IL: IVP, 2003), p. 20.

54 William Cash. 'Did atheist philosopher see God when he 'died'?', http://gonsalves.org/favorite/atheist.htm.

55 F.C. Copleston, *Contemporary Philosophy* (London: Burns & Oates, 1957), p. 9.

56 Hilary Spurling, 'The Wickedest Man in Oxford', www.nytimes.com/books/00/12/24/reviews/001224.24spurlit.html.

57 Anthony Kenny, 'The Wisdom of Not Knowing', *The Philosophers' Magazine*, Issue 37, 1st quarter 2007, p. 39.

58 Ibid.

59 Julian Baggini, 'The Wisdom of Not Knowing', *The Philosophers' Magazine*, Issue 37, 1st quarter 2007, pp. 38–39.

60 Paul Copan and William Lane Craig, 'Preface', *Passionate Conviction: Contemporary Discourses on Christian Apologetics* (Nashville, TN: B&H Academic, 2007), p. vii.

61 F. C. Copleston, *Contemporary Philosophy* (London: Burns & Oates), p. 9.

62 John Hick, 'Theology and Verification' in Basil Mitchell (ed.), *The Philosophy of Religion* (Oxford: Oxford University Press, 1971), p. 69.

63 Ibid., p. 71.

64 Basil Mitchell, 'Reflections on C.S. Lewis, Apologetics, and the Moral Tradition: Basil Mitchell in Conversation with Andrew Walker', in Andrew Walker and James Patrick (eds.), *Rumours of Heaven: Essays in Celebration of C.S. Lewis* (Guildford: Eagle, 1998), p. 19.

65 George Schlesinger, *Religion and Scientific Method* (Boston: D. Reidel, 1997), p. 5.

66 Dawkins, *The God Delusion*, pp. 46, 48.

67 Ibid., p. 361.

68 See 'Intelligent Design', www.newworldencyclopedia.org/entry/Intelligent_design; 'What is Intelligent Design?', www.arn.org/

idfaq/What%20is%20intelligent%20design.htm; 'CSC Top Quest-ions', www.discovery.org/csc/topQuestions.php.

[69] See Peter S. Williams, 'Design and the Humean Touchstone', www.arn.org/docs/williams/pw_humeantouchstone.htm.

[70] Dawkins, *The God Delusion*, p. 50.

[71] Ibid., p. 59.

[72] William Lane Craig, 'Naturalism and Intelligent Design' in Robert B. Stewart (ed.), *Intelligent Design: William A. Dembski and Michael Ruse in Dialogue* (Minneapolis: Fortress, 2007), pp. 70–71.

[73] R. Douglas Geivett, 'The evidential Value of Religious Experience', in Paul Copan and Paul K. Moser (eds.), *The Rationality of Theism* (London: Routledge, 2003), p. 175.

[74] William P. Alston, 'Religious Language and Verificationism', Copan and Moser (eds.), *The Rationality of Theism*, p. 21.

[75] Keith Ward, *God: A Guide for the Perplexed* (Oxford: Oneworld, 2002), p. 184.

[76] Clark, *Philosophers Who Believe*, Introduction, www.calvin.edu/aca-demic/philosophy/writings/pwbintro.htm.

[77] A.J. Ayer, quoted by Keith Ward, *The Turn of the Tide* (London: BBC Publications, 1986), p. 59.

[78] A.J. Ayer, *The Central Questions of Philosophy* (London: Penguin, 1973), pp. 22–34.

[79] A.J. Ayer, *The Listener*, 2 March 1978.

[80] A.J. Ayer in Varghese (ed.), *Great Thinkers on Great Questions*, p. 49.

[81] Tyler Burge, 'Philosophy of Language and Mind', *Philosophical Review* 101 (1992), p. 49.

[82] William Lane Craig, 'Theistic Critiques of Atheism', Martin (ed.), *The Cambridge Companion to Atheism*, p. 69.

[83] William Lane Craig, *Philosophy of Religion: A Reader and Guide* (Edinburgh: Edinburgh University Press, 2002), p. 1.

[84] Alvin Plantinga, *God and Other Minds* (Cornell University Press, 1967), p. 271.

[85] See Trent Dougherty, 'Concise introduction to the Modal Ontological Argument for the Existence of God', www.abarnett.demon.co.uk/atheism/ontol.html.

[86] Roger Scruton, *An Intelligent Person's Guide to Philosophy* (London: Duckworth, 1997), p. 93.

[87] Sam Harris, *Letter To A Christian Nation* (London: Bantam, 2007), p. 55.

88 William L. Rowe, 'The Problem of Evil and Some Varieties of Atheism', *American Philosophical Quarterly* 16 (1979).

89 Michael L. Peterson, William Hasker, Bruce Reichenbach, and David Basinger, *Reason and Religious Belief* (Oxford: Oxford University Press, 1991), p. 97.

90 William Lane Craig, www.leaderu.com/offices/billcraig/docs/craig-nielsen1.html.

91 Paul Draper, 'Seeking But Not Believing' in Daniel Howard Snyder and Paul K. Moser, *Divine Hiddenness: New Essays* (Cambridge: Cambridge University Press, 2002), p. 204

92 Paul Copan, *That's Just Your Interpretation* (Grand Rapids, MI: Baker, 2001), p. 96.

93 See William P. Alston, 'The Inductive Argument from Evil' and Stephen John Wykstra, 'Rowe's Noseeum Arguments from Evil', in Daniel Howard-Snyder (ed.), *The Evidential Problem of Evil* (Indiana University Press, 1996); Gregory E. Ganssle, 'God and Evil', Copan and Moser (eds.), *The Rationality of Theism*, p. 263; Alvin Plantinga, *Warranted Christian Belief* (Oxford: Oxford University Press, 2000).

94 Plantinga, *Warranted Christian Belief*, pp. 462–463.

95 Graham Oppy, 'Review: Suffering Belief', www.infidels.org/library/modern/graham_oppy/weisberger.html.

96 John G. Stackhouse, 'Mind Over Skepticism', http://ctlibrary.com/7937.

97 Ibid.

98 William Lane Craig, 'The Cosmological Argument', in Copan and Moser (eds.), *The Rationality of Theism*, p. 112.

99 John T. Elson, 'Is God Dead?', *Time Magazine*, 8 April 1966.

100 Craig, *Philosophy of Religion: A Reader and Guide*, p. 1.

101 'Modernizing the Case for God', *Time Magazine*, 7 April 1980, pp. 65–66.

102 William Lane Craig, 'The Resurrection of Theism', *Truth Journal*, updated 8 August 1997, www.leaderu.com/truth/3truth01.html.

103 Gary R. Habermas and John F. Ankerberg (eds.), *Resurrected? An Atheist and Theist Dialogue* (Oxford: Rowman & Littlefield, 2005), p. 55.

104 Richard M. Gale, *On The Nature and Existence of God* (Cambridge: Cambridge University Press, 1993), p. 2.

105 Wolfhart Pannenberg, Siemon-Netto, 'God not so dead: Atheism worldwide in decline', www.worldtribune.com/worldtribune/WTARC/2005/cs_atheism_03_03.html.

106 Quentin Smith, 'The Metaphilosophy of Naturalism', Philo Vol. 4, Number 2, 05 January 2002, www.philoonline.org/library/ smith_4_2.htm.

107 Ibid.

108 Ibid.

109 Alister McGrath, www.thersa.org/acrobat/dennett_130306.pdf.

110 J.P. Moreland, quoted by Craig, 'The Resurrection of Theism', www.leaderu.com/truth/3truth0l.html.

111 J.P. Moreland, *Scaling the Secular City* (Grand Rapids, MI: Baker, 1987), p. 11.

112 Roy Abraham Varghese, in Gary R. Habermas, Antony G.N. Flew and Terry L. Miethe, *Did Jesus Rise From the Dead?* (Eugene, OR: Wipf & Stock, 2003), Preface.

113 John Polkinghorne, 'Where is Natural Theology Today?', *Science & Christian Belief* (2006) Vol. 18 No. 2, pp. 170–171.

114 Robert Jastrow, *God and the Astronomers* (New York: W.W. Norton, 1978).

115 Ibid.

116 Michael J. Wilkins and J.P. Moreland, *Jesus Under Fire* (Carlisle: Paternoster, 1995), p. 10.

117 See Roger Forster and Paul Marston, *Reason, Science & Faith* (Crowborough: Monarch, 1999).

118 John West, *Darwin's Conservatives: The Misguided Quest* (Seattle: Discovery Institute, 2006), pp. 73–77.

119 Jerry Fodor, 'Why Pigs Don't Have Wings', *London Review of Books*, 18 October 2007, www.lrb.co.uk/v29/n20/fodo01_.html.

120 Terry L. Miethe in Terry L. Miethe and Anthony Flew, *Does God Exist? A Believer and an Atheist Debate* (London: HarperCollins, 1991), p. 196.

121 Alister McGrath, 'Challenges from Atheism', in Ravi Zacharias (ed.), *Beyond Opinion* (Nashville: Thomas Nelson, 2007), p. 21.

122 Ibid.

123 Ralph McInerny, 'Modern Philosophy And The Turn To Belief In God', Varghese (ed.), *The Intellectuals Speak Out about God*, p. 169.

124 William C. Davies and Michael J. Murray (ed.), *Reason for the Hope Within* (Grand Rapids, MI: Eerdmans, 1999), p. 44.

[125] Ibid., p. 171.

[126] James F. Sennett and Douglas Groothuis (eds.), *In Defence of Natural Theology: A Post-Humean Assessment* (Downers Grove, IL: IVP, 2005), p. 15.

[127] Norman L. Geisler, 'The Collapse of Modern Atheism', in Varghese (ed.), *The Intellectuals Speak Out about God*, p. 129.

[128] Copan and Moser, *The Rationality of Theism*, p. 2.

[129] Antony Flew, *There Is A God: How the World's Most Notorious Atheist Changed His Mind* (New York: Harper One, 2007), p. 29.

[130] Roy Abraham Varghese, *There Is A God*, Preface, p. ix.

[131] Craig J. Hazen, Preface to 'My Pilgrimage from Atheism to Theism: An Exclusive Interview with Former British Atheist Professor Antony Flew', www.biola.edu/antonyflew/flew-interview.pdf.

[132] Comment quoted by Gary R. Habermas, 'My Pilgrimage from Atheism to Theism: An Exclusive Interview with Former British Atheist Professor Antony Flew', www.biola.edu/antonyflew/flew-interview.pdf.

[133] Antony Flew, 'My Pilgrimage from Atheism to Theism: An Exclusive Interview with Former British Atheist Professor Antony Flew', www.biola.edu/antonyflew/flew-interview.pdf.

[134] ABC News, 'Famous Atheist Now Believes In God', abcnews.go.com/US/wireStory?id=315976.

[135] Craig J. Hazen in 'My Pilgrimage from Atheism to Theism: An Exclusive Interview with Former British Atheist Professor Antony Flew', www.biola.edu/antonyflew/flew-interview.pdf.

[136] Jay W. Richards, The Contemporary Argument For Design: An Overview', Paul Copan and William Lane Craig (eds.), *Passionate Conviction*, p. 69.

[137] Flew, *There Is a God*, p. 1.

[138] *Ad hominem* is: 'A Latin phrase meaning "to the person" . . . [The fallacy involves] shifting attention from the point in question to some non-relevant aspect of the person making it' (Nigel Warburton, *Thinking from A to Z* [London: Routledge, 2007], p. 4).

[139] The same acusation was hurled at French existentialist philosopher Jean Paul Sartre when he indicated that he embraced messianic Judaism in his last days (see Jean Paul Sartre, http://nobelists.net/); Ravi Zacharias, *Can Man Live Without God?* (Milton Keynes: Word, 1994), p. 212.

[140] Flew, *There Is A God*, p. 2.

[141] Mark Tauber, http://abetterhope.blogspot.com/2007/11/flew-publishes-his-new-book.html.

[142] Antony Flew, http://abetterhope.blogspot.com/2007/11/flew-publishes-his-new-book.html.

[143] Roy Abraham Varghese, Letter to the Editor, Magazine, *New York Times*, 3 November 2007, http://dangerousidea.blogspot.com/2007/11/varghese-reponds-via-gary-habermas.html.

[144] Tauber, http://abetterhope.blogspot.com/2007/11/flew-publishes-his-new-book.html.

[145] Benjamin Wiker, 'Exclusive Flew Interview', www.tothesource.org/10_30_2007/10_30_2007.htm.

[146] Alvin Plantinga, 'Modern Philosophy And The Turn To Belief In God', in Varghese (ed.), *The Intellectuals Speak Out about God*, p. 165.

[147] Alister E. McGrath, *The Twilight of Atheism: The Rise And Fall of Disbelief in The Modern World* (London: Rider, 2004), p. 174.

[148] Michael Shermer, *How We Believe: The Search for God in an Age of Science* (New York: Freeman, 2000), p. xv.

[149] Tom Flynn, 'Secularism – Will it Survive?', Free Inquiry, October/November 2005, Vol. 25 No. 6, p. 28.

[150] Michael Martin, *ibid*, p. 38.

[151] Ibid.

2. Long Live the New Atheism?

[1] Michel Onfray, *In Defence of Atheism: The Case Against Christianity, Judaism and Islam* (London: Serpent's Tail, 2007), p. 37.

[2] Alister E. McGrath, *The Dawkins Delusion* (London: SPCK, 2007), p. 63.

[3] Gavin Hyman, 'Atheism in Modern History', Michael Martin (ed.), *The Cambridge Companion to Atheism* (Cambridge University Press, 2007), p. 33.

[4] Richard Norman, 'Holy Communion', *New Humanist*, November–December 2007, p. 17.

[5] Tina Beattie, *The New Atheists: The Twilight of Reason and the War on Religion* (London: DLT, 2007), p. 6.

[6] Reported by David Aikman, *The Delusion of Disbelief* (Carol Stream, IL: SaltRiver, 2008), p. 5.

[7] Daniel Dennett, 'The Bright Stuff', www.the-brights.net/vision/essays/dennett_nyt_article.html.

[8] Ann Coulter, *Godless: The Church of Liberalism* (New York: Crown Forum, 2006), p. 268; quoted by Dawkins, *The God Delusion*, p. 321.

⁹ Richard Dawkins, *The God Delusion* (London: Bantam, 2006), p. 27.

¹⁰ David Berlinski, *The Devil's Delusion: Atheism And Its Scientific Pretensions* (New York: Crown Forum, 2008), p. 3.

¹¹ Daniel Dennett, 'The Bright Stuff', www.the-brights.net/vision/essays/dennett_nyt_article.html.

¹² Ibid.

¹³ Christopher Hitchens, *God is Not Great* (London: Atlantic, 2007), p. 5.

¹⁴ Norman, 'Holy Communion', p. 17.

¹⁵ Rod Liddle, 'God's role in politics is not to underwrite bad ideas', *The Spectator*, 15–29 December 2007, p. 18.

¹⁶ Beattie, *The New Atheists*, p. 6.

¹⁷ Richard Dawkins, 'Let there be brights', www.the-brights.net/vision/essays/let_there_be_brights.html.

¹⁸ Matt Purple, 'Religion Must Be Destroyed, Atheist Alliance Declares', www.cnsnews.com/ViewCulture.asp?Page=/Culture/archive/2007 10/CUL20071003a.html.

¹⁹ See Sam Harris, 'The Problem With Atheism', www.samharris.org/site/full_text/aai-lecture-the-problem-with-atheism/.

²⁰ Sam Harris, 'The Problem With Atheism', http://newsweek.washingtonpost.com/onfaith/sam_harris/2007/10/the_problem_with_a theism.html.

²¹ Ibid.

²² Ibid.

²³ Ellen Johnson Responds to 'The End of Atheism', www.humaniststudies.org/enews/?id=317&article=1.

²⁴ Sam Harris, 'Response to my fellow Atheists', www.samharris.org/site/full_text/response-to-my-fellow-atheists/.

²⁵ Ibid.

²⁶ Freeman Dyson, 'Religion from the outside', *New York Review of Books*, 22 June 2006, www.nybooks.com/articles/article-preview?article_id=19090.

²⁷ I will have comparatively little to say about Hitchens, who spends very little time arguing about the existence of God. See John Mark Reynolds, 'Atheism Ranting: The Pity and Poverty of Modern Anti-Theism', www.scriptoriumdaily.com/2007/05/21/atheism-ranting-the-pity-and-poverty-of-modern-anti-theism/.

²⁸ Tom Clark, 'Deny God, Then What?', www.naturalism.org/new_atheism.htm.

[29] Albert Mohler, 'The New Atheism?', www.albertmohler.com/commentary_read.php?cdate=2006-11-21.

[30] John Cornwell, *Darwin's Angel: An Angelic Riposte to The God Delusion* (London: Profile, 2007), pp. 15–16.

[31] *New Humanist* magazine asked readers: '"Are Richard Dawkins and Christopher Hitchens a good thing for humanism?" Over five thousand respondents gave an overwhelming thumbs up to [them]. Seventy-eight percent felt these two leading atheists were providing a much needed vigorous response to religion, 17 percent chose the only slightly less enthusiastic answer that they enliven the debate, while a mere 3 percent dislike their tone. Only 35 people thought they were bad for the humanist cause' (Editorial, *New Humanist*, November–December 2007, p. 3).

[32] Alister E. McGrath, 'Dawkins, God, and the Scientific Enterprise', in Robert B. Stewart (ed.), *Intelligent Design: William A. Dembski and Michael Ruse in Dialogue* (Minneapolis: Fortress, 2007), p. 101.

[33] Michael Ruse, 'Rational Atheism: An open letter to Messers. Dawkins, Dennett, Harris and Hitchens', *Scientific American*, September 2007, pp. 25–26.

[34] http://lfab-uvm.blogspot.com/2007/06/new-atheism-controversy-explained.html.

[35] George Johnson, 'A Free-for-All on Science and Religion', *The New York Times*, 23 November 2006.

[36] See http://beyondbelief2006.org/.

[37] Johnson, 'A Free-for-All on Science and Religion', *The New York Times*, 23 November 2006.

[38] See http://beyondbelief2006.org/About/.

[39] Michael Brooks, 'This Week: Beyond Belief', *New Scientist* 18 November 2006, p. 11, www.newscientist.com/channel/opinion/mg19225780.142-beyond-belief-in-place-of-god.html.

[40] Johnson, 'A Free-for-All on Science and Religion', *The New York Times*, 23 November 2006.

[41] Ibid.

[42] Ibid.

[43] Ibid.

[44] Brooks, 'This Week: Beyond Belief', p. 11.

[45] Michael Reilly, 'Does God have a place in a rational world?', www.newscientist.com/channel/opinion/mg19626294.200-does-god-have-a-place-in-a-rational-world.html.

46 University of Cambridge, Investigating Atheism, www.investigatin-gatheism.info/responses.html.

47 Jonathan Haidt, 'Moral Psychology and the Misunderstanding of Religion', www.edge.org/3rd_culture/haidt07/haidt07_index.html.

48 Tim Crane, 'Should Atheists Be Against Religion?', *Think*, Issue 17/18, Spring 2008, pp. 109, 113.

49 Norman, 'Holy Communion', *New Humanist*, p. 17.

50 Ibid.

51 Ibid., pp. 18–19.

52 Mary Ridell, 'God is not Great', The Guardian, 3 June 2007, http://books.guardian.co.uk/reviews/politicsphilosophyandsociety/0,,2094025,00.html.

53 Daniel Dennett, 'Unbelievable', *Boston Globe*, 13 May 2007, www.boston.com/ae/books/articles/2007/05/13/unbelievable/?page=full.

54 Stephen Prothero, 'The Unbeliever', *The Washington Post*, 6 May 2007, www.washingtonpost.com/wp-dyn/content/artcle/2007/05/03/AR2007050301907.html.

55 Kenan Malik, 'Non-believers can be bigoted too', *The Telegraph*, 11 March 2007, www.telegraph.co.uk/arts/main.jhtml;?xml=/arts/2007/03/11/bohar04.xml.

56 Berlinski, *The Devil's Delusion: Atheism And Its Scientific Pretensions*, p. 3.

57 Michael Shermer, *Science Magazine*, January 2007, http://richard-dawkins.net/article,570,Arguing-for-Atheism,Michael-Shermer-Science-Magazine.

58 Richard Dawkins interviewed by Laurie Taylor, 'Gentle Rotweiller' *New Humanist* (January/February 2007), http://richarddawkins.net/images/LaurieTaylorNewHumanist.pdf.

59 Peter Steinfels, 'Books on Atheism are Raising Hackles in Unlikely Places', *New York Times*, 3 March 2007.

60 Thomas Nagel, *The New Republic*, 'Fear of Religion', www.tnr.com/doc.mhtml?i=20061023&s=nagel102306.

61 H. Allen Orr, 'A Mission to Convert', *New York Review of Books*, 11 January 2007, www.nybooks.com/articles/19775.

62 H. Allen Orr, 'The God Project', *The New Yorker*, 3 April 2006, www.newyorker.com/archive/2006/04/03/060403crbo_books?currentPage=3 .

63 Adam Kirsch, 'If men are from mars, what's God', *New York Sun*, 8 Feb 2006, www.nysun.com/article/27182.

[64] Michael Ruse in Tristan Abbey, 'The Impact of Darwinism', *The Stanford Review*, Volume XL, Issue 7, www.stanfordreview.org/Archive/Volume_XL/Issue_7/Features/features2.shtml.

[65] Michael Ruse, www.uncommondescent.com/archives/844.

[66] Ibid.

[67] Michael Ruse, 'Fighting the Fundamentalists: Chamberlain or Churchill?', *Skeptical Inquirer* Volume 31, No. 2, March/April 2007, pp. 39–40.

[68] Ibid., p. 40.

[69] Ibid., p. 41.

[70] Ibid., p. 41.

[71] Ibid., p. 40.

[72] A.C. Grayling, *The Meaning of Things* (London: Weidenfeld & Nicolson, 2001), p. 7.

[73] A.C. Grayling, *Against All Gods* (London: Oberon Books, 2007), p. 9.

[74] Ibid., p. 7.

[75] Ibid., p. 28.

[76] Ibid., p. 23.

[77] Ibid.

[78] Gary Wolf, 'The Church of the Non-Believers', *Wired Magazine*, November 2006, p. 184, www.wired.com/news/wiredmag/0,71985-0.html?tw=wn_index_1.

[79] Ibid.

[80] Grayling, *Against All Gods*, pp. 7, 15.

[81] Ibid., p. 17, my italics.

[82] Ibid., p. 17.

[83] Ibid., p. 16, my italics.

[84] See Rees Mogg, 'Adopt change after 2000 years? Never!', www.timesonline.co.uk/tol/comment/columnists/william_rees_mogg/article1329412.ece.

[85] Grayling, *Against All Gods*, p. 17.

[86] Ibid, p. 16.

[87] See www.quotationreference.com/quotefinder.php.

[88] A.C. Grayling, *The Meaning of Things*, p. 7, my italics.

[89] Grayling, *Against All Gods*, p. 47.

[90] A.C. Grayling, 'Answering Critics', *The Form of Things: Essays on Life, Ideas and Liberty in the 21st Century* (London: Pheonix, 2007), p. 82.

[91] Ibid.

[92] Ibid.

⁹³ Ibid.

⁹⁴ Ibid., my italics.

⁹⁵ Christopher Hitchens, *God is not Great* (London: Atlantic Books, 2007), p. 12.

⁹⁶ Vox Day, *The Irrational Atheist* (Dallas, TX: Benbella, 2008), p. 178.

⁹⁷ Hitchens, *God is not Great*, p. 13.

⁹⁸ Grayling, *Against All Gods*, p. 47.

⁹⁹ Norman, 'Holy Communion', *New Humanist*, p. 19.

¹⁰⁰ Michael Novak, 'Remembering the Secular Age', *Firth Things*, June/July 2007.

¹⁰¹ Richard Dawkins, 'God v. Science', *Time*, www.time.com/time/magazine/article/0,9171,1555132-1,00.html.

¹⁰² Gavin Wolf, 'The Church of the Non-Believers', *Wired Magazine*, November 2006, p. 193.

¹⁰³ Dennett, 'The Bright Stuff', www.the-brights.net/vision/essays/dennett_nyt_article.html.

¹⁰⁴ This charming phrase is attributed to (but not directly quoted from) Peter Berger by sociologist David Martin, 'Does the Advance of Science Mean Secularisation?', *Science and Christian Belief*, Volume 19 (1) 1-96, April 2007, p. 12.

¹⁰⁵ Dennett's use of 'we' is an 'Appeal to the people: In this fallacy, one argues that if you want to be accepted, included in the group, loved, or respected, then you should accept conclusion X as true. Here the arguer incites group emotions or the enthusiasm of the crowd, appeals to people's vanity or snobbery, or challenges people to jump on the bandwagon to support a conclusion' (J.P. Moreland, *Love Your God With All You Mind* [Colorado Springs, Colorado: NavPress, 1997], p. 121).

¹⁰⁶ Sarah Lyall, 'Building in Iceland? Better Clear it With the Elves First', *New York Times*, www.nytimes.com/2005/07/13/international/europe/13elves.html?ex=1278907200&en=5e99759b563f81fe&ei=5090&partner=rssuserland&emc=rss; see also www.icelandtouristboard.com/elf.html.

¹⁰⁷ A Gallup poll revealed that 32 per cent of adult Americans believe in ghosts, 19 per cent aren't sure, and 48 per cent dismiss the idea outright (see www.theregister.co.uk/2005/07/14/us_ghost_survey/).

3. Is Faith the Root of All Evil?

[1] Richard Dawkins, quoted by Richard Norman, 'Holy Communion', *New Humanist*, November-December 2007, p. 17.

[2] A.C. Grayling, *Against All Gods* (London: Oberon Books, 2007), p. 9.

[3] Gerard J. Hughes in Roy Abraham Varghese (ed.), *Great Thinkers on Great Questions* (Oxford: OneWorld, 1998), p. 111.

[4] Russell Stannard, *Science and Wonders: Conversations about Science and Belief* (London: Faber, 1996), p. 27.

[5] Philip Pullman in *Devout Sceptics: Conversations on Faith and Doubt* (London: Hodder & Stoughton, 2003), p. 125–126.

[6] Bel Mooney and Philip Pullman, *Devout Sceptics: Conversations on Faith and Doubt*, p. 126.

[7] Philip J. Sampson, *Six Modern Myths Challenging Christian Faith* (Leicester: IVP, 2000), p. 133.

[8] Hugh Trevor-Roper, *The European Witch-Craze of the Sixteenth and Seventeenth Centuries* (Penguin, 1969), p. 37.

[9] David Marshall, *The Truth Behind The New Atheism* (Eugene, OR: Harvest House, 2007), p. 161.

[10] Tina Beattie, *The New Atheists* (London: DLT, 2007), p. 60. See also Gustav Henningsen and Bengt Ankarloo (eds.), *Early Modern European Witchcraft: Centres and Peripheries* (Oxford: Clarendon Press, 1990).

[11] Richard Norman, *On Humanism* (London: Routledge, 2004), p. 17.

[12] A.C. Grayling, 'Humanism and Religion', *The Form of Things: Essays on Life, Ideas and Liberty in the 21st Century* (London: Pheonix, 2007), p. 124.

[13] Daniel Dennett, *Breaking the Spell* (London: Penguin, 2007), p. 39.

[14] Sam Harris, 'The Problem With Atheism', http://newsweek.washingtonpost.com/onfaith/sam_harris/2007/10/the_problem_with_atheism.html.

[15] Sam Harris, *Letter to a Christian Nation* (London: Bantam, 2007), p. 46.

[16] Ibid., pp. 8, 25.

[17] Jonathan Haidt, 'Moral Psychology and the Misunderstanding of Religion', www.edge.org/3rd_culture/haidt07/haidt07_index.html.

[18] See Samuel Scheffler, *Consequentialism and Its Critics* (Oxford: Oxford University Press, 1988); J.J.C. Smart and Bernard Williams, *Utilitarianism: For and Against* (Cambridge: Cambridge University Press, 1973); Walter Sinnot-Armstrong, 'Consequentialism', http://plato.stanford.edu/entries/consequentialism/; Stephen Law,

'Killing Mary to Save Jodie', http://virtualatdp.berkeley.edu:8081/philosophy/_2/_/2.

[19] Norman, *On Humanism*, p. 102.

[20] Daniel Dennett, *Darwin's Dangerous Idea* (London: Penguin, 1995), p. 520.

[21] For reviews of *The Root of All Evil?* see Denis Alexander, 'A Clash of Fundamentalisms', www.bethinking.org/resource.php?ID=252; Madeleine Bunting, 'No wonder atheists are angry: they seem ready to believe anything', www.guardian.co.uk/Columnists/Column/0,5673,1681235,00.html; Dave Crofts, 'Review: The Root of All Evil', www.christchurchcentral.co.uk/culture/dawkins_1.html; Neil Davenport, 'Is Religion the Root of all Evil?', www.spikedonline.com/Articles/0000000CAF1A.htm; Nick Pollard, 'The Root of all Evil? – The problem with Richard Dawkin's faith – parts 1 and 2', www.bethinking.org/resource.php?ID=243; www.bethinking. org/resource.php?ID=244; Roger Scruton, 'Dawkins is Wrong About God', www.spectator.co.uk/index.thtml; Alom Shaha, 'The Root of all Anti-Science?', www.spiked-online.com/Articles/0000000CAF20.htm; Keith Ward, 'Faith, hype, and a lack of clarity', www.the-tablet.co.uk/articles/501; Keith Ward, 'Is Religion Dangerous?', http://richarddawkins.net.nyud.net:8080/audio/5live_mayo_ward.mp3.

[22] http://en.wikipedia.org/wiki/The_Root_of_All_Evil%3F.

[23] http://en.wikipedia.org/wiki/The_Root_of_All_Evil%3F.

[24] Richard Dawkins, *The God Delusion* (London: Bantam, 2006), pp. 286, 308, my italics.

[25] Norman, 'Holy Communion', *New Humanist*, November-December 2007, p. 17.

[26] Richard Dawkins, quoted by Norman, 'Holy Communion', *New Humanist*, November-December 2007, p. 17.

[27] Harris, *Letter to a Christian Nation*, p. 33.

[28] Ibid.

[29] Daniel Dennett, 'Is religion a threat to rationality and science?', http://richarddawkins.net/article,2498,Is-religion-a-threat-to-rationality-and-science,Dan-Dennett-Lord-Winston.

[30] J.P. Moreland and William Lane Craig, *Foundations of a Christian Worldview* (Downers Grove Illinois: IVP, 2003), pp. 443–444.

[31] Michael Ruse in Robert B. Stewart (ed.), *Intelligent Design: William A. Dembski & Michael Ruse in Dialogue* (Minneapolis: Fortress, 2007), p. 37.

[32] Richard Dawkins, *The Selfish Gene* (Oxford: Oxford University Press, 1989), p. 198.

[33] See Marino, 'Richard Dawkins: The Biologist Who Fills The Gaps In Our Knowledge With Faith', http://atheistricharddawkins. blogspot.com/ 2007/11/richard-dawkins-biologist-who-fills.html; Peter S. Williams, '"What do you believe is true even though you cannot prove it?" – Comparing Dawkins' Blind Faith with Flew's Evidence', www.arn.org/ docs/williams/pw_comparingdawkinsflew.htm.

[34] This was the Edge centre question for 2005.

[35] Richard Dawkins, *Broadcasting House*, BBC Radio 4, Sunday January, 2005.

[36] Richard Dawkins, from BBC's *The Final Hour*, 14 November 2005, quoted by Andrew Wilson, *Deluded by Dawkins?* (Eastbourne: Kingsway, 2007), p. 96, our italics.

[37] Harris, *Letter to a Christian Nation*, p. 67.

[38] Richard Dawkins, *A Devil's Chaplain* (London: Weidenfeld & Nicolson, 2003), p. 242.

[39] Ibid., p. 242.

[40] Ibid., p. 248.

[41] Carl Sagan, *The Varieties of Scientific Experience* (New York: Penguin, 2006), p. 1.

[42] Ibid., p. 189.

[43] Ibid., p. 249.

[44] Ibid.

[45] Blaise Pascal, Honor Levi (trans.), *Pensées and other writings* (Oxford: Oxford University Press, 1995), 142.

[46] Roy Abraham Varghese, *Great Thinkers On Great Questions* (Oxford: Oneworld, 1998), pp. 3, 5, 11.

[47] James Kelly Clark, *Return to Reason* (Grand Rapids, MI: Eerdmans, 1990), p. 126.

[48] Ibid., p. 131.

[49] Ibid., p. 127.

[50] Ibid., p. 126.

[51] Ibid., p. 130.

[52] Ibid., p. 129.

[53] Roy Clouser, *Knowing with the Heart* (Downers Grove, IL: IVP, 1999), pp. 68–71.

[54] Note that an 'indispensably basic' belief cannot have a plural origin. Belief in God is thus not an *indispensably* basic belief.

[55] Clark, *Return to Reason*, pp. 134–135.

[56] Ibid., p. 135.

[57] Nicholas Wolterstorff, *Reason Within the Bounds of Religion* (Grand Rapids, MI: Eerdmans, 1976), p. 52.

[58] Clark, *Return to Reason*, p. 138.

[59] Alan G. Padgett, 'The Relationship Between Theology and Philosophy', James K. Beilby (ed.), *For Faith and Clarity* (Grand Rapids, MI: Baker, 2006), p. 39.

[60] Marshall, *The Truth Behind The New Atheism*, p. 27.

[61] Dennett, *Breaking the Spell*, p. 238.

[62] Dawkins, *The Selfish Gene*, p. 198.

[63] Norman, 'Holy Communion', *New Humanist*, November-December 2007, p. 18.

[64] Alister McGrath, *Dawkins' God* (Oxford: Blackwell, 2005), pp. 91, 99.

[65] Julian Baggini, *Atheism: A Very Short Introduction* (Oxford University Press, 2003), p. 32.

[66] Grayling, *Against All Gods*, pp. 15–16.

[67] Baggini, *Atheism*, p. 33.

[68] Grayling, 'Humanism and Religion', *The Form of Things*, p. 123.

[69] See Richard Bauckham, *Jesus and the Eyewitnesses: The Gospels as Eyewitness Testimony* (Grand Rapids, MI: Eerdmans, 2006).

[70] Roger Steer, *Letter to an Influential Atheist* (Carlisle: Authentic Lifestyle/Paternoster, 2003), pp. 137–138.

[71] J.P. Moreland, 'Living Smart' in Paul Copan and William Lane Craig (eds.), *Passionate Conviction* (Nashville, Tenessee: B&H Academic, 2007), p. 22.

[72] Ibid., pp. 121–122.

[73] Ibid., pp. 123–124.

[74] Michael J. Langford, *Unblind Faith* (London: SCM, 1982), p. 3.

[75] Tom Price, 'Faith is just about "trusting God" isn't it?', www.bethinking.org/resource.php?ID=132&TopicID=9&CategoryID=8.

[76] Michael J. Wilkins and J.P. Moreland, *Jesus Under Fire – Modern Scholarship Reinvents the Historical Jesus* (Carlisle: Paternoster, 1996), p. 8.

[77] Peter Kreeft and Ronald Tacelli, *Handbook of Christian Apologetics* (Downers Grove, IL: IVP, 1994), p. 22.

[78] Richard L. Purtill, *Reason to Believe* (Grand Rapids, MI: Eerdmans, 1974), http://members.core.com/~tony233/Reason_to_Believe.htm#c.

[79] Grayling, *Against All Gods*, pp. 15–16.

[80] Const. De Fide, II, De Rev., quoted by the *Catholic Encyclopedia*, www.newadvent.org/cathen/01215c.htm.

[81] John Polkinghorne, 'Where is Natural Theology Today?', *Science & Christian Belief*, 2006, 18, p. 169.

[82] Norman L. Geisler, *Philosophy of Religion* (Grand Rapids, MI: Zondervan, 1974), p. 208.

[83] Norman L. Geisler and Winfried Corduan, *Philosophy of Religion* (Grand Rapids, MI: Baker, 1988), p. 86–87.

[84] Norman L. Geisler and Paul D. Feinberg, *Introduction to Philosophy: A Christian Perspective* (Grand Rapids, MI: Baker, 1997), p. 73.

[85] C.S. Lewis, quoted by Norman L. Geisler in the foreword to J.P. Moreland's *Scaling the Secular City* (Grand Rapids, MI: Baker, 1987).

[86] John Mark Reynalds, 'Atheism Ranting: The Pity and Poverty of Modern Anti-Theism', www.scriptoriumdaily.com/2007/05/21/atheism-ranting-the-pity-and-poverty-of-modern-anti-theism/.

[87] Richard Dawkins, 'Religion's Real Child Abuse', *Free Inquiry*, Fall 2002, 22 (4), p. 9.

[88] Ibid.

[89] Ibid.

[90] Ibid.

[91] Ibid.

[92] Ibid., p. 12.

[93] Ibid.

[94] Richard Dawkins, *Unweaving the Rainbow* (London: Penguin, 1998), p. ix.

[95] Peter Atkins, quoted by Richard Dawkins in *Unweaving the Rainbow*, p. ix.

[96] Dawkins, *Unweaving the Rainbow*, p. ix.

[97] Ibid., pp. ix–x.

[98] Dawkins, 'Nick Pollard talks to Dr Richard Dawkins', *Third Way*, April 1995, 18 (3).

[99] Ibid.

[100] Richard Dawkins, 'Afterword', in John Brockman (ed.), *What Is Your Dangerous Idea?* (London: Pocket Books, 2006) , p. 307.

[101] Richard Dawkins, 'God's Utility Function', *Scientific American*, November, 1995, p. 85, my italics.

[102] John F. Haught, *God and the New Atheism: A Critical Response to Dawkins, Harris, and Hitchens* (London: Westminster John Knox Press, 2008), pp. 26–27.

103 Anthony O'Hear, *Beyond Evolution* (Oxford: Oxford University Press, 1999),　p. 103.

104 Dawkins, 'God's Utility Function', *Scientific American*, p. 85, my italics.

105 Dawkins, 'Nick Pollard talks to Dr Richard Dawkins', *Third Way*, April 1995, 18 (3).

106 Purtill, *Reason to Believe*, http://members.core.com/~tony233/Reason_to_Believe.htm#c9.

107 Tom Price, 'Religion Causes Wars', www.bethinking.org/ resource .php?ID=227&TopicID=4&CategoryID=6.

108 Ravi Zacharias, *A Shattered Visage* (Grand Rapids, MI: Baker, 1993), pp. 60–61.

109 Victor Frankl, quoted by Ravi Zacharias, *Can Man Live Without God?* (Milton Keynes: Word, 1994).

110 Adolf Hitler, quoted by John Blanchard, *Does God Believe in Atheists?*, p. 75. See also Dinesh D'Souza, 'Was Hitler a Christian?', www.catholiceducation.org/articles/facts/fm0110.htm.

111 Benito Mussolini, cited in Art Lindsley, C.S. Lewis' *Case for Christ* (Downers Grove, IL: IVP, 2005), p. 155.

112 Michael Ruse, www.uncommondescent.com/index.php/archives/844#more-844.

113 Chapman Cohen, 'Monism and Religion', Christopher Hitchens (ed.), *The Portable Atheist: Essential readings for the Non-Believer* (London: Da Capo Press, 2007), p. 171.

4 – Is Religion Nothing Buttery Short of a Sandwich?

1 Richard Dawkins, *The God Delusion* (London: Bantam, 2006), p. 163.

2 Elizabeth Burns and Stephen Law, *Philosophy for AS and A2* (London: Routledge, 2006), p. 119.

3 Ibid.

4 Ibid., p. 175.

5 Alvin Plantinga, *Warranted Christian Belief* (Oxford: Oxford University Press, 2000), pp. 188–189.

6 Ibid., p. 168.

7 Ibid., pp. ix, 151.

8 Ibid.

9 Ibid.

10 Ibid.

11 Ibid.

12 R. Douglas Geivett and Greg Jesson, 'Plantinga's Externalism and the Terminus of Warrant-Based Epistemology', *Philosophia Christi*, Series 2, Volume 3, Number 2, p. 330.

13 Plantinga, *Warranted Christian Belief*, p. 145.

14 Ibid., pp. 197–198.

15 Geivett and Jesson, 'Plantinga's Externalism and the Terminus of Warrant-Based Epistemology', p. 331.

16 Plantinga, *Warranted Christian Belief*, p. 169.

17 Ibid.

18 Edward O. Wilson, *On Human Nature* (Harvard University Press, 1978), p. 192.

19 Kai Nielson, 'Naturalistic explanations of theistic belief', Michael Martin (ed.), *Cambridge Companion to Atheism* (Cambridge: Cambridge University Press, 2007), p. 403.

20 Richard Dawkins, 'Richard Dawkins explains his latest book', http://id-idea.blogspot.com/2006/09/richard-dawkins-explains-his-latest.html.

21 William P. Alston, *Perceiving God* (Ithaca, NY: Cornell University Press, 1993),   p. 230.

22 William P. Alston, 'God and religious experience', Brian Davies (ed.), *Philosophy of Religion: A Guide to the Subject* (London: Continuum, 2003), pp. 68–69.

23 Daniel Dennett, *Breaking the Spell* (London: Penguin, 2006), p. 53.

24 Ibid., p. 240. It all comes, I think, of being overly impressed with David Hume.

25 Ibid., p. 26.

26 Ibid.

27 John Gray, 'Myths of Meaning: Breaking the Spell & Six Impossible Things Before Breakfast', www.newstatesman.com/200603200044.

28 Jeremy Stangroom, 'Original Sin', *The Philosopher's Magazine*, Issue 35, 3rd quarter 2006, p. 88.

29 Dennett, *Breaking the Spell*, pp. 103, 309, 311.

30 Ibid., p. 103.

31 Ibid., p. 135.

32 Ibid., p. 25.

33 Ibid., p. 242.

34 Ibid., p. 27.

[35] Keith Ward, *Is Religion Dangerous?* (Oxford: Lion, 2006), p. 11.

[36] Richard Dawkins, *A Devil's Chaplain* (London: Weidenfeld & Nicolson, 2003), pp. 211–212.

[37] Ibid., p. 212.

[38] Ibid.

[39] Daniel Dennett, 'The Leibnizian Paradigm', David L. Hull and Michael Ruse (eds.), *The Philosophy of Biology* (Oxford University Press, 1998), p. 49.

[40] John F. Haught, *God and the New Atheists: A Critical Response to Dawkins, Harris, and Hitchens* (London: Westminster John Knox Press, 2008), p. x.

[41] Denis Alexander, Book Review – 'Breaking the Spell: Religion as a Natural Phenomenon,' *Science & Christian Belief*, 18 (2), pp. 206–207.

[42] John O'Leary-Hawthorn, 'Arguments for Atheism', *Reason for the Hope Within* (Grand Rapids, MI: Eerdmans, 1999), p. 134.

[43] C.E.M. Joad, *Guide to Modern Thought* (London: Faber and Faber, 1933), p. 213.

[44] In 2007 Dawkins appeared to back off somewhat from memetics: 'I am not going to utter the 'm' word [memes]; everybody else keeps saying it and then looking at me, and I am going to duck out of that. I used not to think this, but I am increasingly thinking that nothing but confusion arises from confounding genetic evolution with cultural evolution, unless you are very careful about what you are doing and don't talk as though they are somehow just different aspects of the same phenomenon. Or, if they are different aspects of the same phenomenon, then let's hear a good case for regarding them as such' (Richard Dawkins, quoted in Michael Shermer, 'The Skeptic's Chaplain: Richard Dawkins as a Fountainhead of Skepticism', *Skeptic*, 13 (2), 2007, p. 45).

[45] Alister McGrath, *Dawkins' God* (Oxford: Blackwell, 2005), p. 124.

[46] C.S. Lewis, *The Prilgrim's Regress* (London: Fount, 1977), p. 80.

[47] Ibid., p. 93.

[48] cf. Richard Bauckham, *Jesus and the Eyewitnesses: The Gospels as Eyewitness Testimony* (Grand Rapids, MI: Eerdmans, 2006).

[49] cf. 'Christian Lawyers strongly against embryo checks being widened', www.christianconcernforournation.co.uk/Embryo/9may6.php.

[50] cf. Peter S. Williams, 'The Abolition of Man: Reflections on Reductionism With Special Reference to Eugenics', www.lewissociety.org/abolition.php.

[51] Dennett, *Breaking the Spell*, p. 205.

[52] Ward, *Is Religion Dangerous?*, pp. 10–11.

[53] Keith Ward, *The Case for Religion* (Oxford: Oneworld, 2004), p. 33.

[54] Steven Lovell, Unpublished PhD thesis, Chapter 5: 'C.S. Lewis and the Freudian Critique of Religious Belief'.

[55] Ibid.

[56] Ibid.

[57] Ibid.

[58] Ibid.

[59] John Blanchard, *Does God Believe in Atheists?* (Darlington: Evangelical Press, 2000), p. 25.

[60] Ward, *Is Religion Dangerous?*, pp. 12–13.

[61] Edward G. Newing, 'Religions of Pre-Literary Societies' in Norman Anderson (ed.), *The World's Religions* (Downers Grove, IL: IVP, 1975), pp. 11–12.

[62] David C. Downing, *The Most Reluctant Convert: C.S. Lewis' Journey to Faith* (Downers Grove, IL: IVP, 2002), p. 52.

[63] Tina Beattie, *The New Atheists* (London: DLT, 2007), p. 45.

[64] Alister McGrath, *The Twilight of Atheism* (London: Rider & Co, 2005), pp. 71, 73.

[65] Martin Rowson, 'If God proved he existed, I still wouldn't believe in him', *The Spectator*, 8 March 2008, p. 22.

[66] Michel Onfray, *In Defence of Atheism: The Case Against Christianity, Judaism and Islam* (London: Sperent's Tail, 2007), p. 14.

[67] Ibid.

[68] J.P. Moreland, *Scaling the Secular City* (Grand Rapids, MI: Baker, 1987), p. 229.

[69] Christopher Hitchens, *The Portable Atheist: Essential Readings For The Nonbeliever – selected and with introductions by Christopher Hitchens* (London: Da Capo Press, 2007), Introduction, p. xxii.

[70] Thomas Nagel, *The Last Word* (Oxford: Thomas Nelson, 1997), pp. 130–131.

[71] The charge that people believe in God for reasons to do with comfort stands in tension with the results of a survey by Michael Shermer and Frank Sulloway, who asked around 1,000 Americans why they believed in God (if they did) and why they thought other people believed in God. Theists generally claimed they believed because of rational factors – e.g. appreciating the design of the universe (28.6%), or religious experience (20.6%). Only ten percent of theists said they

believed in God because belief is 'comforting, consoling or relieving'; yet the majority of respondents (70.8%) attributed *other people's* belief to *non-rational* factors (i.e. 'It is comforting, relieving, consoling, gives meaning and purpose to life' 26.3%; 'Raised to believe in God' 22.4%; 'Just because/faith/need to believe in something' 13%; 'Fear of death/unknown' 9.1%). cf. Michael Shermer, *How We Believe: The Search for God in an Age of Science* (New York: W.H. Freeman & Co, 2000), p. 84.

[72] cf. Paul C. Vitz, 'The Psychology of Atheism', www.origins.org/truth/1truth12.html and *Faith of the Fatherless: The Psychology of Atheism* (Dallas: Spence, 1999).

[73] C.S. Lewis, *Surprised by Joy* (London: Fount, 1998), pp. 133–134.

[74] Francis Collins, *The Language of God* (London: Free Press, 2006), pp. 15–16.

[75] Aldous Huxley, *Ends and Means* (London: Chatto and Windus, 1969), p. 270.

[76] Glenys Roberts, 'Dangerous Liaison', *Daily Mail*, Saturday, April 12, 2008, pp. 56–57, my italics, www.dailymail.co.uk/pages/live/femail/article.html?in_article_id=559137&in_page_id=1879.

[77] Ibid., p. 57.

[78] cf. Jim Herrick, 'Bertrand Russell: A Passionate Rationalist', www.positiveatheism.org/hist/russell6.htm.

[79] Christopher Hitchens, quoted by David Berlinski, *The Devil's Delusion: Atheism And Its Scientific Pretensions* (New York: Crown Forum, 2008), p. 18.

[80] Dawkins, *The God Delusion*, p. 264.

[81] Memoir of Leonado da Vinci in *The Standard Edition of the Complete Psychological Works of Sigmund Freud* (ed.) J. Strachey (London: Hogarth Press, 1957), vol. 11, p. 123.

[82] Benjamin Beit-Hallahmi, 'Atheists: A Psychological Profile', Michael Martin (ed.), *The Cambridge Companion to Atheism* (Cambridge University Press, 2007), pp. 302–303.

[83] Vitz, 'The Psychology of Atheism', www.origins.org/truth/1truth-12.html.

[84] Ibid.

[85] Jean Paul Sartre, quoted by Carole Seymour-Jones, *A Dangerous Liaison: A Revelatory New Biography of Simone De Beauvoir and Jean Paul Sartre* (London: Century, 2008), p. 43.

[86] Christopher Hitchens: Profile, www.bbc.co.uk/bbcfour/documentaries/profile/christopher_hitchens.shtml; see also 'When Christopher

met Peter', http://books.guardian.co.uk/hay2005/story/ 0,15880, 1495897,00.html#article_continue.

87 C.S. Lewis, 'Bulverism' in *First and Second Things* (London: Fount, 1985).

88 Philip A. Stahl, *Atheism: A Beginner's Handbook* (New York: iUniverse, 2007), p. 81.

89 Bob Holmes, 'In Search of God', *New Scientist*, 21 April 2001, pp. 27–28.

90 See www.bbc.co.uk/science/horizon/2003/godonbrain.shtml.

91 Andrew Newberg, quoted by Holmes, 'In Search of God', *New Scientist*, 21 April 2001, p. 28.

92 Holmes, 'In Search of God', *New Scientist*, 21 April 2001, p. 28.

93 See Roxanne Khamsi, 'Electrical brainstorms busted as source of ghosts', www.nature.com/news/2004/041206/pf/04120610_pf.html.

94 Joe Nickell, 'Mystical Experiences: Magnetic Fields or Suggestibility?', *Skeptical Inquirer*, Volume 29, Issue 5, Sept-ember/October 2005, pp. 14–15.

95 Stephen Jay Gould, quoted by Angus J. Menuge, 'Reductionism, Bane of Christianity and Science', *Philosophia Christi*, Volume 4, Number 1, 2002, p. 182.

96 Bill Broadway, 'Is the capacity for spirituality determined by brain chemistry?', *Washington Post*, www.washingtonpost.com/ac2/wp-dyn/A46793-2004NOV12?language=printer.

97 Elizabeth Day, '"God Gene" discovered by scientist behind gay DNA theory', www.telegraph.co.uk.

98 Dean Hamer, quoted by Albert Mohler, 'The God Gene: Bad Science Meets Bad Theology', www.beliefnet.com/story/154story_ 15458 .htm.

99 Albert Mohler, 'The God Gene: Bad Science Meets Bad Theology', www.beliefnet.com/story/154story_15458.htm.

100 Collins, *The Language of God*, p. 262.

101 Dean Hamer, quoted by Julia C. Keller, 'Twin (City) researchers find genetic roots of religiousness', www.stnews.org/research-424.htm.

102 Broadway, 'Is the capacity for spirituality determined by brain chemistry?', *Washington Post*, www.washingtonpost.com/ac2/wp-dyn/A46793-2004NOV12?language=printer.

103 Dean Zimmer, quoted by Albert Mohler, 'The God Gene: Bad Science Meets Bad Theology', www.beliefnet.com/story/154story_15458 .htm.

[104] Zimmer, quoted by Albert Mohler, 'The God Gene: Bad Science Meets Bad Theology', www.beliefnet.com/story/154story_15458. htm.

[105] Bill Broadway, 'Is the capacity for spirituality determined by brain chemistry?', *Washington Post*, www.washingtonpost.com/ac2/wp-dyn/A46793-2004NOV12?language=printer.

[106] Collins, *The Language of God*, p. 263.

[107] Quoted by Shermer, *How We Believe*, p. 64.

[108] Ibid.

[109] cf. Julia C. Keller, 'Twin (City) researchers find genetic roots of religiousness', www.stnews.org/research-424.htm.

[110] Nancy Segal, *Entwined Lives* (1999), quoted by Shermer, *How We Believe*, p. 64.

[111] Shermer, *How We Believe*, pp. 64–65.

[112] David Stove, *Darwinian Fairytales: Selfish Genes, Errors of Heredity, and Other Fables of Evolution* (New York: Encounter Books, 1995), pp. 183–184.

[113] Collins, *The Language of God*, pp. 262–263.

[114] Dawkins, *The God Delusion*, p. 190.

[115] Phil Zuckerman, 'Contemporary Numbers and Patterns', Michael Martin (ed.), *Cambridge Companion to Atheism* (Cambridge University Press, 2007), pp. 60–61.

[116] John Hick, *Philosophy of Religion* (New Jersey: Prentice Hall, 1963), p. 33.

[117] Mel Thompson, *An Introduction to Philosophy and Ethics* (London: Hodder & Stoughton, 2003), p. 65.

[118] cf. Gregory Koukl, 'Is God Just an Idea?', www.str.org/site/News2?page=NewsArticle&id=6067; Kelly L. Ross, 'Forms of the Genetic Fallacy', www.friesian.com/genetic.htm.

5 – Does Science Explain Everything?

[1] Christopher Hitchens, *God Is Not Great* (London: Atlantic, 2007), pp. 64–65.

[2] Michel Onfray, *In Defence of Atheism: The Case Against Christianity, Judaism and Islam* (London: Serpent's Tale, 2007), pp. 67–68, 81, 83, 95.

[3] Benjamin A. Plotinsky , 'The Fanatical Philosopher', www.city-journal.org/html/rev2007-02-01bp.html.

[4] Daniel Dennett, *Breaking the Spell* (London: Penguin, 2006), p. 103.

5 Anthony Kenny , 'The Wisdom of Not Knowing', *The Philosophers' Magazine*, Issue 37, 1st quarter 2007, p. 38.

6 Dennett, *Breaking the Spell*, p. 26.

7 Ludwig Feuerbach, quoted by Luis Palau, *Is God Relevant?* (London: Hodder & Stoughton, 1997), p. 62.

8 Adolf Hitler, *Table Talk*, quoted by John Cornwell, *Darwin's Angel* (London: Profile, 2007), p. 88.

9 Rudolf Bultmann, *Kerygma and Myth* (New York: Harper & Rowe, 1961), p. 5.

10 Antony O'Hear, *Beyond Evolution* (Oxford: Clarendon Press, 1997), p. 201.

11 Nigel Warburton, *Thinking: From A to Z* (London: Routledge, 1998), p. 19.

12 John Gray, 'Sex, Atheism and Piano Legs' in *Heresies: Against Progress and Other Illusions* (London: Granta, 2004), p. 45.

13 Ibid., p. 46.

14 Kai Nielson, *Does God Exist?* (Amherst, NY: Promethius, 1993), p. 48.

15 Piers Benn, 'Is Atheism a Faith Position?', *Think*, Issue 13, Summer 2006, p. 29.

16 Alvin Plantinga, *Warranted Christian Belief* (Oxford: Oxford University Press, 2000), p. 405.

17 Jim Endersby, 'Evolution myths', *The Times Literary Supplement* (14 March 2007), http://tls.timesonline.co.uk/article/0,,25350–2622681,00.html.

18 Sam Harris, *Letter to a Christian Nation* (London: Bantam Press, 2007), p. 63.

19 Alister McGrath, *Christian Theology: An Introduction* (Oxford: Blackwell, 2001), p. 120.

20 R.C. Sproul, John Gerstner and Arthur Lindsay, *Classical Apologetics* (Grand Rapids, MI: Zondervan/Academic Books, 1984), pp. 9–10.

21 David Ford, *Theology: A Very Short Introduction* (Oxford: Oxford University Press, 1999), p. 19.

22 Alvin Plantinga, 'Evolution and Design', James K. Beilby (ed.), *For Faith and Clarity* (Grand Rapids, MI: Baker, 2006), p. 212.

23 Michael Ruse in David L. Hull and Michael Ruse (eds.), *The Philosophy of Biology* (Oxford: Oxford University Press, 1998), p. 671.

24 Alister McGrath, *The Twilight of Atheism* (London: Rider & Co, 2005), p. 87.

25 Anthony Freeman, *God in Us: A Case for Christian Humanism* (London: SCM Press, 1993), p. 3.

26 Ibid., p. 6.

27 Ibid., p. 9.

28 William Lane Craig, in Lee Strobel, *The Case for Faith* (Grand Rapids, MI: Zondervan, 2000), p. 63.

29 Richard Dawkins, in Russell Stannard, *Science & Wonders* (BBC), p. 72.

30 Douglas Adams, *The Hitch Hiker's Guide to the Galaxy* (London: Pan, 1979), p. 62.

31 Steven Weinberg, inaugural speech at the 'Beyond Belief' conference, 5 November 2006.

32 Blaise Pascal, *Pensées*, 263.

33 Carl Sagan, *The Varieties of Scientific Experience: A Personal View of the Search for God* (London: Penguin, 2006), p. 2.

34 Ibid., p. 5.

35 Ibid.

36 Ibid.

37 On problems with understanding even the origin of the material of which Earth is made, cf. Cornelius Hunter, *Science's Blind Spot : The Unseen Religion of Scientific Naturalism* (Grand Rapids, MI: Brazos, 2007).

38 Carl Sagan, *The Varieties of Scientific Experience: A Personal View of the Search for God* (London: Penguin, 2006), p. 11.

39 C.S. Lewis, *The Discarded Image* (Cambridge: Cambridge University Press, 1994), p. 26.

40 Moses Maimonides, *Guide for the Perplexed*.

41 Sagan, *The Varieties of Scientific Experience*, p. 11.

42 Ibid.

43 Ibid., p. 23.

44 Benjamin Wiker, 'Does Science Point to God?', www.arn.org/docs2/news/doessciencepointtogod040903.htm.

45 Sagan, *The Varieties of Scientific Experience*, p. 24.

46 Ibid.

47 Keith Ward, *Pascal's Fire* (Oxford: Oneworld, 2006), p. 13.

48 Onfray, *In Defence of Atheism*, p. 90.

49 Robert C. Koons, 'Science and Theism: Concord, not conflict', in Paul Copan and Paul K. Moser (eds.), *The Rationality of Theism* (London: Routledge, 2003), p. 73.

50 Nancy Pearcey and Charles Thaxton, *The Soul of Science: Christian Faith and Natural Philosophy* (Wheaton, IL: Crossway, 1994), p. 38.

[51] Galileo Galileo, *Dialogue Concerning the Two Chief World Systems,* trans. S. Drake (University of California Press, 1967), p. 37.

[52] Sagan, *The Varieties of Scientific Experience,* p. 36.

[53] Ibid.

[54] Ibid., p. 37.

[55] Ibid., p. 40.

[56] cf. *The Privileged Planet* (Illustra Media), www.theapologiaproject. org/media/the_privileged_planet.ram; Guillermo Gonzalez and Jay Richards, *The Privileged Planet: How Our Place in the Cosmos Is Designed for Discovery* (Washington, DC: Regnery, 2004); Peter D. Ward and Donald Brownlee, *Rare Earth: Why Complex Life Is Uncommon in the Universe* (New York: Copernicus, 2000); *Journey Toward Creation: Travel Back to When Light First Sprang from Darkness* (Questar, 2003); Peter S. Williams, 'New Planet Discovered – just how "earth-like" is it?', http://idpluspeterswilliams.blogspot.com/2007 /04/new-planet-discovered-just-how-earth.html.

[57] Sagan, *The Varieties of Scientific Experience,* pp. 37–38.

[58] Ronald Numbers, 'Seeing the light – of science', www.salon.com/ books/int/2007/01/02/numbers/index2.html.

[59] J. Bronowski, *The Ascent of Man* (BBC, 1974), p. 213.

[60] Ronald Numbers, 'Seeing the light – of science' www.salon.com/ books/int/2007/01/02/numbers/index3.html.

[61] Steve Fuller, *The Intellectual* (Cambridge: Icon, 2006), pp. 56–57.

[62] John O'Leary-Hawthorn, 'Arguments for Atheism', *Reason for the Hope Within* (Grand Rapids, MI: Eerdmans, 1999), p. 121.

[63] Dennett, *Breaking the Spell,* p. 61. Dennett displays lamentable prejudice when he writes in his final endnotes that: 'William Dembski, the author of numerous books and articles attacking evolutionary theory, often complains loudly that his "scientific" work is not treated with respect by working biologists. As coeditor of *Unapologetic Apologetics: Meeting the Challenges of Theological Studies* (2002), he can find the reason for this in his own practices' (p. 412). So now we know: anyone with any connection to apologetics (or is it theology?) couldn't possibly produce any genuinely scientific work, and that work couldn't possibly merit serious consideration; even if the person in question (Dembski) has seven degrees, including a PhD in mathematics and a PhD in the philosophy of science (both from the University of Chicago), and even if the work in question is published by Cambridge University Press as part of the peer-reviewed

monograph series, *Cambridge Studies in Probability, Induction, and Decision Theory* (as was Dembski's groundbreaking book *The Design Inference*). I wonder if the above note about Dembski is one of those 'little jokes, quite innocuous in context' that Dennett predicts 'will be brandished to demonstrate my "intolerance", my "disrespect," my anti-Christian . . . "bias"?' (p. 412). I encourage readers to read Dennett's comments in context for themselves and to make up their own minds.

[64] cf. 'Peer Reviewed & Peer Edited Scientific Publications Supporting the Theory of Intelligent Design', www.discovery.org/scripts/viewDB/index.php?command=view&id=2640&program=CSC%20-%20Scientific%20Research%20and%20Scholarship%20-%20Science; 'Discovery Institute: Books by Centre Fellows', www.discovery.org/csc/books/.

[65] cf. 'A Scientific Dissent from Darwinism', www.dissentfromdawin.org/.

[66] cf. Lyle Jensen, http://intelligentdesign.podomatic.com/enclsure/2007-07-23T10_49_05-07_00.mp3.

[67] cf. Phillip Skell, http://intelligentdesign.podomatic.com/enclsure/2007-11-26T11_25_30-08_00.mp3.

[68] cf. 'Nobel Laureate given standing ovation after slamming Darwinism during a graduation ceremony', www.uncommondescent.com/education/historical-anecdote-2004-nobel-laureate-given-standing-ovation-after-slamming-darwinism/.

[69] cf. www.arn.org/docs2/news/100scientists0929.htm; www.reviewevolution.com/press/pressRelease_100Scientists.php.

[70] 'Brief of Amici Curiae Biologists and Other Scientists in Support of Appellants', reproduced in John G. West, *Darwin's Conservatives: The Misguided Quest* (Centre for Science & Culture, 2006), pp. 115–122.

[71] Francis Fukuyama, *Our Posthuman Future* (London: Profile, 2002), p. 152.

[72] Dominic J. Balestra, 'Science and Religion' in Brian Davies OP (ed.), *Philosophy of Religion: A Guide to the Subject* (London: Continuumm, 2003), pp. 327, 343–344.

[73] Ibid., p. 350.

[74] We can distinguish between hard-line methodological naturalism (HMN) and soft methodological naturalism (SMN). HMN holds that science must not appeal to personal agency of any sort in its

explanations; whereas SMN holds that while science can appeal to personal agency in its explanations, it cannot appeal to supernatural agency. Intelligent design theory is incompatible with HMN, but then so are many subjects whose scientific credentials are uncontroversial (e.g. SETI, archaeology, cryptography, forensic science, parapsychology, psychology and sociology). Intelligent design theory is compatible with SMN.

[75] Richard Dawkins in 'God vs. Science', *Time Magazine*, Sunday, 5 November 2006, www.time.com/time/printout/0,8816,1555132, 00.html.

[76] Josef Pieper, *In Defence of Philosophy* (San Francisco: Ignatius, 2000), p. 95.

[77] Richard Dawkins, *Daily Telegraph*, 31 August 1993.

[78] Francis Collins, *The Language of God* (New York: Free Press, 2006), p. 229.

[79] Laurence Krauss, quoted by Brooks, 'This Week: Beyond Belief', *New Scientist*, 18 November 2006, p. 11.

[80] Kai Nielson, 'Naturalistic explanations of theistic belief', in *A Companion to the Philosophy of Religion* (Oxford: Blackwell, 1999), p. 402.

[81] Robert C. Koons, 'Science and theism: Concord not conflict', in Paul Copan and Paul K. Moser (eds.), *The Rationality of Theism* (London: Routledge, 2003), pp. 76–77.

[82] Steven Weinberg, 'Confronting O'Brian' in Clifton Fadiman (ed.), p. 265.

[83] Peter Atkins, in a 1998 debate at Oxford University, quoted by John Blanchard, *Is God Past His Sell-By Date?*, p. 61.

[84] Freeman, *God in Us*, p. 10.

[85] Stephen Weinberg, 'What About God?', in Christopher Hitchens (ed.), *The Portable Atheist: Essential Readings for the Non-Believer* (London: Da Capo Press, 2007), p. 372.

[86] Ned Block, 'Consciousness', in *A Companion to Philosophy of Mind* (ed.) Samuel Guttenplan (Oxford: Blackwell, 1994), p. 211.

[87] Ned Block, www.edge.org/q2005/q05_3.html.

[88] Ibid.

[89] Atkins, in a 1998 debate at Oxford University, quoted by John Blanchard, *Is God Past His Sell-By Date?*, p. 61.

[90] Steve Jones, *The Language of Genes* (London: Harper Collins), p. xi.

[91] Stephen Hawking, *Black Holes and Baby Universes* (London: Bantam Books), p. 90. Victor Stenger's attempt to answer this question in *God: The Failed Hypothesis* reveals his lack of philosophical acumen:

'many systems of particles are unstable, that is, have limited life-times as they undergo spontaneous phase transitions to more complex structures of lower energy. Since "nothing" is as simple as it gets, we cannot expect it to be very stable. It would likely undergo a spontaneous phase transition to something more complicated, like a universe containing matter.' ('Cosmic Evidence' from *God: The Failed Hypothesis*, in Christopher Hitchens (ed.), *The Portable Atheist* [Cambridge, MA: Da Capo Press, 2007], p. 326.) The description 'simple' can only be predicated of something (something simple), not of nothing. Nothing is not a maximally simple *something*! To what, exactly, does Stenger's 'it' refer when he says that 'we cannot expect *it* to be very stable' and '*It* would likely undergo a spontaneous phase transition . . .'? Either 'it' refers to something or to nothing. If 'it' refers to something, it does not refer to nothing. If 'it' refers to nothing, this is to say that it does not refer to anything, not to say that 'nothing' is a something to which 'it' refers! Stenger is treating 'nothing' like Lewis Caroll's 'nobody' who passed Alice upon the road! *What*, exactly, does Stenger suppose to undergo a process of a phase transition, spontaneous or otherwise? And if we take Stenger's quotation marks around 'nothing' as referring back to his attempt to argue that the existence of matter is a free lunch because the negative gravitational energy of the universe exactly cancels out the positive energy represented by matter, such that 'the total energy of the universe is zero' (Ibid., p. 314), then one simply has to point out that an overall energy measurement of zero obtained by averaging figures that apply to two aspects of an undoubtedly real universe does not thereby equal an ontological 'nothing'! As mathematician George Ellis comments, 'This speculative theory, which apparently presumes that the laws of physics existed in some Platonic domain before space and time came into being, does not deal with the ultimate issues of creation or existence, and is certainly not proven science' ('Case not Proven', http://physicsworld.com/cws/article/print/27736). See also Benjamin Wiker, 'The Atheist's Bench-warmer', www.discovery.org/a/4220; William Lane Craig vs. Victor Stenger, 'Theism vs. Non-Theism', www.bringyou.to/Craig StengerDebate.mp3.

92 Mikuláš Blazek and Miroslav Karaba, 'Several Open Problems in Physics and Cosmology', www.metanexus.net/conferences/pdf/conference2006/Blazek_Karaba.pdf (my italics).

[93] Erwin Schrödinger, 'Nature and the Greeks', quoted by John Blanchard, *Is God Past His Sell-By Date?* (Darlington: Evangelical Press, 2002), p. 66.

[94] J.P. Moreland, *Christianity and the Nature of Science* (Grand Rapids, MI: Baker, 1998), p. 45.

[95] Del Ratzsch, 'Science and Design', www.galilean-library.org/ratzsch.html.

[96] Charles Hartshorne in Gary R. Habermas, Antony G.N. Flew and Terry L. Miethe, *Did Jesus Rise From the Dead?* (Eugene, OR: Wipf & Stock, 2003), p. 138.

[97] Fraser Watts, *The Times*, 10 December 1994.

[98] Guillermo Gonzalez and Jay W. Richards, *The Privilaged Planet* (Washington, DC: Regnery, 2004), p. 228.

[99] J.J. Haldane, *Atheism & Theism* (Oxford: Blackwell, 1996), p. 92.

[100] A.C. Grayling, *The Meaning of Things: Applying Philosophy to Life* (Weidenfeld & Nicolson, 2001), p. 122.

[101] Ibid.

[102] C.S. Lewis, *The Pilgrims Regress* (London: Fount, 1977), p. 48.

[103] Peter Atkins, 1998 debate in Oxford, quoted by John Blanchard, *Does God Believe in Atheists?* (Darlington: Evangelical Press, 2000), p. 436.

[104] Ludwig Feuerbach, quoted by Blanchard, *Does God Believe in Atheists?*, p. 62.

[105] Friedrich Nietzsche, quoted by McGrath, *The Twilight of Atheism*, p. 149.

[106] McGrath, Ibid.

[107] Nietzsche, quoted by McGrath, *ibid*.

[108] Kai Nielson, 'Religiosity and Powerlessness': Part III of 'The Resurgence of Fundamentalism', in *The Humanist*, 37:46, May–June 1977, p. 46.

[109] Michael Ruse, 'Fighting the Fundamentalists', *Skeptical Inquirer*, 31 (2), March/April 2007, p. 40.

[110] C.S. Lewis, *The Problem of Pain* (London: Fount, 2002), p. 134.

[111] C.S. Lewis, *Surprised by Joy* (London: Fount, 1998)

[112] Peter Kreeft, *The Journey* (Downers Grove, IL: IVP, 1996), p. 75.

[113] David Martin, 'Does the Advance of Science Mean Secularisation?', *Science & Christian Belief*, 19 (1), April 2007, p. 14.

6 – A Significant Absence of Evidence?

1. Paul Kurtz, 'Creating Secular and Humanist Alternatives to Religion' in *Free Inquiry*, August/September 2006, 26 (5), p. 7.

2. Richard Dawkins, 'Richard Dawkins: you Ask The Questions Special', *Independent*, 5 December 2006, http://news.independent.co.uk/people/profiles/article2037496.ece.

3. H.L. Mencken, quoted by Alistair Cooke in *Clifton Fadiman* (ed.), p. 123.

4. Piers Benn, 'Is Atheism A Faith Position?', *Think*, Issue 13, Summer 2006, p. 27.

5. Richard Dawkins, *The God Delusion* (London: Bantam Press, 2006), p. 59.

6. Richard Dawkins, *The Blind Watchmaker* (London: Penguin, 1990), Preface, p. x.

7. Paul Kurtz and Edwin H. Wilson, *Humanist Manifesto* II (1973), www.americanhumanist.org/about/manifesto2.php.

8. Antony Flew and T.T. Miethe, *Does God Exist? A Believer And An Atheist Debate* (Harper SanFrancisco, 1991), p. 19.

9. Ibid.

10. Keith Parsons, 'Is there a case for Christian theism?' in J.P. Moreland and Kai Nielson, *Does God Exist? The Debate Between Theists and Atheists* (Amherts, NY: Prometheus, 1993), p. 192.

11. Kai Nielson, 'Naturalistic explanations of theistic belief', *A Companion to the Philosophy of Religion* (Oxford: Blackwell, 1999) , p. 403.

12. Alvin Plantinga, *Warranted Christian Belief* (Oxford: Oxford University Press, 2000), p. 242.

13. William Lane Craig, 'The Evidence for Christianity', www.bethinking.org/resource.php?ID=100&TopicID=&CategoryID. On Kant, cf. Norman L. Geisler, *Christian Apologetics* (Grand Rapids, MI: Baker, 1976).

14. See R. Douglas Geivett and Gary R. Habermas (eds.), *In Defence of Miracles* (Leicester: Apollos, 1997); James F. Sennett and Douglas Groothuis (eds.), *In Defence of Natural Theology: A Post-Humean Assessment* (Downers Grove, IL: IVP, 2005); Richard Swinburne, 'The Argument from Design' in R. Douglas Geivett and Brendan Sweetman (eds.), *Contemporary Perspectives on Religious Epistemology* (Oxford: Oxford University Press, 1992); Charles Taliaferro and Anders Hendrickson, 'Hume's Racism and His Case Against the Miraculous', *Philosophia Christi*, Volume 4, Number 2, 2002; Peter S.

Williams, 'Design and the Humean Touchstone', www.arn.org/docs/williams/pw_humeantouchstone.htm.

[15] Kai Nielson, 'Naturalistic explanations of theistic belief', *A Companion to the Philosophy of Religion*, p. 404.

[16] James F. Sennett and Douglas Groothuis, *In Defence of Natural Theology: A Post-Humean Assessment*, p. 15.

[17] Nicholas Capaldi, *David Hume* (Hall & Co, 1975), chapter 9; see also Dave Armstrong, 'Was Skeptical Philosopher David Hume an Atheist?', http://ic.net/~erasmus/RAZ515.HTM.

[18] John Perry and Michael Bratman, *Introduction to Philosophy: Classical and Contemporary Readings* (Oxford: Oxford University Press, 1998).

[19] See Richard Swinburne, 'The Argument from Design', in R. Douglas Geivett and Brendan Sweetman (eds.), *Contemporary Perspectives on Religious Epistemology* (Oxford: Oxford University Press, 1992); Brain Davies, *An Introduction to the Philosophy of Religion*, new edition (Oxford: Oxford University Press, 1993).

[20] David Hume, *An Enquiry Concerning Human Understanding*, 136.

[21] cf. Richard Swinburne, *The Existence of God*, 2nd edition, appendix A, (Oxford: Clarendon Press, 1994).

[22] cf. Paul Copan, 'Can Michael Martin be a Moral Realist? Sic et Non', www.paulcopan.com/articles/pdf/Michael-Martin-a-moral-realist.pdf; Paul Copan, 'Morality and Meaning Without God: Another Failed Attempt – A review Essay on *Atheism, Morality, and Meaning*', www.paulcopan.com/articles/pdf/Morality-Meaning. pdf; Paul Copan, 'The Necessity of God: A book review of *The Impossibility of God* by Michael Martin and Ricki Monnier, editors (Prometheus Books, 2003)', www.paulcopan.com/articles/pdf/Necessity-of-God.pdf; The Fernandes-Martin Debate, www.infidels.org/library/ modern/michael_martin/fernandes-martin/index.shtml; J.P. Moreland and Gary R. Habermas, *Beyond Death: Exploring the Evidence for Immortality* (Wheaton, IL: Crossway, 1998); James Patrick Holding, 'Michael Martin on the Problem of Evil', www.tektonics.org/lp/martinm02.html; James Patrick Holding, 'Rebuttals of Michael Martin's *The Case Against Christianity*', www.tektonics .org/lp/martincacex.html; www.tektonics.org/lp/martincac2 .html; www.tektonics.org/lp/martincac04.html; www.tektonics .org/lp/martincac06.html and www. tektonics.org/lp/martincac07.html; Stephen E. Parrish, 'The Case Against Christianity: A Summary Critique', http://www.equip.org/free/DH230.pdf;

Centre for Reformed Theology and Apologetics: Responses to Atheist Philosopher, Michael Martin (mainly by John Frame), www.reformed.org/apologetics/index.html?mainframe=/apologetics/martin_TAG.html.

23 Edward Feser, *Philosophy of Mind: A Short Introduction* (Oxford: Oneworld, 2005), p. 64.

24 Robert C. Koons, 'Science and Theism: Concord, not Conflict', in Paul Copan and Paul K. Moser (eds.), *The Rationality of Theism* (London: Routledge, 2003), p. 73.

25 John Humphrys, 'The Return of God?', www.telegraph.co.uk/news/main.jhtml?xml=/news/2007/03/03/nrgod03.xml.

26 Lewis Wolpert, 'The Hard Cell', *Third Way*, March 2007, p. 16.

27 Ibid., p. 17.

28 Tom Price, 'Craig vs. Wolpert', http://abetterhope.blogspot.com/2007/02/william-lane-craig-vs-lewis-wolpert.html.

29 John Humphrys 'The Return of God?', www.telegraph.co.uk/news/main.jhtml?xml=/news/2007/03/03/nrgod03.xml.

30 William Lane Craig, Newsletter, March 2007, www.reasonable-faith.org/site/News2?page=NewsArticle&id=5491.

31 Lewis Wolpert, 'The Hard Cell', *Third Way*, March 2007, p. 18.

32 Ibid., p. 17.

33 Ibid.

34 Ibid.

35 Ibid., p. 18.

36 Ibid., p. 17.

37 Ibid., p. 16.

38 Antony Flew, *There Is A God* (New York: Harper One, 2007), pp. 86–88.

39 Wolpert, 'The Hard Cell', *Third Way*, March 2007, p. 18.

40 Ibid.

41 Franklin Harold, *The Way of the Cell: Molecules, Organisms, and the Order of Life* (New York: Oxford University Press, 2003), p. 254.

42 Ibid.

43 William Lane Craig, 'Naturalism and Intelligent Design', in Robert B. Stewart (ed.), *Intelligent Design: William A. Dembski & Michael Ruse in Dialogue* (Minneapolis: Fortress, 2007), pp. 66, 71.

44 Dawkins, *The Blind Watchmaker*, p. 151, my emphasis.

45 Richard Lewontin, 'Billions and Billions of Demons', *New York Review of Books*, 9 January 1997.

[46] Ibid., my italics.
[47] Antony Flew, *Philosophy Now*, Issue 47, August/September 2004, p. 22.
[48] Ibid.
[49] Dawkins, *The God Delusion*, p. 137.
[50] Robert Shapiro, 'A replicator was not involved in the origin of life', in *IUBMB Life* 49 (2000), pp. 173–175.
[51] Stuart Pullen, *Intelligent Design or Evolution? Why the Origin of Life and the Evolution of Molecular Knowledge Imply Design* (Raleigh, NC: Intelligent Design Books, 2005), pp. 8–9.
[52] Paul Davies, *New Scientist*, November 2006, p. 35.
[53] Gregg Easterbrook, *Wired*, February 2007, p. 108.
[54] Reported by Tom Woodward, *Darwin Strikes Back: Defending the Science of Intelligent Design* (Grand Rapids, MI: Baker, 2006), p. 134.
[55] Dawkins, *The God Delusion*, pp. 138–139.
[56] Richard Dawkins, *Climbing Mount Improbable* (London: Penguin, 1997), my emphasis.
[57] Stephen C. Meyer, 'Evidence for design in Physics and Biology', in *Science and Evidence for Design in the Universe* (San Francisco: Ignatius, 2000), p. 75.
[58] Dean L. Overman, *A Case Against Accident and Self-Organization* (Oxford: Rowman & Littlefield, 1997), p. 63.
[59] David Swift, *Evolution Under the Microscope* (Stirling: Leigton Academic, 2002), p. 344.
[60] Fazale Rana and Hugh Ross, *Origins of Life* (Colorado Springs: NavPress, 2004), p. 163. See also www.sciencedaily.com/releases/1999/12/991213052506.htm.
[61] Jonathan Sarfati with Mike Matthews, *Refuting Evolution 2* (Green Forest, AR: Master Books, 2002), p. 155.
[62] Rana and Ross, *Origins of Life*, pp. 162, 165, my italics.
[63] Paul Davies, *The Fifth Miracle: The Search for the Origins of Life* (London: Penguin, 1998), pp. 64–65.
[64] Swift, *Evolution Under the Microscope*, p. 139.
[65] Davies, *The Fifth Miracle*, pp. 64–65.
[66] Danny R. Faulkner in John F. Ashton (ed.), *On the Seventh Day* (Green Forrest: Master Books, 2002), p. 107.
[67] cf. Hugh Ross, 'Fine Tuning of Physical Life Support Body', www.reasons.org/resources/apologetics/design_evidences/20020502_solar_system_design.shtml?main and 'Probability for a Life Support Body',

www.reasons.org/resources/ apologetics/ design_evidences/
20020502_life_support_body_prob.shtml? main.

[68] Hugh Ross, 'Astronomical Evidences for a Personal, Transcendent God', pp. 169–170.

[69] Guillermo Gonzalez and Jay W. Richards, *Privileged Planet* (Washington, DC: Regnery Publishing, 2004), p. 341.

[70] Peter Ward and Don Brownlee, *Rare Earth* (New York: Springer-Verlag, 2000), pp. 35, 37.

[71] Dawkins, *The God Delusion*, p. 71.

[72] Ibid.

[73] Richard Dawkins, *OP-ED, Free Inquiry*, October/November 2004, Vol. 24 No. 6, pp. 11–12.

[74] J.T. Trevors and D. L. Abel, 'Three subsets of sequence complexity and their relevance to biopolymeric information', *Theoretical Biology and Medical Modelling* (2005, 2:29), www.pubmedcentral.nih.gov/articlerender.fcgi?artid=1208958.

[75] Fred Hoyle and Chandra Wickramasinghe, *Evolution from Space* (Dent, 1981), pp. 24–148.

[76] Dawkins, OP-ED, *Free Inquiry*, October/November 2004, Vol. 24 No. 6, pp. 11–12.

[77] cf. Peter S. Williams, 'The Design Inference from Specified Complexity Defended by Scholars Outside the Intelligent Design Movement – A Critical Review', *Philosophia Christi*, Volume 9, Number 2, 2007, pp. 407–428.

[78] Wolpert, 'The Hard Cell', *Third Way*, March 2007, p. 17.

[79] John O'Leary-Hawthorne, 'Arguments for Atheism' in Michael J. Murray (ed.), *Reason for the Hope Within* (Grand Rapids, MI: Eerdmans, 1999), p. 124.

[80] Ibid., p. 51.

[81] Keith Ward, *The Case for Religion* (Oxford: Oneworld, 2004), p. 29.

[82] Scot A. Shalkowski, 'Atheological Apologetics' in R. Douglas Geivett and Brendan Sweetman (eds.), *Contemporary Perspectives on Religious Epistemology* (Oxford: Oxford University Press, 1992), pp. 63–70.

[83] Robert A. Harris, *The Integration of Faith and Learning: A Worldview Approach* (Eugene, OR: Cascade, 2004), p. 83.

[84] Richard Norman, *On Humanism* (London: Routledge, 2004), p. 16.

[85] Antony Flew, *The Presumption of Atheism* (London: Pemberton, 1976), p. 14.

[86] Paul Copan, 'The Presumptuousness of Atheism', www.rzim.org/publications/essay_arttext.php?id=3.

[87] Kai Nielsen, *Reason and Practice* (New York: Harper & Row, 1971), pp. 143–144.

[88] Paul Copan, 'The Presumptuousness of Atheism', www.rzim.org/publications/essay_arttext.php?id=3.

[89] Steven Lovell, 'Evidence and Atheism', www.csl-philosophy.co.uk/.

[90] William Rowe 'Reflections on the Craig-Flew Debate' in Stan W. Wallace (ed.), *Does God Exist? The Craig-Flew Debate* (London: Ashgate, 2003), pp. 70–71.

[91] J.P. Moreland and William Lane Criag, *Philosophical Foundations for a Christian Worldview* (Downers Grove, IL: IVP, 2003), p. 157.

[92] Ibid., p. 158.

[93] J.J.C. Smart, *Atheism & Theism* (Oxford: Blackwell, 1996), pp. 50–51.

[94] Robert A. Harries, *The Integration of Faith and Learning* (Eugene, OR: Cascade Books, 2004), p. 82.

[85] Michael J. Murray, 'Seek and You will Find', in *God and the Philosophers* (ed.) Thomas V. Morris (Oxford: Oxford University Press, 1994), p. 69.

[86] Ibid., p. 69.

[87] Ibid., p. 70.

7 – The Emperor Has No Clothes: Natural Theology and the God Hypothesis

[1] Jim Walker, 'Book Review: The God Delusion', http//nobeliefs.com/dawkins4.htm.

[2] Richard Dawkins, *The God Delusion* (London: Bantam, 2006), p. 5.

[3] Ibid., pp. 5–6.

[4] Ibid., p. 6.

[5] James Swingle, www.noneuclideancafe.com/issues/vol2_issue1_Fall2006/reviews.htm#Dawkins.

[6] P.Z. Myers, www.seedmagazine.com/news/2006/10/bad_religion.php.

[7] Jim Walker, 'Book Review: The God Delusion', http://nobeliefs.com/dawkins4.htm.

[8] Terry Eagleton, *London Review of Books*, Vol. 28 No. 20, 19 October 2006.

9 John Cornwell, 'A Question of Respect', www.timesonline.co.uk/ article/0,,2102-2375182.html.

10 Dawkins, *The God Delusion*, pp. 132, 230, 231, 293.

11 Stephen Law, *The War for Children's Minds* (London: Routledge, 2006), p. 23.

12 Antony Latham, *The Naked Emperor: Darwinism Exposed* (London: Janus, 2005), p. 243.

13 Barney Zwartz, 'The God Delusion', www.theage.com.au.news/ book-reviews/the-god-delusion/2006/11/24/1164341.

14 Alister McGrath, 'The Dawkins Delusion', www.theosthinktank. co.uk/The_Dawkins_Delusion.aspx?ArticleID=50&PageID=11&Ref PageID=5.

15 Alister McGrath, *Dawkins' God* (Oxford: Blackwell, 2005), pp. 83–84.

16 Terry Eagleton, 'Lunging, Flailing, Mispunching', *London Review of Books*, Vol. 28 No. 20, 19 October 2006, www.lrb.co.uk/v28/n20/ eagl01_.html.

17 Jim Holt, 'A passionate atheist's case against religion', *International Herald Tribune*, Saturday-Sunday, October 21–22, 2006, p. 10.

18 Richard Swinburne, 'Evidence for God' in Gillian Ryeland (ed.), *Beyond Reasonable Doubt: Evidence for God in the 1990s* (Norwich: The Canterbury Press, 1991), pp. 13–14.

19 Ibid., p. 14.

20 H.H. Price, quoted by Charles Taliaferro, *Contemporary Philosophy of Religion* (Oxford: Blackwell, 2001), p. 272.

21 Dawkins, *The God Delusion*, p. 90.

22 Ibid., p. 92.

23 Thomas Aquinas, 'Whether God Exists?' from *Summa Theologica*, www.newadvent.org/summa/100203.htm.

24 Dawkins, *The God Delusion*, p. 77.

25 Ibid.

26 David Berlinski, *The Devil's Delusion: Atheism And Its Scientific Pretensions* (New York: Crown Forum, 2008), p. 68.

27 Dawkins, *The God Delusion*, p. 77.

28 J.L. Mackie, *The Miracle of Theism* (Oxford: Oxford University Press, 1982), p. 7.

29 Sam Harris, *Letter to a Christian Nation* (London: Bantam, 2006), pp. 72–73. Attacking how an argument 'more or less' goes doesn't cut the philosophical mustard.

30 Daniel Dennett, *Breaking the Spell* (London: Penguin, 2006), p. 242.

[31] For example, cf. Norman L. Geisler, *Christian Apologetics* (Grand Rapids, MI: Baker, 1995), in which Geisler argues both that 'The theist need not claim that everything has a cause' (p. 238) and that 'a self-caused being is impossible' (p. 241).

[32] Including Julian Baggini, Richard Dawkins, Daniel Dennett, Sam Harris and Nigel Warburton.

[33] It is worth noting that none of our atheists critique a quoted cosmological argument; and that they all present their summary as if it represented the core of an entire class of theistic argument that in reality comes in at least three distinct versions (e.g. Thomistic, Leibnitzian and Kalam arguments).

[34] A.C. Grayling, *Against All Gods* (London: Oberon Books, 2007), p. 34.

[35] cf. A. C. Grayling, 'Understanding Realism', http://acgrayling.com/Realism/realism.html.

[36] Dawkins, *The God Delusion*, p. 80.

[37] Ibid.

[38] Ibid., p. 81.

[39] Ibid., p. 82.

[40] Stephen T. Davis, 'The ontological argument' in Paul Copan and Paul K. Moser (eds.), *The Rationality of Theism* (London: Routledge, 2003), p. 94.

[41] Dawkins, *The God Delusion*, p. 83.

[42] Christopher Hitchens, *God Is Not Great* (London: Atlantic, 20907), p. 265.

[43] Immanuel Kant, *Critique of Pure Reason* (ed.) Norman Kemp Smith (Macmillan, 1929), p. 61.

[44] Charles Hartshorne, 'A Recent Ontological Argument' in Chad Meister (ed.), *The Philosophy of Religion Reader* (London: Routledge, 2008), p. 311.

[45] Davis, 'The ontological argument' in Paul Copan and Paul K. Moser (eds.), *The Rationality of Theism*, pp. 98–99.

[46] Keith Yandell, 'David Hume on Meaning, Verification and Natural Theology' in James F. Sennett and Douglas Groothuis (eds.), *In Defence of Natural Theology: A Post-Humean Assessment* (Downers Grove: IVP, 2005), p. 72.

[47] Jim Holt, 'Beyond Belief', *New York Times*; see also Trent Dougherty, 'Concise Introduction to the Modal Ontological Argument for the Existence of God', www.abarnett.demon.co.uk/atheism/ contol.html.

⁴⁸ Alvin Plantinga, *God, Freedom and Evil* (Grand Rapids, MI: Eerdmans, 1977), from Michael Peterson et al., *Philosophy of Religion: Selected Readings* (Oxford: Oxford University Press, 1996), p. 158.

⁴⁹ Ibid., p. 163.

⁵⁰ Ibid., p. 159.

⁵¹ Michael Peterson et al., *Reason and Religious Belief* (Oxford: Oxford University Press, 1991), p. 73.

⁵² C. Stephen Evans, *Philosophy of Religion* (Downers Grove, IL: IVP, 1982), p. 50.

⁵³ On the coherence of the concept of God, cf. Thomas V. Morris, *Our Idea of God* (Notre Dame, IN: University of Notre Dame Press, 1991) and Charles Taliaferro, 'The Possibility of God' in Paul Copan and Paul K. Moser (eds.), *The Rationality of Theism* (London: Routledge, 2003).

⁵⁴ Hartshorne, 'A Recent Ontological Argument' in Meister (ed.), *The Philosophy of Religion Reader*, p. 311.

⁵⁵ Charles Taliaferro, *Contemporary Philosophy of Religion* (Oxford: Blackwell, 2001), p. 381.

⁵⁶ Alvin Plantinga, *The Nature of Necessity* (Oxford: Clarendon Press, 1978), p. 221.

⁵⁷ Alvin Plantinga, *God, Freedom and Evil* (Grand Rapids, MI: Eerdmans, 1974), p. 163.

⁵⁸ Josef Seifert in Roy Abraham Varghese (ed.), *Great Thinkers On Great Questions* (Oxford: Oneworld, 1998), p. 131.

⁵⁹ Taliaferro, *Contemporary Philosophy of Religion*, p. 379.

⁶⁰ Trent Dougherty, 'Concise Introduction to the Modal Ontological Argument for the Existence of God', www.abarnett.demon.co.uk/ atheism/ontol.html.

⁶¹ Thomas Aquinas, *Summa Theologica*, www.newadvent.org/ summa/ 100203.htm.

⁶² Dawkins, *The God Delusion*, p. 79.

⁶³ cf. Christopher F. J. Martin, 'The Fourth Way', http://users.colloqui- um.co.uk/~BARRETT/Viae4.htm.

⁶⁴ E.L. Mascall, *He Who Is* (London: Longmans, 1954), p. 53.

⁶⁵ Paul Copan, *True For You But Not For Me* (Minneapolis, MN: Bethany House, 1998), p. 45.

⁶⁶ Paul Copan, 'A Moral Argument', in Paul Copan and William Lane Craig (eds.), *Passionate Conviction: Contemporary Discourses on Christian Apologetics* (Nashville, TN: B&H Academic), pp. 85–86.

[67] Richard Dawkins, 'God's Utility Function', *Scientific American*, November, 1995, p. 85, my italics.

[68] Dawkins, *The God Delusion*, p. 232.

[69] Antony Flew, *There Is A God* (New York: HarperOne, 2007), p. 95.

[70] Dawkins, *The God Delusion*, p. 141.

[71] Ibid., p. 136.

[72] Ibid.

[73] Ibid.

[74] Ibid.

[75] Tom Woodward, *Darwin Strikes Back* (Grand Rapids, MI: Baker, 2006), p. 160.

[76] Dawkins, *The God Delusion*, p. 141.

[77] Jimmy H. Davies and Harry L. Poe, *Designer Universe* (Nashville, TN: Broadman & Holman, 2002), p. 110.

[78] Dawkins, *The God Delusion*, pp. 144–145.

[79] Ibid., p. 145.

[80] Guillermo Gonzalez, 'Home Alone in the Universe', www.arn. org/docs/gonzalez/gg_homealone_.htm.

[81] Richard Swinburne, 'The Argument from Design', mind.ucsd.edu/ syllabi/02–03/01w/readings/swinburne-design.pdf.

[82] Dawkins, *The God Delusion*, p. 366.

[83] Ibid., p. 145.

[84] Ibid., p. 136.

[85] Gonzalez, 'Home Alone in the Universe', www.arn.org/docs/gonzalez/gg_homealone_.htm.

[86] After all, the designer might have made more than one universe. Hence the existence of multiple universes is logically compatible with the existence of a universe designer.

[87] Nothing depends upon the traditional Shakespearian reference here – the argument works just as well if we imagine unearthing an alien text on a distant planet.

[88] Paul Davies, *The Goldilocks Enigma: Why is the universe just right for life?* (London: Penguin, 2007), pp. 231–232, 237.

[89] Robin Collins, 'Design and the Many Worlds Hypothesis', http://home.messiah.edu/~rcollins/finetune/Craig7.htm.

[90] Flew, *There is a God*, pp. 118–119. Brian Green, physicist and mathematician at Columbia University, and author of *The Fabric of the Cosmos*, points out that positing unlimited probabilistic resources is a science stopper: 'If true, the idea of a multiverse would be . . . a rich and

astounding upheaval, but one with potentially hazardous consequences. Beyond the inherent difficulty in assessing its validity, when
should we allow the multiverse framework to be invoked in lieu of a
more traditional scientific explanation? Had this idea surfaced a hundred years ago, might researchers have chalked up various mysteries
to how things just happen to be in our corner of the multiverse and not
pressed on to discover all the wondrous science of the last century?
. . . The danger, if the multiverse idea takes root, is that researchers may
too quickly give up the search for underlying explanations. When
faced with seemingly inexplicable observations, researchers may
invoke the framework of the multiverse prematurely – proclaiming
some phenomenon or other to merely reflect conditions in our own
bubble universe and thereby failing to discover the deeper understanding that awaits us' ('The Multiverse', in John Brockman (ed.),
What's Your Dangerous Idea? [London: Pocket Books, 2006], pp.
120–121).

[91] Hitchens, *God Is Not Great*, p. 71.

[92] Dawkins, *The God Delusion*, p. 157.

[93] Richard Norman thinks that 'Dawkins has an excellent reply to this
argument [i.e. the fine-tuning argument]. He argues that whatever
the explanation of the initial conditions may be, God is not a good
explanation, because the existence of a hugely powerful intelligence
who knows all the physical constants and scientific laws is even more
difficult to explain than the things it is supposed to account for'
('Holy Communion', *New Humanist*, November–December 2007,
p. 18).

[94] Dawkins, *The God Delusion*, pp. 157–158.

[95] Jakob Wolf, 'A Critique of "Theistic Evolution" As a Supplementary
Model of the Relationship between Darwinian Theory and Religion',
www.iscid.org/papers/Wolf_TheisticEvolution_011505.pdf.

[96] Dawkins, *The God Delusion*, pp. 157–158.

[97] Jay Richards, quoted by Dembski, *No Free Lunch* (Oxford: Rowman &
Littlefield, 2001), p. 255.

[98] William Lane Craig, 'Why I Believe in God', in Norman L. Geisler
and Paul K. Hoffman (eds.), *Why I Am A Christian* (Grand Rapids, MI:
Baker, 2001), p. 73.

[99] Alvin Plantinga, 'The Dawkins Confusion', www.christianitytoday.
com/bc/2007/002/1.21.html.

[100] Dawkins, *The God Delusion*, p. 109.

[101] Ibid., p. 73.

[102] Mike King, *The God Delusion Revisited* (Lulu, 2007), p. 49.

[103] Tom Woodward, *Darwin Strikes Back* (Grand Rapids, MI: Baker, 2006), p. 166.

[104] Dawkins, *The God Delusion*, p. 147.

[105] Flew, *There is a God*, p. 111.

[106] Berlinski, *The Devil's Delusion*, p. 142.

[107] James E. Taylor, *Introducing Apologetics: Cultivating Christian Commitment* (Grand Rapids, MI: Baker, 2006), p. 139.

[108] 'A category error occurs when someone acts as though some object had properties which it does not or cannot have. The reason why it cannot have those properties is because the properties belong to objects in some other category or class.' (See http://atheism.about.com/library/glossary/general/bldef_categoryerror.htm).

[109] Alvin Plantinga, 'The Dawkins Confusion', www.christianitytoday.com/bc/2007/002/1.21.html.

[110] Richard Swinburne, http://users.ox.ac.uk/~orie0087/frameset-pdfs.shtml.

[111] cf. Jay Wesley Richards, 'Divine Simplicity: The Good, the Bad, and the Ugly', in James K. Beilby (ed.), *For Faith and Clarity: Philosophical Contributions to Christian Theology* (Grand Rapids, MI: Baker Academic, 2006).

[112] J.P. Moreland and William Lane Craig, *Philosophical Foundations For A Christian Worldview* (Downers Grove, IL: IVP, 2003), p. 490.

[113] Thomas Nagel, quoted by Paul Nelson, 'Thomas Nagel Critiques Dawkins: The Design-Cannot-Possibly-Be-True Argument', www.idthefuture.com/2006/10/nagel_on_dawkins.html.

[114] Alvin Plantinga, 'The Dawkins Confusion', www.christianitytoday.com/bc/2007/002/1.21.html.

[115] Tim Gebhart, 'Book Review – Atheist Manifesto II: The God Delusion by Richard Dawkins', http://blogcritics.org/archives/2006/10/31/085317.php.

[116] Dawkins, *The God Delusion*, p. 5.

[117] Ibid., p. 6.

[118] Ibid., p. 5.

[119] Thomas Nagel, *The New Republic*, 'Fear of Religion', www.tnr.com/doc.mhtml?i=20061023&s=nagel102306.

[120] Jeremy Pierce, prosblogion.ektopos.com/archives/2006/10/dawkins_review.html.

121 Dawkins, *The God Delusion*, p. 77.

122 Ibid., p. 59.

123 Jay Tolson, 'The New Unbelievers', www.templeton-cambridge. org/fellows/tolson/publications/2006.11.05/the_new_unbelievers/.

124 Richard Dawkins quoted by Nicky Gumbel, 'Is God a delusion?', *Alpha News*, March-June 2008, p. 15.

125 Gregory Clark, 'Reasons to Disagree With Richard Dawkins – Politely', www.case.edu.au/uploads/media/clarke-dawkins-op-ed.pdf.

Conclusion: 'None Shall Pass'

1 Paul Copan, 'Interview with Paul Copan: Is Yaweh a Moral Monster?', www.epsociety.org/blog/2008/04/interview-with-paul-copan-is-yahweh.asp.

2 Becky Garrison, *The New Atheist Crusaders And Their Unholy Grail* (Nashville: Thomas Nelson, 2007), p. 26.

3 Richard Norman, 'Holy Communion', *New Humanist*, November-December 2007, pp. 16–17.

6 cf. 'TheBlackKnight'www.youtube.com/watch?v=kNKSzmM44g-E&feature=related.

5 Ibid.

6 Ibid.

7 Peter Berkowitz, 'The New New Atheism', *The Wall Street Journal* Editorial Page, 16 July 2007.

8 cf. 'She's a Witch', www.youtube.com/watch?v=zrzMhU_4m-g&feature=related.

9 John F. Haught, *God and the New Atheism: A Critical Response to Dawkins, Harris, and Hitchens* (London: Westminster John Knox Press, 2008) p. 25.

10 Michael Licona in Lee Strobel, *The Case for Jesus* (Grand Rapids, MI: Zondervan, 2007), p. 143.

11 Colin Tudge, 'Review: God's Undertaker: Has Science Buried God?', http://books.guardian.co.uk/reviews/politicsphilosophyandsociety/0,,2223841,00.html.

12 Michael Novak, 'Lonely Atheists of the Global Village', www.aei.org/publications/filter.all,pubID.25770/pub_detail.asp.

[13] Alvin Plantinga, 'Two Dozen or so Theistic Arguments', www.calvin.edu/academic/philosophy/virtual_library/articles/plantinga_alvin/two_dozen_or_so_theistic_arguments.pdf.

[14] Invited to debate Professor William Lane Craig in 2007, Dawkins replied: 'I've never heard of William Craig. A debate with him might look good on his resume, but it wouldn't look good on mine!' cf. William Lane Craig, 'The New Atheism: 2 of 2', www.rfmedia.org/RF_audio_video/RF_podcast/The_New_Atheism.mp3; Victor Reppert, 'Dawkins Ducks Craig', http://dangerousidea.blogspot.com/2007/01/dawkins-ducks-craig.html; Tom Price, 'Dawkins has a conversation', www.damaris.org/content/content.php?type=5&id=530. It is astonishing that today's leading public atheist has 'never heard' of one of today's leading theistic philosophers (especially when Craig is the leading contemporary advocate of the *Kalam* version of the cosmological argument). Nor would it take much effort to find out about Craig and to see that debating a scholar who has shared platforms with the likes of John Dominic Crossan, Daniel Dennett, Theodore Drange, Paul Draper, Bart Ehrman, Antony Flew, Paul Kurtz, Gerd Lüdemann, Kai Nielson, Keith Parsons, Massimo Pigliucci, Quentin Smith, Walter Sinnott-Armstrong, Victor Stenger and Richard Taylor would look good on anyone's CV! Indeed, I know the organizer of the 2007 Craig tour of England, who issued the invitation to Dawkins to debate Craig, and I know that his invitation included information about Craig. Craig ended up debating Lewis Wolpert under the chairmanship of John Humphrys. Perhaps Wolpert doesn't care about his CV?!

[15] Alvin Plantinga, 'The Dawkins Confusion', *Books & Culture*, March/April 2007, www.christianitytoday.com/bc/2007/002/1.21.html.

[16] Michael Ruse, *Isis*, December 2007.

[17] As Richard L. Purtill warns, 'many treatments of arguments for God's existence take some very old and very short treatment of the proofs for God's existence, and then follow this with later criticisms, some written by present-day philosophers. Now even if the old version of the argument is essentially correct, as it may be, the impression given (sometimes, I fear, intentionally) is that of a historical progression: Long ago this is how men thought they could argue for God's existence, but then such and such criticisms were discovered. But in fact both arguments and objections have been long debated.

Also the language used and the assumptions made by an older philo-sophical text create difficulties in understanding and appreciating the argument. A particular favorite for this tactic is the version of five arguments for God's existence given by St. Thomas Aquinas in a very long work, which was a sort of philosophical and theological ency-clopedia, called the *Summa Theologica*. This version covers only about a page of print and was never intended as a full-scale version of the arguments, only as a sort of reminder for those who knew them already. It was addressed to philosophers who might or might not be Christians but who agreed with Aquinas about certain ways of doing philosophy and certain philosophical positions, mostly derived from the Greek philosopher Aristotle. Terms like "cause" and "motion" are used in senses that are no longer familiar; and with all due respect to the Saint, some of the arguments are ambiguously put and at least one is put in such a way as to be seriously incomplete if not just plain invalid. This is all to the good for those who want a good brief state-ment of the arguments so that they can proceed to their real business of refuting them' (*Reason to Believe* [Grand Rapids, MI: Eerdmans, 1974]), http://members.core.com/~tony233/Reason_to_Believe. htm#c7.

[18] Richard Dawkins, 'God's Utility Function', *Scientific American*, November, 1995, p. 85, my italics.

[19] Julian Baggini, *Atheism: A Very Short Introduction* (Oxford: Oxford University Press, 2003), pp. 41–51.

[20] Novak, 'Lonely Atheists of the Global Village', www.aei.org/publi-cations/filter.all,pubID.25770/pub_detail.asp.

[21] Norman, 'Holy Communion', *New Humanist*, pp. 16–17, my italics.

[22] Novak, 'Lonely Atheists of the Global Village', www.aei.org/publi-cations/filter.all,pubID.25770/pub_detail.asp.

[23] Ibid.

[24] Douglas Groothuis, 'Who Designed the Designer? A Dialogue On Richard Dawkins's The God Delusion', *Think*, Issue Sixteen, Winter 2008, p. 35.

[25] A.C. Grayling, *The Meaning of Things: Applying Philosophy to Life* (London: Weidenfeld & Nicolson, 2001), p. 25.

[26] Fr Andrew SDC, Margaret Pepper (ed.), *The Macmillan Dictionary of Religious Quotations* (London: Macmillan, 1996), p. 161.

[27] John Humphrys, *In God We Doubt* (London: Hodder & Stoughton, 2007), pp. 16–17.

28 I remain unmoved by any case for atheism with which I am acquainted; but I cheerfully concede that there are scholars outside the realm of popular atheology, surveyed herein, who are capable of mounting more intellectually responsible and sophisticated challenges to theism. John Schellenberg and Quentin Smith spring to mind as examples. These scholars propound anti-theistic arguments that I consider unsound, but which make what I consider to be far subtler, interesting and understandable mistakes than those made, for example, by the New Atheists. But that, as they say, is a different story. cf. Daniel Howard-Snyder and Paul K. Moser (eds.), *Divine Hiddenness: New Essays* (Cambridge: Cambridge University Press, 2002); Quentin Smith and William Lane Craig, *Theism, Atheism and Big Bang Cosmology* (Oxford: Clarendon Press, 1995); Chad Meister (ed.), *The Philosophy of Religion Reader* (London: Routledge, 2008).

Appendix

1 Daniel Dennett, *Breaking the Spell* (London: Penguin, 2007), p. 164.

2 Antony Flew, *There Is A God: How the World's Most Notorious Atheist Changed His Mind* (New York: HarperOne, 2007), p. 157.

3 Ibid., pp. 185–186.

4 Richard Dawkins, *The God Delusion* (London: Bantam, 2006), pp. 37–97.

5 Francis Collins, *The Language of God* (New York: Free Press, 2006), p. 223.

6 Craig L. Blomberg, *The Historical Reliability of the Gospels* (Leicester: IVP, 2008).

7 Norman L. Geisler and Frank Turek, *I Don't Have Enough Faith To Be An Atheist* (Wheaton, IL: Crossway, 2004), p. 225.

8 cf. John Wenham, *Christ and the Bible* (Grand Rapids, MI: Baker, 1984), pp. 186–187.

9 Quoted by Norman L. Geisler and Peter Bocchino, *Unshakeable Foundations* (Eugene, Oregon: Bethany House, 2001), p. 258.

10 Winfried Corduan, *No Doubt About It* (Nashville, TN: Broadman & Homan, 1997), p. 193.

11 N.T. Wright, Foreword, F.F. Bruce, *The New Testament Documents: Are They Reliable?* (Grand Rapids, MI: Eerdmans, 2000), p. x.

12 Geilser and Bocchino, *Unshakeable Foundations*, p. 257.

13 cf. www.itsee.bham.ac.uk/projects/sinaiticus/.

14 cf. http://en.wikipedia.org/wiki/Codex_Ephraemi_Rescriptus.

15 cf. http://en.wikipedia.org/wiki/Chester_Beatty_Papyri.

16 cf. http://en.wikipedia.org/wiki/Bodmer_Papyri.

17 cf. http://en.wikipedia.org/wiki/Papyrus_52.

18 cf. '7Q5', http://en.wikipedia.org/wiki/7Q5 and Daniel B. Wallace, '7Q5: The Earliest NT Papyrus?', www.bible.org/page.php?page_id=1196,

19 Antony Flew in Terry L. Miethe (ed.), *Did Jesus Rise From the Dead? The Resurrection Debate* (Eugene, OR: Wipf & Stock, 2003), p. 66.

20 cf. Ralph O. Muncaster, *Examine the Evidence: Exploring the Case for Christianity* (Eugene, OR: Harvest House, 2004), p. 226.

21 Ibid.

22 Geilser and Bocchino, *Unshakeable Foundations*, p. 121.

23 Gregory A. Boyd, *Letters From a Skeptic* (Downers Grove, IL: IVP, 2000), p. 95.

24 F.F. Bruce, *The New Testament Documents: Are They Reliable?* (Downers Grove, IL: IVP, 2006), p. 17.

25 J.P. Moreland, *Scaling the Secular City* (Grand Rapids, MI: Baker, 1987), p. 151.

26 Carsten Peter Thiede, *Jesus: Life or Legend?* (Oxford: Lion, 1990), p. 9.

27 Moreland, *Scaling the Secular City*, p. 137.

28 cf. Josh McDowell and Bill Wilson, *He Walked Among Us* (Alpha, 2000), pp. 118–119.

29 R.T. France, *The Evidence for Jesus* (London: Hodder & Stoughton, 1986), pp. 122, 124.

30 Walter A. Elwell and Robert W. Yarbrough, *Encountering the New Testament* (Grand Rapids, MI: Baker, 1998), p. 75.

31 Craig L. Blomberg, *Jesus and the Gospels* (Leicester: Apollos, 1997), p. 365.

32 Craig L. Blomberg, 'Where Do We Start Studying Jesus?', *Jesus Under Fire* (Carlisle: Paternoster, 1995), p. 28.

33 R.T. France, *The Evidence for Jesus* (London: Hodder & Stoughton, 1986), p. 121.

34 Graham Stanton, *The Gospels and Jesus* (Oxford University Press, 1993), p. 35.

35 Ibid., p. 101.

36 Moreland, *Scaling the Secular City*, p. 148.

37 Alister McGrath, *Jesus: Who He Is and Why He Matters* (Leicester: IVP, 1994), p. 69.

[38] Moreland, *Scaling the Secular City*, p. 148.

[39] Ibid., pp.148–149.

[40] Ibid., p. 149.

[41] Ibid., pp. 149–150.

[42] Terry L. Miethe and Gary R. Habermas, *Why Believe?* (Joplin, MO: College Press, 1993), p. 267.

[43] Ibid., p. 267.

[44] J. Jeremias, 'Easter: The earliest tradition and the earliest interpretation', in *New Testament Theology*, (Charles Scribner's Sons, 1971), p. 306.

[45] Miethe and Habermas, *Why Believe?*, pp. 267–268.

[46] Craig L. Blomberg, *Jesus and the Gospels*, p. 381.

[47] Miethe and Habermas, *Why Believe?*, p. 269.

[48] Michel Onfray, *In Defence of Atheism: The Case Against Christianity, Judaism and Islam* (London: Serpent's Tail, 2007), p. 115.

[49] Gary R. Habermas, 'Why I Believe the New Testament is Historically Reliable', www.apologetics.com/default.jsp?bodycontent=/articles/historical_apologetics/habermas-nt.html.

[50] Geisler and Turek, *I Don't Have Enough Faith to be an Atheist*, p. 223.

[51] Blomberg, *The Historical Reliability of the Gospels*, p. 251.

[52] Norman L. Geisler, *Christian Apologetics* (Grand Rapids, MI: Baker, 1995), pp. 325–326.

[53] Muncaster, *Examine the Evidence*, p. 267.

[54] cf. Muncaster, *Examine the Evidence*, p. 273.

[55] Moreland, *Scaling the Secular City*, p. 156.

[56] Paul Copan, "True For You, But Not For Me" – *Defeating the Slogans that leave Christians Speechless* (Eugene, OR: Bethany House, 1998), p. 103.

[57] Blomberg, *The Historical Reliability of the Gospels*, p. 381.

[58] Copan, *True For You, But Not For*, p. 117.

[59] William Lane Craig, *Are You There, God?* (RZIM, 1999), p. 41.

[60] N.T. Wright and M. Borg, *The Meaning of Jesus: Two Visions* (San Francisco: HarperSan Francisco, 1998), p. 166.

[61] John Rist, 'Where Else?', *Philosophers Who Believe* (Leicester: IVP, 1993), pp. 100–101.

[62] Mike King, *The God Delusion Revisited* (Lulu, 2007), p. 63. See also Michael J. Murray and Michael Rea, *An Introduction to the Philosophy of Religion* (Cambridge: Cambridge University Press, 2008), pp. 76–80.

[63] William Lane Craig, 'Christ and Miracles' in *To Everyone an Answer* (Downers Grove, IL: IVP, 2004), p. 142. See also Francis J. Beckwith,

David Hume's Argument Against Miracles: A Critical Analysis (Larkam, MD: University Press of America, 1989); Francis J. Beckwith, 'Theism, Miracles, And the Modern Mind' in Paul Copan and Paul K. Moser (eds.), *The Rationality of Theism* (London: Routledge, 2003); Winfried Corduan, 'Miracles' in Francis J. Beckwith, William Lane Craig, and J.P. Moreland (eds.), *To Everyone An Answer: A Case for the Christian Worldview* (Downers Grove IL: IVP, 2004); Stephen T. Davis, *Risen Indeed* (Grand Rapids, MI: Eerdmans, 1993); C. Stephen Evans, *Philosophy of Religion: Thinking About Faith* (Downers Grove, IL: IVP, 2001); R. Douglas Geivett, 'Why I Believe in the Possibility of Miracles' in Norman L. Geisler and Paul K. Hoffman (eds.), *Why I Am A Christian: Leading Thinkers Explain Why They Believe* (Grand Rapids, MI: Baker, 20062); R. Douglas Geivett amd Gary R. Habermas (eds.), *In Defence of Miracles: A Comprehensive Case for God's Action In History* (Leicester: Apollos, 1997); C.S. Lewis, *Miracles* (London: Fount, 2002); Michael J. Murray and Michael Rea, *An Introduction to the Philosophy of Religion* (Cambridge: Cambridge University Press, 2008), pp. 201–208.

[64] John Earman, *Hume's Abject Failure* (Oxford University Press, 2000), p. 70.

[65] Flew, *There Is A God*, p. 157.

[66] Craig, 'Christ and Miracles' in *To Everyone an Answer*, p. 142.

[67] Onfray, *In Defence of Atheism*, p. 77.

[68] R.T. France, 'The Gospels as Historical Sources for Jesus, the Founder of Christianity,' *Truth* 1 (1985), 86.

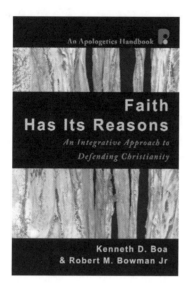

Faith Has Its Reasons

An Integrative Approach to Defending Christianity

Kenneth Boa and Robert Bowman Jr.

Winner of the Gold Medallion Book Award

A wealth of information to help Christians present their faith with intelligence. Ever since the apostle Paul addressed the Stoic and Epicurean philosophers in Athens relating the Christian worldview to a non-Christian world has been a challenge.

Boa and Bowman consider very different apologetic approaches such as evidentialism and presuppositionalism and argue that the strengths of the different apologetic schools of thought can be combined into an integrative approach that enables a strong case to be made for Christianity. This book is essential reading for anyone interested in the rationality of Christian faith.

Kenneth D. Boa is the President of Reflections Ministries.
Robert M. Bowman, Jr, is the President of the Center for Biblical Apologetics, California.

978-1-932805-34-5

The Case for Angels

Peter S. Williams

Do angels really exist, or are they merely literary and figurative devices on the page? What kind of creatures are angels supposed to be? Is their existence even possible and, if so, how do we know whether they actually exist? Williams employs the resources of contemporary philosophy in defence of a traditional Christian angelology. In discussion with naturalistic sceptism, New Age belief and Christian doubt, he highlights the importance of worldview pre-suppositions in determining attitudes towards angels, and enlarges upon the 'culture' war emerging between theism and metaphysical naturalism.

Peter S. Williams works for the Damaris Trust.

978-1-84227-169-8

Think God, Think Science

Conversations on Life, the Universe and Faith

Michael Pfundner in discussion with Ernest Lucas

Has science killed God? How, if at all, are we to 'think God' in the scientific twenty-first century? That question is at the heart of this introductory yet intelligent book in which Michael Pfundner talks to biblical scholar and biochemist, Ernest Lucas. The conversation engages three broad areas:

- *The Sky*: as our scientific understanding of the universe – its vastness, its age, and its origins – has increased, have the stars stopped declaring the glory of God?
- *The Cell*: What place is there for a good creator amidst the random genetic mutations and brutal processes of neo-Darwinian evolution? How can mere 'naked apes' think of themselves as being made in the image of God? Did Genesis get it wrong?
- *The Faith*: Has the recent work of historians and archaeologists undermined traditional Christian belief in the historical reliability of the gospels and in Jesus' resurrection?

Ernest Lucas argues that modern science is fully compatible with Christian theology and Scripture.

This is a wonderfully inspiring book! An immensely valuable – and readable – contribution to the field.' – **John Bryant**, Professor of Genetics, Exeter University

Ernest Lucas is Vice-Principal and Tutor in Biblical Studies, Bristol Baptist College; Michael Pfunder is Bible & Church Development Officer, Bible Society, UK.

978-1-84227-609-9

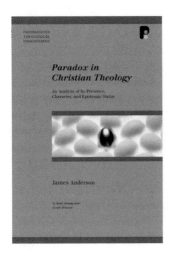

Paradox in Christian Theology

An Analysis of Its Presence, Character, and Epistemic Status

James Anderson

Does traditional creedal Christianity involve paradoxical doctrines, that is, doctrines which present the appearance (at least) of logical inconsistency? If so, what is the nature of these paradoxes and why do they arise? What is the relationship between 'paradox' and, 'mystery' in theological theorizing? And what are the implications for the rationality, or otherwise, of orthodox Christian beliefs? In *Paradox in Christian Theology*, James Anderson argues that the doctrines of the Trinity and the Incarnation, as derived from Scripture and formulated in the ecumenical creeds, are indeed paradoxical. But this conclusion, he contends, need not imply that Christians who believe these doctrines are irrational in doing so. In support of this claim, Anderson develops and defends a model of understanding paradoxical Christian doctrines according to which the presence of such doctrines is unsurprising and adherence to paradoxical doctrines can be entirely reasonable. As such, the phenomenon of theological paradox cannot be considered as a serious intellectual obstacle to belief in Christianity. The case presented in this book has significant implications for the practice of systematic theology, biblical exegesis, and Christian apologetics.

> 'In defending the ineluctable presence of paradox in theology, James Anderson argues that attempts to avoid this will result in formulations that are inadequate to the articulation of core Christian doctrines. What is particularly striking about this study is its accomplished engagement of important recent work in analytic philosophy of religion.' – **David Fergusson**, University of Edinburgh

978-1-84227-462-0

Debating Darwin

Two Debates: Is Darwinism True and Does it Matter?

Graeme Finlay, Stephen Lloyd, Stephen Pattemore and David Swift

Christians continue to disagree about whether Darwinism should be baptised into our theology or rejected as anti-Christian. This book is aimed at Christians on both sides of the debate and hopes to further discussion by giving space for an open airing of the case both ways. Two distinct questions are under the microscope.

1. Is Darwinism compatible with orthodox Christian faith?
2. Does the scientific evidence support Darwinism?

The book begins with a simple explanation of the neo-Darwinian theory of evolution. Stephen Lloyd then opens the first debate by making a theological and biblical case against Darwinism. He is met in 'battle' by Graeme Finlay and Stephen Patterson who argue that Christian Scripture and theology are compatible with Darwinism. Each set of authors then has a chance to respond to their opponents. In the second debate David Swift argues that whilst the science does support micro-evolution by natural selection it does not support macro-evolution. In fact, he says, the science *undermines* neo-Darwinian claims. 'Not so!' says Graeme Finlay, who argues that the latest work in genetics demonstrates the truth of neo-Darwinism beyond reasonable doubt. Swift and Finlay then interact with each other. This book will not tell readers what to think but it will inform the more intelligent debate.

978-1-932805-619-8